THE DREIFUS

THE DREYFUS AFFAIR

Honour and Politics in the *Belle Époque*

Martin P. Johnson
Northern Illinois University

St. Martin's Press
New York

THE DREYFUS AFFAIR

Copyright © 1999 by Martin P. Johnson

St. Martin's Press, Scholarly and Reference Division, 175 Fifth Avenue, New York, N.Y. 10010

First published in the United States of America in 1999

This book is printed on paper suitable for recycling and made from fully managed and sustained forest sources.

Printed in Hong Kong

ISBN 0–312–22158–4 clothbound
ISBN 0–312–22159–2 paperback

Library of Congress Cataloging-in-Publication Data
Johnson, Martin Phillip, 1959–
The Dreyfus affair : honour and politics in the Belle Époque /
Martin P. Johnson.
p.   cm.
Includes bibliographical references and index.
ISBN 0–312–22158–4 (cloth)
ISBN 0–312–22159–2 (pbk.)
1. Dreyfus, Alfred, 1859–1935.   2. France—Ethnic relations. 3.
Trials (Treason)—France—Political aspects.   4.
Antisemitism—France—History—19th century.   5. France—Politics
and government—1870–1940—Public opinion.   6. Public
opinion—France.   7. France. Armée Officers—Biography.   I. Title.
DC354.8 .J64   1999
944.081'2'092—dc21   98–48285
                                                                      CIP

CONTENTS

CHRONOLOGY

1894   Late September: Henry brings the *bordereau* to the Statistical Section.

15 October: Du Paty interrogates and arrests Dreyfus.

22 December: Dreyfus convicted.

1895   5 January: Ceremonial degradation of Dreyfus at the Ecole Militaire.

April: Dreyfus arrives at Devil's Island.

1896   Mid-March: Henry brings the *petit bleu* to the Statistical Section.

Late August: Investigating the *petit bleu*, Picquart determines that Esterhazy wrote the *bordereau*.

September: Picquart informs Gonse and Boisdeffre of his discovery; Mathieu plants a false story in the press that Dreyfus has escaped; Dreyfus placed in chains.

October: Picquart sent from Paris; Henry begins wholesale fabrications.

1897   June: Picquart confers with his lawyer Leblois.

13 July: Leblois convinces Scheurer-Kestner that Dreyfus is innocent.

October: Scheurer-Kestner meets with high officials; Du Paty warns Esterhazy, beginning the 'collusion'.

15 November: Mathieu publicly denounces Esterhazy as the author of the *bordereau*.

1898   Mid-January: Esterhazy acquitted; Zola publishes *J'accuse*; riots and demonstrations across France.

23 February: Zola found guilty of libel.

July: Minister of War Cavaignac reads the 'false Henry' to the Chamber; Picquart denounces it as a forgery; Picquart arrested; Zola flees to Britain.

13 August: The 'false Henry' is discovered to be a forgery.

30 August: Cavaignac interrogates and arrests Henry who then commits suicide.

1 September: Esterhazy flees to Britain.

September: Cavaignac resigns; Brisson government refers Lucy Dreyfus's request for revision to the appeals court.

1899   23 February:. Déroulède's attempted coup.

June: Appeals court annuls Dreyfus's conviction and remands him for retrial; President Loubet attacked at Auteuil racetrack; Zola returns to France; Picquart freed.

22 June: Waldeck-Rousseau forms government of 'Republican defence'.

9 September: Dreyfus found guilty by court martial at Rennes.

19 September: Dreyfus pardoned.

1900   December: Amnesty law passed.

1903   April: Jaurès revives the Affair in a speech to the Chamber; Minister of War André begins a new investigation.

November: Dreyfus requests revision of the Rennes verdict.

1904   March: Appeals court undertakes review of the Rennes verdict.

1906   July: Rennes verdict annulled without remand for retrial; Dreyfus reinstated to the army with promotion and awarded the Legion of Honour.

PREFACE

In January 1998, at the centenary of Emile Zola's *J'accuse*, an article that inaugurated the most turbulent period of the Dreyfus Affair, Prime Minister Lionel Jospin upbraided his opponents in the Chamber of Deputies for the historical misjudgements of their party. 'Everyone knows that the left was Dreyfusard', he chided, 'everyone knows that the right was anti-Dreyfusard'. He similarly evoked the right's alleged resistance to the abolition of slavery. Shouting 'Shame!' and 'Resign!' several opposition deputies rushed towards the rostrum with raised fists while ushers leapt forward to prevent an assault on the prime minister. Most deputies of the right then walked out, while those of the left applauded Jospin's scolding. One hundred years had passed, yet the Affair sparked by the trial of an obscure army officer could still provoke violence and conflict.

The Dreyfus Affair comprises attempted assassinations, suicides, perjury, forgeries, invective, stunning reversals, and abortive *coups d'état*, involving the honour and destiny of an individual and of France. It is also a fascinating detective story with profound political and social consequences; little wonder, then, that participants, observers, and scholars have often succumbed to the temptation of trying to find some secret key to unlock the enigmas of the Affair. Many contemporaries believed that the case exposed a vast Judaeo-Masonic syndicate responsible for the nation's ills;[1] others thought Dreyfus was the casualty of a Jesuitical–military cabal determined to return France to a past of superstition and oppression. In the years since, some have found the key to the Affair in a French army operation to mislead the Germans about a new artillery piece, or as a grand hoax perpetrated to fend off a threatened progressive income tax, or as the echo of treason by the highest ranking officer in France.[2] For all sides the Affair became a litmus test of patriotism or republicanism, of rationality or morality. In current scholarship the Affair has attained the rank of those few historical events (Vichy, Vietnam) about which it is not permitted to arrive at an erroneous conclusion: the officer in charge of French army archives was forced from his post in 1994 after writing that Dreyfus's innocence is the 'hypothesis' accepted by most historians.

A tale of mysteries and secrets, the Affair reveals the preoccupations and divisions of France and Europe at the turn of the century. At the centre is the unjust imprisonment upon Devil's Island of Captain Alfred Dreyfus, a Jew convicted of a crime he did not commit, who was in part the victim of an ancient prejudice. As the gravest crisis of the Third Republic the Dreyfus Affair transformed French politics, recasting the struggle between order and movement that has characterized France since the Revolution. As a crucial episode in the history of racial nationalism it marked the transition from traditional to racial anti-Semitism, foreshadowing the horrors of the twentieth century. And as a prolonged and explosive contest for human rights and judicial equity it engaged academics, writers, and artists as self-conscious 'intellectuals' in French politics for the first time, opening a new mode of involvement for those who claimed moral authority by virtue of erudition or sensibility.

Over the twelve years from 1894 to 1906 the Affair acted as a kind of X-ray, revealing (and aggravating) fractures in French politics and society; it divided families, friends, political groups, and intellectuals. Behind these fissures a set of larger tensions exacerbated the crisis: national insecurity felt by many French when facing an increasingly powerful Germany; economic and social dislocations largely responsible for the rising tide of anti-Semitism; the threat posed to the established order by 'cosmopolitan' groups such as Jews (held responsible for corrupting France during the Panama scandal, 1892–93), anarchists (who assassinated President Sadie Carnot in 1893), and socialists (beneficiaries of unprecedented success in the 1893 elections). Meanwhile, radical republicans implemented thoroughgoing anti-clericalism, culminating with the exclusion of clergy from schools and the separation of church and state in 1905. Against this backdrop a half-dozen spectacular trials associated with the Dreyfus Affair transfixed public opinion, while numerous duels between partisans expressed the depth of personal identification with the affair. The fundamental question was not in fact the guilt of one man, it was the identity of France: its political form and dominant values. Republic or authoritarian state? Secular liberalism or clerical traditionalism?

Equality for all citizens or exclusion of cultural aliens? The Affair thrived upon these simple oppositions. For virtually all French engaged in national life it provided clearly defined heroes and villains, certainty of conviction, and a sense of shared devotion to a high and important cause.

Rather than follow Prime Minister Jospin and distribute praise or blame for such dedication, it may be more fruitful to explore the circumstances that led people of intelligence and good will to opposing conclusions; indeed, this paradox accounts for much of the tragedy of the Affair. On all sides it is possible to distinguish moderates and radicals. Many began as mere revisionists who questioned the legality of the verdict, but moved in time to a belief in Dreyfus's innocence, making them full Dreyfusards. In contrast, simple anti-revisionists opposed further judicial inquiries because they were not warranted by the facts, while radical anti-Dreyfusards were ideologically committed to a war against Jews, Freemasons, or Protestants, as well as the decadent Republic that did their bidding. Still, the practical overlap in these labels renders them near synonyms, and they are generally used here interchangeably; whatever the label, the Affair commanded enthusiasm and sacrifice. Great questions of moral truth and transcendent justice will always surround the Affair, and unresolvable mysteries will always trouble students of the case. We shall instead pursue a more attainable objective: understanding why the trial of one man became the *Affaire*, with all its consequences.

1

IN SEARCH OF A TRAITOR (1894)

...I am however sending you, Monsieur, some interesting information.[1]

The explosive Affair that would agitate France for a decade began in
late September 1894 when Major Hubert-Joseph Henry of the French
intelligence service collected a batch of documents taken from the
German embassy. This was so routine that the method of collection
came to be called 'the ordinary path', meaning that Henry simply
paid the cleaning woman to hand over the contents of embassy waste-
baskets. Usually little of interest was found, although occasionally the
refuse brought startling insights into the activities and personalities
of the German diplomatic corps in Paris. For instance, Colonel Maximilien von Schwartzkoppen, the military attaché, enjoyed liaisons with
many admirers who sent him letters of sometimes bracing frankness.
One such admirer was evidently the Italian military attaché in Paris,
Colonel Alessandro Panizzardi. As part of their duties the two men
exchanged military information, but perhaps to confuse prying eyes
they interposed affectionate messages, often exchanging and femi-
nising their names, so that Henry encountered messages such as,
'Dear Maximilien, am I still your Alexandrine?', 'A thousand saluta-
tions from the girl who loves you so', or, 'My little green dog, I'm
returning to you [several documents]. Farewell, my little Loulou. Your
bugger.'[2] Major Henry, at least, was enough convinced of the sincerity
of these sentiments to consider blackmailing Schwartzkoppen but his

1

superiors in the intelligence service demurred; however serious the contest between France and Germany, notions of honour still proscribed the rules of the game.

On this autumn day Commandant Henry did not find any messages from 'Maximilienne' or 'Alexandrine' amid the embassy detritus, but something even more remarkable: a torn *bordereau*, or note, which began, 'Without news indicating that you wish to see me, I am however sending you, *Monsieur*, some interesting information.' The *bordereau* then listed five documents the writer was forwarding to military attaché Schwartzkoppen, none of which has ever come to light, on matters such as the functioning of the French 120 millimetre cannon, troop deployments, and a new artillery manual. There was no signature, and the note merely concluded with, 'I am leaving on manoeuvres.' Henry had discovered that a traitor, evidently a French officer, was delivering secrets to the German army. The struggle over the identity of this traitor led France into a paroxysm of recrimination and violence.

Yet before there was a Dreyfus Affair, there was the case of the *bordereau*, the note whose origin and authenticity incited countless trials, debates, and speculations. When the contents of the *bordereau* became public in 1896 Schwartzkoppen told his superiors he had never received it, much less thrown it into his wastebasket, and even in his personal notes published long after his death he never deviated from that position.[3] He was, however, conducting espionage without the knowledge of his ambassador – the previous military attaché had been removed for exactly the same activity – and in any case might not have wanted to admit his incompetence in simply discarding such an incriminating document. In addition, Schwartzkoppen may have thought that had he acknowledged the authenticity of the *bordereau* he would also have to admit to his flirtatious correspondence with Panizzardi and other compromising letters that also arrived by the 'ordinary path'. Joseph Reinach, the first and still most exhaustive historian of the Affair, developed an alternative provenance for the *bordereau*, arguing that a French agent removed it from the concierge's lodge at the embassy before it could have been delivered to Schwartzkoppen's office. This version, rejected by most recent students of the case, allowed Reinach to maintain that Major Henry was actually a partner in treason with the writer of the *bordereau*; Henry could not destroy it when it came into his hands because the agent who stole it would have known of its contents and importance.[4]

Thus, from its first moments the Dreyfus Affair presents such complexities that even the most sure-footed may be excused for sometimes losing their way. Although a central figure in the Affair, Henry was not a collaborator in treason, but a soldier who had proved his courage on the battlefields of the Franco-Prussian War (1870–1871) and in imperial struggles from Tunisia to Tonkin. Forty-eight years old, from solid peasant stock, his lack of polish and education and his ignorance of foreign languages prevented him from attaining higher positions in French army intelligence. Yet his large frame and confident, powerful personality suited him for dealing with the shady characters who furnished so much dubious and genuine information on foreign agents and diplomats. His suicide in 1898 proved that he was literally willing to die for his conception of duty and honour, both his own and that of his superiors in the intelligence office he served with such vigour.

Henry brought the *bordereau* to the attention of his colleagues in the Section de Statistique, the euphemistic title of the intelligence service, on 27 September 1894. Colonel Jean-Conrad Sandherr, head of the Statistical Section, and the handful of other officers in the service seemed to be impressed first of all with the range of information offered in the documents listed in the *bordereau*, implying that the author was an officer of the General Staff. They also believed that the information was highly confidential and difficult to obtain, and indeed the *bordereau* stated as much. Moreover, the language used in the *bordereau* to discuss a new cannon suggested to an artillery officer among them that the author was also in the artillery. While seemingly reasonable, these erroneous assumptions coloured the entire investigation, leading to ever more serious miscalculations.

The *bordereau* troubled Colonel Sandherr and the officers of the Statistical Section all the more because this was by no means the first espionage case to disrupt the French army. Indeed the alarm and consternation at the highest levels of the army can only be understood when placed in the context of the intelligence wars *belle époque*. Over the previous few years nearly a dozen French soldiers and civilians had been convicted of communicating technical or military secrets to foreign powers. French and foreign intelligence services also waged sustained campaigns of misinformation, resorting to disguise, forgery, impersonation, and seduction. When Henry discovered the new treason Colonel Sandherr was directing an elaborate ruse to mislead Germany about the very cannon mentioned in the *bordereau*. Under

the minister of war's supervision Sandherr was also compiling lists of
military-age foreign nationals and resident aliens in France who would
be interned in case of war, part of what has been called the 'xenophobic style' of the 1890s.[5]

Most of the spies and traitors apprehended in this veritable war of
secrets were accused of complicity with Germany, which over the last
thirty years had supplanted Great Britain as France's most feared
enemy. After humiliating defeat in the Franco-Prussian War France in
1871 had ceded Alsace and parts of Lorraine to the newly formed
German Empire, a source of permanent outrage for French nationalists. Until 1890 Otto von Bismarck's adept diplomacy had prevented
France from allying with another great power, the only hope if France
were to defeat the more powerful Germany and regain the lost
provinces. In addition, imperial rivalry in East Africa and Asia
perturbed Anglo-French relations, while conflicting French and Italian
ambitions in North Africa explained at least in part why
Schwartzkoppen and Panizzardi worked so intimately together. Thus
revanchistes – those in France who sought to avenge 1871 – were heart-
ened when Kaiser Wilhelm II dismissed Bismarck in 1890, and elated
when Russia, concerned over modifications in German foreign policy,
finally succumbed to French pursuit and agreed to a series of military and diplomatic accords beginning in 1892. The emerging Franco-
Russian Alliance was still untested in 1894, however, and fear of
German power fuelled much of the passionate obsession displayed by
the officers of the Statistical Section as they sought the officer who
had passed secrets to the national enemy.

For just over a week the inquiry yielded no leads. Sandherr
searched in vain through the archives of the Statistical Section for
other examples of the same handwriting, and a photograph of the
bordereau was circulated to the department chiefs of the General Staff
with equally negligible results. On 6 October 1894, however, Lieutenant-Colonel Marquis Albert d'Aboville posited a further set of
assumptions about its author that led directly to the arrest of the
presumed culprit. Like the other officers, d'Aboville, who had just
returned from leave, appears to have independently concluded that
the traitor was probably an artillery officer associated with the General
Staff. Yet he also speculated that only *stagiaires*, officers in training
who passed in stages through the four departments of the General
Staff, would have access to the wide range of apparently secret information mentioned in the document. D'Aboville and his superior,

Colonel Pierre Fabre, then consulted a list of current *stagiaires* and their attention immediately fell upon one about whom Fabre had once given a bad report: Artillery Captain Alfred Dreyfus. 'An imperfect officer,' Fabre had written the year before, 'very intelligent and highly gifted, but pretentious, who does not fulfil from the standpoint of character, conscience, and manner of service, the conditions necessary for employment with the General Staff of the Army.' D'Aboville and Fabre found a remarkable similarity between the *bordereau* and a specimen of writing by Dreyfus found in the General Staff files. When they informed Colonel Sandherr, who did not know Dreyfus well but had seen him about the offices of the General Staff, Sandherr struck his head with his hand and cried, 'I should have known!'

Why did officers of the Statistical Section and the General Staff find it so easy to believe that Dreyfus was the traitor? Certainly most of the answer lies in the unfortunate way Dreyfus fitted the profile imagined over the previous week: an artillery officer and *stagiaire* attached to the General Staff whose writing appeared to match the *bordereau*. And there was more. Sandherr and the Statistical Section had known since spring of a traitor whom Schwartzkoppen described as 'that scoundrel D' (*ce canaille de D*) in a letter to Panizzardi. That the *bordereau* had not already been associated with the 'scoundrel D' document may explain Sandherr's reaction upon hearing Dreyfus's name. But d'Aboville, Fabre, and Sandherr were also prepared to accuse Dreyfus because of who he was, for none was ignorant that he was a Jew at a time when anti-Semitism and race consciousness in France had reached alarming proportions.

The Dreyfus Affair occurred at a critical moment in the history of anti-Semitism, when doctrines of biological determinism and radical nationalism transformed traditional anti-Semitism into the racist ideology familiar to the late nineteenth and early twentieth centuries. Traditional anti-Semitism rested mainly upon religious and cultural foundations such as differences in devotional practices and language, and anti-Semitic writers often castigated Jews for their obstinacy in refusing to adopt Christianity and for remaining outside the larger cultural community. Traditional anti-Semitism also derived from perceived economic grievances. Jews were often prohibited from owning land, and even where this was legally possible periodic expulsions and other persecutions rendered liquid forms of wealth more desirable. Thus Jews became highly overrepresented in certain economic activities, such as money-lending and peddling, making

them targets of popular and official wrath when times were hard.
Nineteenth-century socialists such as Charles Fourier and Pierre-
Joseph Proudhon associated Jews and capitalism, creating fertile soil
for anti-Semitism on the left to match the traditional religious anti-
Semitism of the right. Traditional anti-Semitism was not so much a
political philosophy as a cultural temperament.

The multiple roots of traditional anti-Semitism meant that Jews
could be held responsible for any calamity, whether it be plague,
unemployment, indebtedness, famine – or national degeneration.
Once social Darwinists began asserting that the struggle for survival
determined relations among social groups and nations as well as
species, anti-Semites increasingly cast Jews as a threat to racial purity
and national strength. Even in the early nineteenth century romantic
nationalists had defined a nation as the noble and unique product
of soil, history, and blood. By the later part of the century anti-
Semites like Wilhelm Marr in Germany could declare that 'genuine
nationhood is the race'.[6] Traditional anti-Semitism considered Jews
a malevolent threat that could be overcome by assimilation if Jews
accepted the religion and culture of the larger community. Racial
anti-Semitism saw Jews as biologically alien parasites that had to be
eliminated by expulsion or extermination. Such sentiments flour-
ished particularly among nationalities that felt threatened in the
struggle for survival. As an organized political movement anti-
Semitism failed in the confident and burgeoning German Empire,
but thrived among anxious German-speakers in the multinational
Austro-Hungarian Empire.[7]

In France, where one eminent scholar has noted that anti-Semitism
was 'as French as croissants',[8] the 85,000 Jews made up an insignificant proportion of the 39 million population, but anti-Semites successfully associated the Jewish threat with the German threat. Until the
arrival of Jews from Russia and Poland in the late nineteenth century
nearly all French Jews came from or lived in Alsace, and generally
spoke some form of German as their native tongue. The late 1880s
and early 1890s witnessed a remarkable rise in anti-Semitic books,
pamphlets, newspapers, and organizations, sparked by the tremendous success of Edouard Drumont's *La France Juive*, published in
1886. Drumont's 1,200 page tome purported to reveal the hidden
truth of history: that the Jews and those in their pay had caused every
disaster, defeat, and humiliation suffered by France. This was a
powerful message in a nation still traumatized by the débâcle of 1871.

In the 1880s and 90s social and political changes increased the fears of those concerned with French national decline. The rising economic and military power of Germany contributed to a pervasive psychology of national insecurity in France. Germany's population was nearly half as large again as that of France, and was growing much more rapidly. Since 1871 countless books, magazines, and newspaper articles had bemoaned the low French birth-rate, and the conservative and Catholic press especially found the main causes to be a general collapse of morals, the rejection of religious guidance by the secular Third Republic, and the disruption of the traditional social order. Alcoholism, homosexuality, feminism, and myriad other modern ills were alleged to have sapped the moral fibre of the Gallic race. Opponents on the left and right of the supposedly degenerate Republic had momentarily rallied to the quasi-bonapartism represented by General Georges Boulanger in the mid-1880s, united in part by anti-Semitism.[9] Boulanger's flight and subsequent suicide abruptly ended the episode, but the discontent behind Boulangism did not vanish. In the early 1890s Drumont and others exploited this discontent during the financial scandal surrounding a failed Panama canal project, asserting that Jews had corrupted French political elites.

Already anti-Semitism had affected Dreyfus's military career. In the summer of 1892 Dreyfus had nightmares over his fears that one of his instructors at the Ecole de Guerre, General Pierre Bonnefond, was treating him and other Jews unfairly. His fears were realised when Bonnefond, who Dreyfus said did not want a Jew on the General Staff, gave him a poor evaluation, lowering his class rank from third to ninth. Dreyfus took the unusual step of lodging a formal protest, asking, 'is a Jewish officer not capable of serving his country as well as any other soldier?'[10] The timing of this incident was not accidental, as it was the high point of the Panama scandal that had given new momentum to the anti-Semitic movement. Drumont's newspaper *La Libre Parole* was also issuing a series of articles pretending to expose Jewish contamination of the military. 'Already the rulers in finance and in the bureaucracy, dictating their decrees to the judiciary', Drumont railed, 'they will become the definitive rulers of France the day they command the Army.' Jews and others responded by challenging Drumont and his associates to duels, one of which resulted in the death of the Jewish army captain Armand Mayer. In reaction, perhaps 20,000 mourners attended Mayer's funeral as a protest against anti-Semitism, and the government stated that distinguishing

among Catholics, Protestants, and Jews in the army was 'a crime
against the nation'. Yet the poisonous political and cultural climate
continued to affect Dreyfus when he became a *stagiaire*. 'Anti-Semitic
prejudices were already abroad in the General Staff', Major Georges
Picquart later recalled, so he assigned Dreyfus to duties that did not
involve military secrets in order to avoid 'certain embarrassments'.
Most of the key investigating officers did not conceal their anti-
Semitism: Henry read *La Libre Parole*; Fabre's evaluation appears to
have been largely prompted by anti-Semitism; another officer later
noted 'there are some situations in which persons who are not incontrovertibly French ought not to be placed';[11] Sandherr was notoriously hostile to Jews, and had even refused to have Dreyfus assigned
to his service; and just one week after Dreyfus's name was first
mentioned in the case d'Aboville warned against the efforts of 'upper
Jewdom' to help Dreyfus.

There was also another way in which who Dreyfus was affected his
fate. At his trial many officers testified in various ways that Dreyfus
boasted of his accomplishments and of his family's wealth, and that
he was not well liked by his fellow officers.[12] Perhaps for this reason,
or because he was a Jew, he lacked a patron in the General Staff,
which was a necessity in the French army as then constituted.
Accusing him would not incur the wrath of a highly placed mentor,
something that was not true of others who had been momentarily
suspected. Furthermore, the officers on the case seemed to genuinely
believe that the handwriting evidence was unassailable, although their
assumption that they were competent to make such a determination
was both arrogant and erroneous. Finally, strong career and instit-
utional imperatives propelled the rush to judgement. Although the
investigation was only a week old, the belief that the traitor 'D' was
in their midst had long troubled the highest officers of the army;
ferreting out the culprit might help one's career, and would certainly
remove a potential source of trouble for the army, not to mention a
threat to the nation.

The precise weight of these factors in the final determination to
focus on Dreyfus can never be known. On the one hand those who
interpret the Affair as a struggle between justice and prejudice, virtue
and iniquity, often emphasize the role of anti-Semitism even at the
earliest moments of the case. On the other, those who view the Affair
as a series of errors in reasoning or judgement often minimize the
importance of racism and xenophobia. It is fair to say that the inter-

ested officers did not search for a Jewish traitor and then hit upon Dreyfus; however, given their mistaken assumptions about the author of the *bordereau*, once Dreyfus's name was found upon the list of *stagiaires* their prejudices led them to assume the worst. All this does not yet constitute a conspiracy against Dreyfus, although it helps explain why there was little serious consideration of other suspects. Most of the pieces seemed to fit, and those that did not would soon be made to do so.

Once Dreyfus was linked to the *bordereau* on 6 October events moved with a fatal inevitability. Sandherr had already begun compiling documents from the Statistical Section archive which appeared related to the *bordereau*, either by virtue of the information covered or even the words employed. At some point the 'scoundrel D' letter was added to the file, and would become one of the most powerful pieces of evidence used against Dreyfus, despite the fact that nothing indicated Dreyfus was 'D' or even that it was the actual initial of the agent who passed the military plans. After all, Schwartzkoppen himself used the false name Alexandrine to sign 'the scoundrel D' letter to Panizzardi (He had also added a postscript: 'Don't bugger too much!').[13] On the evening of 6 October, after consulting with Minister of War Auguste Mercier, Chief of Staff General Raoul de Boisdeffre appointed Boisdeffre's cousin and amateur graphologist, Major Marquis Mercier Du Paty de Clam, to compare the handwriting and help with the still unofficial investigation into Dreyfus. After working all day Sunday, 7 October, Du Paty declared that the handwriting of the *bordereau* resembled that of Dreyfus enough to warrant continued investigation. Still, neither Sandherr nor his immediate superior, General Charles-Arthur Gonse, was willing to order that Dreyfus be watched without the authorization of Chief of Staff Boisdeffre, who had left Paris. This was less a sign of uncertainty than of understandable prudence in committing the General Staff to a full judicial inquiry into a fellow officer without explicit approval from the highest levels. Everyone knew that the case would have important diplomatic and political ramifications, since it involved not only the German military attaché but an officer of the General Staff. The nationalist press could be expected to have a field day excoriating the government and army for harbouring another traitor. Indeed, General Félix Saussier, the military governor of Paris and commander-in-chief of French forces, thought the army could ill afford another scandal. He also worried that Jewish financial interests would exact revenge for the prosecution of Dreyfus, demonstrating how pervasive was the consciousness of Dreyfus's heritage. Saussier assumed, as did most anti-Semites, that Jews formed a distinct group and would be loyal to their clan rather than the state. 'Better to send this Dreyfus to get killed in Africa', was Saussier's advice.

   Minister of War Mercier was of another mind. On Wednesday, 10 October, he separately told President of the Republic Jean Casimir-Périer and Prime Minister Charles Dupuy that a traitor had been uncovered. Like Saussier, Dupuy counselled prudence, in particular because the evidence seemed thin. Perhaps as a temporizing measure, or to restrain Mercier, Dupuy convened a meeting of the cabinet members most directly affected by cases of espionage. With no other evidence than Du Paty's somewhat ambiguous guesswork Mercier told the assembled ministers that handwriting analysis had revealed the name of the traitor. Only Foreign Minister Gabriel Hanotaux closely questioned Mercier. Hanotaux objected that the *bordereau* had been obtained illegally and that the violation of the German embassy inherent in the 'ordinary path' would be a cause for justified complaints from the German government. Diplomatic imperatives forbade prosecuting Dreyfus on such evidence, and Hanotaux even opposed continuing the investigation. Yet in the absence of support from the other ministers Hanotaux could only induce Mercier to agree not to arrest the suspect, whose name was never mentioned, unless more compelling evidence surfaced. Hanotaux was so concerned that he went to Mercier's home later that day and reiterated his arguments. At that point Mercier added a new reason for not ending the inquiry: so many knew of the case that not to proceed would appear to be conniving at treason. The inquiry was only two weeks old but had already developed a kind of independent momentum.

   After the meeting of the ministers on 11 October Mercier summoned Sandherr's immediate superior, General Charles-Arthur Gonse, to demand that he produce more evidence, an odd request since Mercier had just assured his colleagues that there was no doubt of the traitor's identity. Yet that was the crux of the problem faced by Mercier: he and the other officers were convinced that Dreyfus was guilty, but they had no proof that would stand up under judicial scrutiny. At the same time that Mercier demanded further proofs he proceeded with arrangements to arrest Dreyfus as if the arrest were unconnected to the investigation. It was only that day that a professional graphologist who worked for the Bank of France, Alfred Gobert, had been asked to compare the handwriting of the *bordereau* to that Dreyfus. When presenting Gobert with the documents, Chief of Staff Boisdeffre and other officers insisted that the suspect had written the *bordereau*, saying that there existed additional evidence against him, probably referring to the 'scoundrel D' letter and other documents accumulating in Sandherr's file on the case. In addition, General Gonse twice visited Gobert as he analysed the documents. While perfectly legitimate in the eyes of the officers, such actions suggest a certain willingness to prejudice Gobert's opinion, the first appearance of the bad faith, falsifications, and illegalities that would increasingly characterize the investigation and subsequent trial.

Mercier probably knew of the 'scoundrel D' letter by this time, which may in his eyes have constituted the new evidence required for an arrest under his agreement with Minister of Foreign Affairs Hanotaux. At some point Mercier showed the document to Hanotaux, but could not overcome his objections. On Friday, 12 October, before Gobert had rendered his judgement, Chief of Staff Boisdeffre, acting upon Mercier's orders, told Du Paty to arrest Dreyfus the following Monday. Their conversation demonstrates that the investigating officers understood the explosive implications of the case, for Du Paty later claimed to have objected to his cousin, 'you are going to poison my life' and requested that an officer without family responsibilities be given the assignment, as if it were front-line duty. Boisdeffre insisted, allegedly pointing out that 'you don't come from a Jesuit school, you don't have Jewish connections'.[14] Boisdeffre wanted no partisan or sectarian recriminations, although he clearly expected them.

Gobert announced his findings the next morning: while there were significant similarities between the *bordereau* and the writings by the suspect, 'the anonymous incriminating letter might be that of another person'. The case against the presumed traitor could never succeed on the basis of such doubtful evidence, but Gobert's opinion was given little credence. General Gonse had already remarked that Gobert had asked the name of the suspect, which was withheld, but Gobert had ascertained it from the documents and the *Annuaire militaire*. In addition, the investigating officers believed that Dreyfus had had dealings with Gobert's employer, the Bank of France. Dreyfus always denied this, but could there be some connection between the expert and the suspect? Gonse thought as much, and even before Gobert had completed his examination Gonse had asked for the

opinion of another consultant, Alphonse Bertillon, who will be one
of the more diverting figures in the Affair. Bertillon directed the Judicial Identification Division of the Paris Prefecture of Police but was
not a trained or practising graphologist. He was famous for devel-
oping a new method of identifying individuals based upon precise
body measurements which in 1892 had helped solve the spectacular
case of the anarchist bomber Ravachol. Convinced of his crimino-
logical genius, Bertillon later developed the bizarre theory that
Dreyfus had forged his own handwriting by a method of almost
demoniacal complexity. However, on this first occasion the army
consulted Bertillon he was almost reticent. 'If one sets aside the
hypothesis of a document forged with the greatest care', he wrote in
an opinion delivered a few hours after that of Gobert, 'it appears
manifest to us that the same person wrote the texts communicated
to us and the incriminating document.' Bertillon's later theory would
be developed precisely because there were so many divergences in
the handwriting of the two sets of documents that Bertillon came to
believe Dreyfus had in fact forged the *bordereau* with the greatest care.
Bertillon's analysis squarely contradicted Gobert's, who categorically
asserted that the *bordereau* was written in a natural style, implying
that such a forgery was impossible.

The divided opinions of the handwriting consultants did not alter
the plan to arrest Dreyfus. According to Du Paty, Mercier told him
at a final meeting on Sunday, 14 October, in the presence of Boisdeffre, Sandherr, and several others, that the president and prime
minister had decided 'this affair cannot be suppressed, and that a
crime like this cannot go unpunished'. Mercier had most probably
not seen the president and prime minister – Prime Minister Dupuy
had counselled prudence even before the handwriting consultants
had been heard from – but there is no convincing reason why Du
Paty should fabricate such a story. No doubt Mercier invoked the
highest political authorities in order to overcome Du Paty's obvious
reluctance, the first sign of Mercier's willingness to alter the truth
that will later allow him to commit outright illegalities. Mercier's
statement also reveals his state of mind on the eve of the arrest of
Dreyfus. Whether or not Mercier had actually spoken with the two
politicians, for him the question was not whether Dreyfus was guilty,
but only whether the case should be suppressed as Military Governor
Saussier and Foreign Minister Hanotaux had counselled.

Mercier's decision on 12 October to have Dreyfus arrested, in retrospect the point of no return in the case, probably reflected a number
of considerations. Foremost was the conviction among the investigating officers that only Dreyfus could have written the *bordereau*. Yet
the decision did not rest upon the evidence alone, for the evidence
was not only circumstantial and incomplete, it was contradictory.
While some have found Mercier's decision fully justifiable, Mercier
was acting like a man pressed for time, harried by considerations that
were only tangentially related to the facts of the investigation.[15]
Having affirmed to his ministerial colleagues on 11 October that he
knew the name of the culprit, Mercier had effectively staked his
personal credibility and competence on the outcome of the inquiry.
And unfortunately for Dreyfus, Auguste Mercier was a man almost
constitutionally incapable of admitting an error. His career had been
made in the field, not the offices of the General Staff, for he had
served with distinction in the French expedition to Mexico in 1867
and the Franco-Prussian War. While a Catholic, he was not particularly devout – he married an English Protestant – and he had a reputation as a 'republican general' at a time when such was not easily
found in the French army, which perhaps had recommended him to
Casimir-Périer and Dupuy, in whose cabinets he served. Only one of
the many ironies of the Dreyfus Affair is that a republican general,
not overtly anti-Semitic, initiated the worst political crisis of the Third
Republic and a wave of anti-Semitism.

By October 1894 Mercier had been minister of war nearly two years
and was coming under increasing criticism. In the summer he had
arranged for the disposition of 60,000 conscripts without first gaining
the president's approval; Casimir-Périer had got his back up and
called a special cabinet meeting, while the nationalist press declared
that the republican general was denuding French fortresses. Then an
inventor named Turpin threatened to sell the secret of a new explosive to the Germans after Mercier had refused to purchase it,
providing more fuel for criticism in some quarters. Meanwhile, a
scandal had erupted over alleged cheating on the entrance exam to
the French army college Saint-Cyr, and some journalists accused
Mercier of quashing the investigation because his son had entered the
college that year. Finally, at the same moment the *bordereau* was
causing such dismay among the General Staff, the anti-Semitic press
was denouncing Mercier for having asked for a review of a court-
martial verdict removing a Jewish doctor from the reserves. Already

Jules Roche, a conservative deputy and member of the military budget committee, had announced that he was going to question the minister of war before the Chamber regarding the 60,000 troops. Mercier may have feared that Prime Minister Dupuy would be more than willing to jettison his troublesome minister of war to assuage such powerful critics. Thus Mercier may have wanted to present the country with the traitor before the Chamber met as a concrete sign of his vigilance and effectiveness, so maligned in recent months. Mercier may also have hurried the arrest of Dreyfus from fear that the press would hear of the newest case of treason and start another campaign against him that could cost his cabinet post.

Arresting an officer of the General Staff was a serious matter. Unfortunately, although he was a brilliant officer who had graduated second from the prestigious and demanding Ecole Polytechnique, Du Paty also had a taste for dramatics. Mindful of the paucity of evidence, he carefully arranged every detail to induce the suspect to confess in a moment of panic or despair. On Saturday Dreyfus was summoned to appear for inspection the following Monday at 9 am in civilian dress, so that no one would remark upon a uniformed officer being conducted to the Cherche-Midi military prison. That morning d'Aboville was dispatched to Major Forzinetti, the prison governor, to prepare for the arrival of the prisoner. After telling Forzinetti the name and rank of the accused and the charges against him, d'Aboville pointedly asked Forzinetti to agree on his word of honour to obey all instructions, both written and oral, regarding the prisoner. Given that such obedience could be expected this was a strange request, but it had a purpose, for d'Aboville carried orders directly from Mercier which if not illegal were certainly irregular. First, Forzinetti was not to inform General Saussier of the incarceration, even though regulations stipulated that Saussier had to approve all prison internments. Also, the accused officer was to be treated as a common convict, even though this contradicted the military code. D'Aboville also instructed Forzinetti to hold the prisoner in the strictest solitary confinement. Lastly, according to Forzinetti, d'Aboville 'put me on my guard against the probable efforts of "upper Jewdom" as soon as they should hear of the imprisonment'.[16]

Dreyfus appeared for inspection on 15 October as requested, and was immediately caught in Du Paty's web. Instead of finding fellow officers waiting for review, he met Commandant Du Paty in uniform. At the end of the room stood three men in civilian dress to whom

Dreyfus was not introduced: Armand Cochefert, the head of French political police, who was helping Du Paty; his secretary; and Félix Gribelin, archivist for the Statistical Section. Major Henry was positioned behind a curtain, perhaps because it was felt he had a right to be part of the arrest because he had discovered the *bordereau* but his overt presence would warn Dreyfus that the game was up. Du Paty announced that the general was detained and asked whether Dreyfus would write a note for him since he had cut his finger. As Dreyfus sat in a chair indicated Du Paty sat close by and then watched Dreyfus's hand as he filled out a routine inspection form – perhaps so that the observers could see how he wrote normally – and then as he wrote the message Du Paty dictated. A mirror had been placed so that the men could see Dreyfus's face. The first part of the dictation loosely repeated the opening paragraph of the *bordereau*; Dreyfus wrote this section without any sign of distress. Then when Du Paty dictated the list of documents enumerated in the *bordereau* the wording became almost exactly the same. Dreyfus was in the midst of a sentence when Du Paty exclaimed sharply, 'You tremble, Captain!' Dreyfus was surprised by the commandant's vehement hostility and later denied trembling, but not wanting to contradict Du Paty he merely said that his fingers were cold. Either just before or after Du Paty's exclamation Dreyfus made his first of two mistakes, leaving a small blot on the page. Perhaps this had given Du Paty a pretext, for he later admitted Dreyfus had not trembled and that his remark was intended to shake Dreyfus's assurance. As Dreyfus continued to write Du Paty interrupted again, saying, 'Pay attention. This is important', but Dreyfus simply continued writing. After a few more sentences Du Paty concluded that Dreyfus had 'regained his composure', which apparently had never been lost, and rose from his chair. Gripping Dreyfus on the shoulder he loudly announced, 'I arrest you in the name of the law. You are accused of the crime of high treason.'

'A thunderbolt striking at my feet would not have produced a more violent emotion', Dreyfus later recalled, 'I blurted out disconnected sentences, protesting against so infamous an accusation, which nothing in my life could have given rise to.'[17] Du Paty thought his reaction theatrical, which more appropriately describes his own preparations, and read aloud the text of the law against treason, which stated inaccurately that the punishment was death. He then revealed a revolver that had lain hidden upon the table. The evening before, Mercier had consented to allowing the suspect to kill himself,

no doubt the quickest and quietest solution to the problem of the
traitor. Despite Du Paty's careful arrangements, Dreyfus refused to
confess or commit suicide. 'I want to live to establish my innocence',
he declared, 'I can see that a horrendous plot has been fomented
against me.' Dreyfus mentioned Bonnefond's bad report against him
at the Ecole de Guerre; in the context of Drumont's assertions an
anti-Semitic conspiracy seemed one explanation, but Dreyfus also
believed for a time that the vengeance of some former mistress might
be behind his arrest.[18] Dreyfus was not told of the *bordereau*, but the
four men questioned him in detail about his knowledge of the information mentioned in it. Even as he heatedly denied the charges his
somewhat stiff personality revealed itself, for his interrogators found
him detached and inwardly controlled, his external agitation merely
a polished liar's pose. After two hours of interrogation Henry was
called in to escort Dreyfus to Cherche-Midi, along the way feigning
ignorance of what had transpired in another attempt to trick the
suspect into an indiscreet admission. The cell door closed upon
Dreyfus sometime in the early afternoon of Monday, 15 October
1894. He would not see his family for six weeks, and he would not
be freed for five years.

The dramatic staging for the arrest was not intended to determine
whether Dreyfus was guilty, but to find proof that he was. Such elaborate preparations for a confession or suicide demonstrate that even
Du Paty knew the evidence was weak. Indeed, two weeks later Du
Paty wrote a report that advised Dreyfus be released, not because he
was innocent, but because there was so little evidence of guilt. The
officers of the Statistical Section, the General Staff, and Minister of
War Mercier himself had become convinced of Dreyfus's guilt on the
basis of a flawed investigation rife with hasty assumptions, prejudice,
and a remarkable lack of common sense. Initially hypothetical deduc-
tions quickly became rigid orthodoxy, and discussion of the case led
to a kind of collective certainty among the investigating officers that
overcame any individual doubts. Because of the panic in the General
Staff and Mercier's delicate political situation the inquiry had been
rushed to completion in less than three weeks, preventing balanced
judgement or reasoned assessment of the contradictory evidence.

The lack of interest of the investigating officers in the question of
the alleged traitor's motive is particularly enlightening, revealing
again the powerful subterranean role of anti-Semitism in the initial
investigation. Motive was little discussed among the investigating offi-

cers, and the official prosecution report written on the eve of Dreyfus's trial did not even mention the subject. On one occasion Major Picquart, who would much later become Dreyfus's only champion on the General Staff, asked Du Paty what he thought Dreyfus had gained by his crime. Du Paty replied that the German government had hidden a large payment as an insurance settlement on a recently burned factory owned by the Dreyfus family. This motive was not taken very seriously even by the investigating officers, and was only mentioned in passing at Dreyfus's trial. On another occasion Du Paty argued that Dreyfus acted from prideful anger and frustrated ambition over Bonnefond's negative evaluation, but this, too, was not insisted upon in the indictment or at the trial. It was apparently assumed that every Jew was a potential traitor; how else to account for the treason of a wealthy man whose wife had brought a dowry of 200,000 francs? Anti-Semitism not only helps account for why Dreyfus was singled out among the other *stagiaires*, but provided the reason for a seemingly motiveless crime.

Up to the point that Dreyfus was arrested the lack of evidence, combined with certainty of Dreyfus's guilt – based in part upon anti-Semitic prejudice – had led only to a tendentious reading of the facts. As the next phase of the investigation proceeded, however, the officers of the Statistical Section and Minister of War Mercier himself embarked on a cycle of falsifications and outright felonies in order to assure a conviction and then to prevent an appeal. Already officers of the General Staff, including Chief of Staff Boisdeffre, had attempted – perhaps unconsciously – to influence Gobert's opinion. Mercier had probably lied to Du Paty about the support of the government, and then had issued orders of questionable propriety to Forzinetti. Dreyfus's misfortune was not only that he became a suspect due to errors aggravated by prejudice. He had also fallen under the power of men who would stop at little to assure that their judgement was unquestioned and their 'honour' unsullied.

2

A TRIAL, AN EXILE (1894–1895)

There is a traitor, and it is not I![1]

Alfred Dreyfus was by most accounts a reserved man, but when the cell door closed behind him on 15 October he lost all control. Hurling himself against the walls he shouted with wild rage. 'I screamed with pain', Dreyfus later recalled, 'paced in my cell, banged my head against the walls.' Prison warden Forzinetti calmed him only with great difficulty, writing later that 'he looked like a madman; his eyes were bloodshot, and the things in his room had been upset'.[2] From this time Forzinetti doubted Dreyfus's guilt, and as Dreyfus later noted with gratitude, he did all he could within the limits of his duty to ease Dreyfus's imprisonment. Still, in the first days Dreyfus was illegally treated as a common convict as Mercier had ordered, until Forzinetti was able to have the order rescinded. For three days Dreyfus was kept in the strictest solitary confinement, and the guards had orders not to speak to him under any circumstances; even after that he spoke only with Forzinetti or Du Paty. He had been told nothing of the evidence against him, and was given no news of his wife and family.

Du Paty evidently hoped that the long days in isolation after the sudden arrest and imprisonment would break Dreyfus's will and prepare his guilty conscience for confession. If so he was only half mistaken, for after nine days Dreyfus appeared to be on the verge of a complete mental collapse. Nightmares disturbed his sleep, and he could eat only a thin soup. Eventually Forzinetti, 'anxious as to my own responsibility', disregarded Mercier's orders as well as his own

word of honour and on 24 October reported his fears to his superior, Military Governor Saussier. Not wanting to become involved in
such a murky affair, Saussier told Forzinetti to speak with the chief
of staff. 'You are on the wrong track', Forzinetti told Boisdeffre, 'this
officer is not guilty.' Boisdeffre permitted the prison doctor to see
Dreyfus, and the medications he prescribed appear to have helped,
although Dreyfus was still subject to outbursts and despair.

Dreyfus's wife Lucie Hadamard Dreyfus was in nearly as bad a state.
After the arrest Du Paty had gone to search the Dreyfus home, telling
Lucie only that her husband had been imprisoned. 'One word, a
single word uttered by you and he will be ruined', he cautioned, 'the
only way to save him is by silence.'[3] Later, Du Paty would also tell
her that her silence alone could prevent a great European war. For
the next two weeks Lucie knew nothing of the specific charges nor
even where Alfred was imprisoned; she was alone with her grief and
anxieties, her isolation broken only by a single note from her husband:
'I assure you of my honour and affection.'[4] The wording of even this
brief message, however, revealed Alfred's twin concern for his honour
and his family that will be the obsession of his life for the next twelve
years. As has been aptly stated, the Dreyfus case was also 'a family
affair', the intersection of an entire family's fate with the deepest political and cultural currents of the *belle époque*.[5] The story of the Dreyfus
family during the Affair illustrates one destiny for Jews in France and
Europe at the moment when modern anti-Semitism emerged. If
Dreyfus's family and heritage helped make him a victim, however,
they also powerfully contributed to his eventual vindication.

Alfred Dreyfus's grandfather and great-grandfather had been
pedlars in Alsace, which lies along the ancient Rhine frontier that has
divided Europe since Roman times. In part because it was a border
region it harboured a relatively large Jewish population, many of
whom, like those who would take the name Dreÿfuss, had lived in
the area for centuries. Rioting and violence against Jews erupted at
almost predictable moments, as when a war or crop failure threatened the region. Most recently, Jews were killed or their property
destroyed during the French Revolution and the upheavals of 1848
and 1870–71, as well as on occasions of local crises. And despite the
emancipation of French Jews in 1791 recognizing their legal and
political equality with other citizens, Jews in Alsace also had to
confront the commonplace marks of discrimination that were taken
for granted in the nineteenth century.

When Alfred was born in 1859 his father Raphael was well on the way to earning a fortune as a textile manufacturer in the city of Mulhouse, an important French industrial centre. Like many newly wealthy couples he and his wife Jeanette, who had helped support the household as a seamstress, wanted their children to have advantages they had lacked, and spared little expense in their upbringing and education. As the youngest of six children, including three brothers who could be expected to continue the family business, Alfred from an early age had been marked for more than an industrialist's career. His grandfather and great-grandfather had spoken a local Jewish-Alsatian dialect, and Raphael spoke a form of German as his first language as well as a heavily accented French, which prevented the family from mixing with the best families in the highly chauvinistic town, including the best Jewish families. Even Alfred's elder siblings spoke mainly German, but the younger children learned French. When father Raphael changed the spelling of his family name to Dreyfus the classic process of acculturation was nearly complete.

Looking back at his childhood Dreyfus recalled that 'my first sorrow was the Franco-Prussian War. It has never faded from my memory.'[6] Dreyfus was eleven when soldiers from Prussia and other German states occupied Alsace and Lorraine in 1870, and he vividly recalled German troops marching in the streets of Mulhouse. The memory was all the more powerful because the Dreyfus family felt it had to lock the doors against demonstrators who shouted 'Down with the Prussians of the Interior', meaning in fact Jews, Protestants, and others held responsible for undermining the nation. Under the Treaty of Frankfurt (1871) the German Empire annexed the provinces but residents could opt for French citizenship if they emigrated, leaving behind their homes, businesses, workshops, and farms. For financial reasons Raphael did not believe he could afford to leave, but he did not want his sons wearing a German uniform when they reached the age for obligatory military service. Fortunately Jacques, the eldest son, had already served in the French army and so was exempted from German conscription. This allowed Raphael to arrange for Jacques to run the factory as a German citizen, while he, his wife, and their other children moved across the border to opt for France, joining perhaps 150,000 others from the region who made the same choice. Eventually most of the family received permission to return to Mulhouse, but in their hearts they, and Alfred, remained French and Alsatian rather than German.

The surest mark of Dreyfus's patriotism is that from an early age he made a career in the French army the central goal of his life. After attending preparatory schools in Paris, Dreyfus passed the *baccalauréat* in 1876, an honour attained by only half who sat for the exam. In 1878 he was admitted to the Ecole Polytechnique, the most prestigious of the *grandes écoles*, as the 182nd entrant of 236; when he graduated in 1880 he ranked 32nd. He then entered the army as a second lieutenant and spent the next ten years at various artillery camps and schools. His somewhat rigid manner and unsympathetic exterior did not win him many close friends in these years, but evaluations by his superiors reveal that he was considered intelligent, capable, and extremely hard-working. He also further developed that almost obsessive regard for duty and honour that seems to have been a feature of his personality since his youth. 'The army should not only be a school of duty and honour alone', he wrote at that time, 'but also a school of high morality.'[7] One can only imagine the tortures he endured when he later found his own honour and morality in question; as Dreyfus later wrote to his wife, 'to have worked all my life with the sole aim of wreaking revenge against the infamous ravisher who abducted our beloved Alsace, and to see oneself accused of betraying this country, no, my darling, my mind refuses to comprehend'.[8] In 1890 he entered the Ecole de Guerre (ranked 67 of 81), the highest training institute in the army, which virtually guaranteed its top graduates a place on the General Staff. Even with General Bonnefond's negative evaluation he passed ninth out of the Ecole de Guerre and was made a *stagiaire*; he held the rank of captain and was nearing the end of his apprenticeship at the General Staff when the discovery of the *bordereau* interrupted a promising career.

Having left Dreyfus alone for three days after his arrest, Du Paty finally continued his interrogation on 18 October, giving free rein to his imagination in concocting new ways to bewilder and disconcert the prisoner. He had Dreyfus write and rewrite portions of the *bordereau* while sitting, standing, lying down, with gloves on and off; he placed fragments of photographs of the *bordereau* and Dreyfus's own handwriting in a hat and had Dreyfus attempt to pick out his own handwriting from the rest – and Dreyfus always succeeded; he even sought to surprise Dreyfus in the dark of night by flashing a strong light in his face and peppering him with questions – but Forzinetti refused to allow such dishonourable proceedings. As Dreyfus dryly observed, 'that my brain did not give way during these endless days and nights was not the fault of Commandant Du Paty'.[9] At times Dreyfus contemplated suicide, but his twin concerns for his family and his honour conquered his despair.

Meanwhile, the Statistical Section had employed one of its agents, François Guénée, to ferret out incriminating personal information about Dreyfus. From his sources in gambling dens and brothels Guénée discovered that a man named Dreyfus had contracted large gambling debts and had frequented women of easy virtue who had questionable connections with foreign agents. Another inquiry by the Prefecture of Police established that this was a different individual, but the second report was either accidentally or intentionally mislaid. Guénée's attitude towards his work may be understood by his remark when later explaining the confusion of names, 'this information could refer as easily to Dreyfus as to another. But as he alone was inculpated, everything fell upon him.'[10] Guénée's report weighed heavily with Du Paty and later at Dreyfus's trial. Du Paty went so far as to assert that a man who betrays his wife – and Dreyfus had had a number of adventures both before and after his marriage – is necessarily capable of betraying his country.

In addition, Du Paty consulted three new handwriting experts. One confirmed Gobert's opinion that the *bordereau* was written in a natural hand and was equally adamant in not ascribing it to Dreyfus. Another sided with Bertillon, finding that the *bordereau* appeared to have been written by Dreyfus in a disguised hand; the third determined simply that Dreyfus had indeed written the *bordereau*. The two-to-three division of the handwriting consultants and the lack of evidence corroborating Dreyfus's guilt after three weeks of feverish investigation induced even Du Paty to question whether to proceed with a trial. On 31 October he gave his final report to Boisdeffre and Mercier: while he personally was convinced of Dreyfus's guilt, there might not be sufficient grounds for a court martial. Despite this report by the main investigator, Mercier did not hesitate. Fortified no doubt by the 'scoundrel D' letter from Schwartzkoppen that seemingly implicated Dreyfus, Du Paty's better-informed superior overruled him. On 3 November, after a cabinet meeting in which Mercier again affirmed unequivocally the suspect's guilt, the ministers approved proceeding with an official indictment.

The cabinet's decision to move forward was rendered almost automatic by the sudden eruption of the case of the *bordereau* into the public arena. Up to the end of October the investigation was known only to the highest political and military officials, but on the 29th Drumont's *La Libre Parole* asked cryptically whether it was true that 'an extremely important arrest has taken place by military order'. By 31 October all of Paris had heard that a Jew named Alfred Dreyfus had been accused of high treason. Already Drumont and others began accusing the government of protecting the alleged culprit because he was Jewish. The news of Dreyfus's imprisonment may have been leaked by one of the investigators – perhaps Henry – to induce Mercier to continue the investigation despite Du Paty's well-known doubts, but Mercier needed no prompting because he was convinced Dreyfus was guilty. The unwanted publicity did have the effect, however, of immeasurably raising the stakes. Mercier had previously argued that too many knew of the investigation into the *bordereau* and Dreyfus not to arrest him; the press leaks and public interest in early November exponentially increased the dynamic of internal momentum in the case. From this moment on the Affair developed in two separate but inextricably connected arenas: in the sphere of public opinion and debate, and behind the scenes in the closed world of army offices and backroom politics. At this critical juncture, Deputy Roche on 6 November closely questioned Mercier before the Chamber of Deputies about his demobilization orders of the previous summer. Some predicted the minister of war's imminent fall. The pressure upon the Statistical Section to provide evidence against Dreyfus intensified, both because the investigators were convinced of his guilt, and because Mercier could not afford to have this case end without a conviction.

Who initiated the forging of incriminating evidence is not known, but the first outright illegality – as opposed to the error and prejudice of the initial investigation – dates from November, after this secret case of alleged treason had become a public scandal. Agent Guénée of the Statistical Section edited and embellished several old reports by an informant in the Spanish embassy, the Marquis de Val-Carlos, to suggest that there was a traitor 'in the offices of the General Staff', and that his contact was the military attaché in the German embassy. Val-Carlos himself later denied saying anything contained in the reports. One of the Affair's most careful historians believed it certain that Major Henry and Colonel Sandherr connived at the falsification, and it is indeed difficult to see how Guénée alone could have removed the old reports from the archive and substituted the new ones without being discovered by the archivist Gribelin in what was after all a locked

and guarded office.[11] Very likely the same person or persons responsible for the forged Guénée Val-Carlos reports – and Sandherr seems
indicated – also 'mislaid' the Prefecture of Police report contradicting
Guénée's tendentious and erroneous report on Dreyfus's alleged
double life of gambling and womanizing. It is not at all clear, however,
that Minister of War Mercier, Chief of Staff Boisdeffre, Vice-Chief
Gonse, or even Commandant Du Paty (who was, after all, Boisdeffre's
man, and was not attached to the Statistical Section) knew of the fabrication or of the 'lost' file. The Guénée falsification and other illegalities later helped convince the original inner circle of Dreyfusards,
including Alfred himself, his brother Mathieu, and Joseph Reinach,
that Henry was an accomplice of the traitor, but more likely the officers of the Statistical Section were simply assuring that the verdict
corresponded to their certainty of Dreyfus's guilt. They could not
know that they had taken the first steps towards a new débâcle for
the reputation of the French army.

The emergence of the case into the public arena also meant that it
was useless to make Lucie Dreyfus keep silent. On 31 October she
was finally allowed to telegraph her husband's family, and Mathieu,
Alfred's closest brother, immediately came to Paris. Mathieu, who
himself had sought a career in the army but had failed at the Ecole
Polytechnique, quickly set about organizing his brother's defence. He
was the person most responsible for Dreyfus's eventual exoneration;
the task would consume his life for the next five years. Anti-
Dreyfusards would come to speak of a cabal, of a vast Dreyfusard
syndicate financed with Jewish money and directed against the army
and France, and Mathieu's tireless efforts did include acts of doubtful
propriety such as bribing petty clerks, inspiring false newspaper
stories, and leaking judicial documents. But as the most active Dreyfusard, Mathieu was not so much directing a cabal as defending his
brother with any weapon at hand, calling upon all the friends and
connections his wealthy family could muster. His first thought was to
engage a prominent lawyer whose reputation would give weight to
the defence. He sought out René Waldeck-Rousseau, a future prime
minister and the foremost legal talent of the time, who politely
refused; defending a Jew for treason was not politically wise. Mathieu
then turned to Edgar Demange, who only accepted the case after
looking into the army's dossier and finding no substance to the
charges. Demange was perhaps a better advocate for Dreyfus than
Waldeck-Rousseau would have been, since Demange's reputation for

prudence, his well-known Catholic devotion, and his conservative politics inoculated him against the worst invective of the anti-Dreyfusards. What is more, in 1892 Demange had defended the man who had killed the Jewish officer Armand Mayer in a duel, and so could not credibly be accused of philo-Semitism. Coincidentally, Demange had also defended the man who murdered a former intimate of Dreyfus, and Dreyfus had given written testimony in the case. Having secured counsel for his younger brother, Mathieu also collected a handful of officers and others as character witnesses, including the Grand Rabbi of France, Zadoc Khan. For anti-Semites, d'Aboville's warnings about the efforts of 'upper Jewdom' to save Dreyfus could not have received stronger confirmation.

Throughout November Major Bexon d'Ormescheville prepared the official indictment, seconded by Du Paty. The long delay before the trial provided ample opportunity for the press to indulge in the wildest speculation, *La Libre Parole* being among the most venomous. 'Judas sold the compassion and love of God', it declared, 'Dreyfus has sold Germany our mobilization plans.' *La Croix*, the widely distributed journal of the Assumptionist Order, asserted that 'the frightful Jews, vomited up into France by the ghettos of Germany, can barely jabber our language'.[12] While most of the largest Parisian dailies refrained from such attacks, few questioned Dreyfus's guilt. Mathieu tried to place favourable stories in the less hostile papers, but was usually rebuffed. The nationalist and anti-Semitic press also railed against Mercier, and the allegedly corrupt government more generally, for harbouring and protecting enemies of the nation. Perhaps feeling his position in the government already in doubt, Mercier responded by telling *Le Figaro* that Dreyfus's guilt was 'absolute, certain', a highly improper declaration that publicly committed Mercier's prestige and career to the outcome of the case. This crushing condemnation finally raised the objection in some quarters that, as one paper put it, 'even a Jew had a right to be innocent'. While the content of the *bordereau* remained secret, it became known publicly that the accusation rested upon one contested document, and the generally sober *La France Militaire* went so far as to declare that 'this case has been so awkwardly, so foolishly undertaken'.[13] Attacked from all sides, the actions of Mercier and the officers of the Statistical Section suggest that they grew even more determined that Dreyfus should be convicted.

See page 28

The public uproar surrounding the nascent Affair also caused serious diplomatic complications for the government. The insults and insinuations hurled at Germany in general and his embassy in particular scandalized German Ambassador Count Georg von Münster, who knew nothing of Schwartzkoppen's activities. Both he and the Italian ambassador declared truthfully that their embassies had never had any dealings with Dreyfus, but these denials did not carry much weight with the public or the press. Matters grew serious when Mercier, in his interview with Le Figaro on 28 November, stated that neither Italy nor Austria-Hungary was implicated, which amounted to an official and public accusation against Germany. The government forced Mercier to deny his interview, but several times in late November and mid-December Münster protested both the tone of the French press and the government's timidity in defending the German embassy from unfounded attacks. In order to justify his illegalities Mercier would much later claim that for a moment in late 1894 or early 1895 France and Germany stood at the brink of war. The press furore over the case certainly complicated the government's relations with Germany, but at no time was there a serious breach, much less any threat of conflict. Mercier's legend simply continued the evocation of national security for self-serving purposes begun when Du Paty enjoined Lucie Dreyfus to silence about her husband's arrest, alleging the threat of a European war.

On 3 December d'Ormescheville completed his report outlining the case against Dreyfus, and given Mercier's public declarations it is not surprising that the indictment systematically interpreted the evidence in the most damning fashion for the accused. D'Ormescheville stated as a fact that the traitor had to be an officer of the artillery since three of the documents mentioned in the bordereau concerned the artillery. He dismissed Gobert's conclusion that Dreyfus might not have written the bordereau because Gobert might have some connection to Dreyfus through the Bank of France, while he discounted Pelletier's similar report because Pelletier had not consulted with Bertillon. D'Ormescheville asserted that Dreyfus had a suspicious attitude, 'like one who practises spying', and even his intelligence and knowledge of foreign languages were used against him, as they 'fitted him for the shameful mission'. D'Ormescheville also made much of Dreyfus's alleged trembling when copying Du Paty's dictation, presented d'Aboville's remarks about the similarity of Dreyfus's writing to that of the bordereau as if he were an expert, and asserted that Dreyfus 'frequented several Paris clubs where there is much gambling'. The most damaging evidence in the report came from the three handwriting consultants who agreed Dreyfus wrote the *bordereau*, and from d'Ormescheville's demonstration that Dreyfus could have had access to all the material mentioned in it. Still, the weakness of the case was such that after Demange saw the report he told Mathieu, 'if Captain Dreyfus were not Jewish he would not be at Cherche-Midi'. On the basis of this report Dreyfus was formally charged with having 'delivered to a foreign power a certain number of confidential documents relating to national defence, thus enabling them to undertake a war with France'.

With the end of the inquiry Dreyfus was finally able to consult Demange in person. From his prison cell Dreyfus helped direct Mathieu and Demange's inquiries, piecing together fragments of information gleaned from his interviews with Du Paty in order to suggest possible avenues of investigation for the agents Mathieu and Demange had hired. Given the contested evidence all three were cautiously hopeful of acquittal if the proceedings were public, so that the lack of proof would be apparent to all. Upon Demange's urging Waldeck-Rousseau spoke to President Casimir-Périer about the need for a public trial, but Mercier was known to want a closed trial to preserve the nation's secrets.

The court martial of Alfred Dreyfus opened on 19 December 1894 before a courtroom crowded with spectators. Mathieu had difficulty finding a place to stand at the back of the room; Lucie remained at home. The first question before the seven-officer tribunal was whether to proceed in public, and Demange only had time to state publicly that his client was being tried on the basis of a single document before the tribunal retired to consider the issue. The jury of officers soon returned and declared the trial closed to the public, so that throughout the proceedings only the lawyers, witnesses, and official observers of the Prefecture of Police (the Prefect himself, Louis Lépine) and Ministry of War (Major Picquart) were allowed to attend. Unfortunately the events of the trial must be assembled from the notes and recollections of the various participants, since there is no steno-graphic record. Among the first prosecution witnesses were Du Paty and Bertillon, who apparently made a bad impression with the court. Du Paty asserted that Dreyfus had trembled with guilt when writing the *bordereau* dictated to him the day of his arrest, but since the docu-ment showed no sign of trembling Du Paty then argued that Dreyfus was calm because he had been tipped off. At another point he declared that he could read Dreyfus's agitation from the movement of his foot, and so the defence called a doctor who testified that the beating of the heart cannot be detected in such a manner. Bertillon bewildered some observers when he outlined a convoluted theory that Dreyfus had written the *bordereau* in a disguised hand using the handwriting of his wife and Mathieu as models; for his part, President Casimir-Périer thought Bertillon a madman. Bertillon's assertion that Germany had paid Dreyfus 500,000 francs appeared equally questionable. Several officers testified that Dreyfus had been overly inquisitive, had lurked about offices in which he had no business, or had displayed a suspicious and unreliable character. Archivist Gribelin and Major Henry, both attached to the Statistical Section, used information from the erroneous Guénée reports to paint Dreyfus as a gambler and womanizer. Defence witnesses instead depicted a father, husband, soldier, and man of impeccable behaviour and honour. Demange's courtroom skills appeared to be having their effect, for after several days of testimony Major Picquart reported that 'the affair was proceeding rather poorly', and Prefect of Police Lépine thought Dreyfus would be acquitted.[14]

The officers of the Statistical Section and Minister of War Mercier were evidently just as uneasy about the outcome, for in the last days of the trial they launched two initiatives that appear to have been crucial to the ultimate conviction. First, Major Henry asked a friend on the tribunal to have him recalled for further testimony regarding reports of a traitor in the army. In dramatic tones Henry then told the court that 'an absolutely honourable person' had confided to him in the spring that there was a traitor on the General Staff, and had later identified the officer by name. Turning and pointing to Dreyfus, Henry loudly proclaimed: 'That man is the traitor!'[15] Dreyfus leaped to his feet demanding to know the name of his accuser, while Demange objected to admitting such anonymous evidence. Henry replied that 'there are secrets in an officer's head that even his kepi should not know', and the presiding officer merely asked Henry to affirm on his honour that his allegations were true. It is not likely a simple coincidence that Henry based this theatrical denunciation upon the forged Guénée Val-Carlos report. Henry's use of the forgery in this manner suggests that he knew it was false, because this allowed the allegations in the report to be introduced without producing the document as evidence, or calling Val-Carlos as a witness. Yet Henry did not perjure himself to protect the real author of the *bordereau*, his alleged partner in treason, for his testimony was part of a larger effort.

The second method employed by Mercier and the Statistical Section to influence the verdict was even more blatantly illegal. After the tribunal retired to consider the verdict, Mercier ordered Du Paty to give an envelope to the presiding officer, the infamous 'secret dossier' selected from the archives of the intelligence bureau. The exact composition of the secret dossier is unclear, but it probably contained a biographical sketch detailing Dreyfus's alleged espionage since 1892 and also four supporting documents: a note from Panizzardi to Schwartzkoppen that mentioned 'a friend', presumed to be Dreyfus; Schwartzkoppen's note to Panizzardi referring to 'that scoundrel D' who was also supposed to be Dreyfus; a confused note written by Schwartzkoppen suggesting that a French officer had offered to spy for him; and the falsified Guénée reports alleging that Val-Carlos had warned of a traitor in the offices of the General Staff. The officers of the tribunal were not lawyers, and did not even question this information presented by the minister of war. After they read the secret dossier Du Paty returned it to Mercier. Having suborned justice Mercier then compounded his crime by attempting to destroy the evidence, burning the biographical sketch and ordering Sandherr to disperse the documents within the intelligence bureau's archive. Instead, Sandherr kept the secret dossier intact, perhaps realizing that it would be useful should questions arise about the case in the future. Over the course of the Affair the dossier would grow to well over 1,000 documents, many of them fabricated or falsified.

It is difficult to see why the secret dossier was communicated to the judges in this illegal manner except to prevent its contents from being subject to rigorous examination, as it contained no information damaging to the security of the state. Several years later Mercier said that producing the documents in open court would have run the risk of war with Germany: 'between the safety of my country and judicial crime, I chose the crime'.[16] Yet the *bordereau* was at least as sensitive as any of the documents in the secret dossier, and it was admitted to evidence in the normal manner. Mercier may well have believed he was protecting the security of the state, but he certainly was also safeguarding his own interests. His actions suggest that he knew the secret dossier comprised a falsified document and sought to prevent the defence from discovering that fact, or at the very least that he hoped

Mercier continues coverup.

Most corrupt

to prevent the defence from demonstrating the lack of connection between the documents and Dreyfus.

Communicating the dossier was only the final and most corrupt action in a series of moves intended to produce a conviction despite weak evidence and no known motive. It has been suggested that the nationalist and anti-Semitic press 'forced Mercier into crime',[17] but it was really Mercier who had painted himself into a corner by precipitously arresting an officer and then assuring his colleagues in the cabinet that he had found the guilty party. Mercier's public declaration of Dreyfus's guilt and his tampering with the trial became almost inevitable once he had staked his prestige and career on a conviction.

The secret dossier may not have been decisive, for two of the judges later said it was of only minor importance. One scholar has suggested instead that Dreyfus was the victim of a military political culture in which conformity took the place of thought.[18] Whatever the reason, on 22 December 1894 the court unanimously convicted Dreyfus. Demange broke into tears upon hearing the news, but Alfred, as always so acutely aware of honour and appearances, listened stoically to the sentence: deportation and imprisonment for life. It was the heaviest sentence possible, the death penalty for political crimes having been abolished in 1848. When left alone in his cell, however, Dreyfus again fell subject to a violent fit, pounding his head against the wall and crying that 'my only crime is to have been born a Jew', one of the few times Dreyfus openly associated his case with anti-Semitism. So rigorously logical, with so much faith in reason, Dreyfus could not comprehend that seven fellow officers should find him guilty on such flimsy evidence. His letters at this time are filled with the thought of suicide. 'It seems to me that at times I am the victim of an awful nightmare', he wrote to Lucie the day after the verdict, 'my bitterness is such, my heart so bruised, that I should already have got rid of this sad life if memory of you had not hindered me... I do not fear death, but the thought of contempt is terrible.' And always the same commandment: 'search for the truth; move Earth and Heaven to discover it; sink in the effort, if need be, all our fortune, to rehabilitate my name'. This seemingly cold man found solace only in the love of his wife and the thought of vindicating his honour. Before the trial Dreyfus had written that he was unbowed by his travail, but afterwards his letters reveal a man reeling under a destiny that he could not understand, returning again and again to the same themes, the same concerns: his love for his family, his desire for vindication. His letters also reflected a new anxiety, for he knew another test was ahead: his ceremonial expulsion from the army, the ritual of public degradation. 'I shall draw the force I still need for that awful day from the deep well of your love, from the affection of you all; from the memory of our dear children; from the supreme hope that some day the truth will come to light.'

Meanwhile, the verdict was welcomed by every shade of opinion and hailed in the press. Jean Jaurès, the great socialist tribune, complained in the Chamber that Dreyfus was spared the death penalty only because he was a rich bourgeois Jew; his attack on the government was so intemperate that the Chamber voted a censure with temporary exclusion from the hall. The unanimity of the verdict reassured the republican and moderate press. 'Justice was done, and it was well done', according to *Le Temps*. Yet the anti-Semitic, royalist, and much of the Catholic press knew no bounds. 'Out of France, Jews!' Drumont's *La Libre Parole* proclaimed the day of the verdict, 'France for the French!' *Le Soleil*, the journal of the Orleanist pretender to the throne, declared that 'Dreyfus is a man without a country, a man from a specific race; he is not French'. The verdict swept away any doubts about Mercier, who was hailed as the saviour of French honour. In this atmosphere of hatred the Dreyfus and Hadamard families felt insecure and isolated, some changing addresses, others sending children to safer havens, all remaining indoors as much as possible. Mathieu recalled that acquaintances fled at their approach, 'no hand was held out to us, and every door was obstinately closed'.[19]

The army rejected Dreyfus's appeal, presented by his sister, which repeated a phrase Demange and Alfred himself had used: 'think of the martyrdom of this man whose only crime is to have been born a Jew'. Mercier's attitude may be measured by his proposal to the Chamber that the death penalty be reinstated for treason. He was so convinced of Dreyfus's guilt that after the appeal was rejected he sent Du Paty to try one last time to procure a confession. Du Paty told Dreyfus that if he confessed the conditions of his imprisonment could be lightened, his wife and family could join him in deportation, for example. Du Paty repeated a suggestion he had made several times in the course of the investigation, that perhaps Dreyfus had been trying to trick the Germans by giving them documents of little worth in exchange for more valuable information. When Dreyfus vehemently denied it all, Du Paty cried, 'if you are innocent, then you are the greatest martyr of all time!' 'Yes, I am a martyr', replied Dreyfus, 'and I hope that the future will prove it to you.' No doubt fearing that Du Paty might denature his denials into a confession, Dreyfus later wrote a long account of the interview to Demange, and a shorter note to Mercier affirming his innocence and asking, 'in the name of my honour, which I hope will be restored to me one day', that Mercier continue the inquiry into the case in order to find the real culprit.

On 2 January 1895 Lucie was finally allowed to visit Alfred, some twelve weeks after he had left home the morning of 15 October for what he had thought was a routine inspection. Separated by two metal grills they could not even touch each other's hand; for a moment Lucie had to be supported by warden Forzinetti, while Dreyfus was so overcome that the meeting had to be cut short. 'My limbs trembled beneath me when I went down to meet you... even now my hand is still trembling, I am terribly shaken by our meeting', he wrote moments later, 'I had to hide myself, so that I might cry a little.' Forzinetti was so affected that he convinced General Saussier to allow the two to meet in the future without being separated, although Forzinetti and a guard were always in attendance.

The worst was yet to come. On 5 January 1895 Dreyfus was brought to the Ecole Militaire which he had known well in happier times when attending the Ecole de Guerre. In the courtyard soldiers from every regiment of the Paris garrison had assembled to witness the ceremonial degradation of an officer convicted of treason. At one end of the square stood officials, invited guests, journalists, and those able to somehow procure a ticket of admission. A large crowd pressed against the grills separating the courtyard from the street, crying, 'Coward', 'Judas', and 'Death to the Jew'. Four soldiers with sabres drawn escorted Dreyfus to the centre of the courtyard, where the presiding general awaited on horseback to declare Dreyfus expelled from the army. Determined to keep his head high and bearing erect, Dreyfus shouted to all that could hear, 'Soldiers, they are degrading an innocent man. Soldiers, they are dishonouring an innocent man. Long live France! Long live the Army!'[20] An officer ripped the red stripes and emblems of rank from Dreyfus's uniform, then broke Dreyfus's sword over his knee. Dreyfus was then paraded around the courtyard before the silent soldiers and the vociferous crowd. In front of the journalists Dreyfus cried again, 'You will say to all of France that I am innocent!' But voices from the crowd responded 'Death to the traitor!' and 'Dirty Jew!' Some saw in the stiff posture and toneless voice further evidence of traitorous hypocrisy, but the reporter for the *New York Herald* believed 'Dreyfus had in every respect the appearance of a man protesting against a great injustice'. Theodore Herzl, an Austrian Jew who was even then laying the foundations of modern Zionism, covered the event for a Viennese newspaper. He tended to think Dreyfus guilty, but the race hatred he witnessed only confirmed his desire for a Jewish state as the only way to secure Jews against persecution. Others came to differing conclusions. Reflecting upon the ceremony, Colonel Sandherr remarked, 'this race [the Jews] has neither patriotism, nor honour, nor pride. For centuries they have done nothing but betray.' According to Maurice Barrès, the nationalist author and political figure, 'Dreyfus does not belong to our Nation, and consequently how could he betray it? The homeland of the Jews is where their money draws the greatest interest.'[21] With some of the most literate and cultivated figures of France expressing such sentiments it is easier to understand the blood-lust of the crowd beyond the grills of the Ecole Militaire. Finally, Dreyfus was taken to prison to await deportation. Writing to Lucie that day of those who had insulted him Dreyfus confided, 'in their place I could not have contained my contempt for an officer who I had been told was a traitor. But alas! there is the tragedy. There is a traitor, but it is not I!' Injured to his core by the public humiliation, Dreyfus cried and grieved, wept and railed against his fate. 'I may have the courage of a soldier, but I ask myself have I the heroic soul of the martyr?' The next five years would answer that question.

Dreyfus had shrewdly taken advantage of the degradation ceremony as his only chance to proclaim publicly his innocence. It is therefore cruelly ironic that even before the sun had set that day the rumour of an alleged confession by the traitor had spread across Paris and had even been reported in several evening newspapers.[22] The rumour was based upon a conversation Dreyfus had with one of his guards, Captain Lebrun-Renault, during an hour's wait for the ceremony to begin. Tense with anxiety and dread, in broken phrases interspersed with long silences Dreyfus had evidently told Lebrun-Renault of the *bordereau*, found 'in a cabinet at an embassy', according to one well-informed report of the conversation, and that he had been convicted solely on the finding of three out of five handwriting experts.[23] Dreyfus then mentioned Du Paty's question about whether Dreyfus had tried to trick the agents of this foreign power by giving them some unimportant information in exchange for more valuable secrets.

That Dreyfus in no way confessed is proven by Lebrun-Renault's official account of his day's duties: 'nothing to report'. As garbled
accounts of the conversation circulated in the course of the day,
however, Dreyfus's denial of any contact with enemy agents was
distorted by either malice or mischance into a 'confession' of contacts
with Germany and duly reported as such in the press. That night
amidst the dancing and songs at the Moulin-Rouge Lebrun-Renault
told his tale to all who would listen, including a journalist for *Le
Figaro*. These reports alarmed the army command. The next morning,
Sunday, the imprudent Lebrun-Renault was awakened just after dawn
and brought before Minister of War Mercier. Whatever Lebrun-
Renault told Mercier about what Dreyfus said it did not constitute a
confession, for Mercier ordered Lebrun-Renault not to speak to the
press. Certainly Mercier would have had a very different response if
Lebrun-Renault had reported that Dreyfus made anything like an
avowal of guilt. Later that morning the unfortunate captain, who by
this time must have been extremely concerned about the trouble he
had got into, was even questioned by Prime Minister Dupuy and President Casimir-Périer, who again commanded silence. Mercier was no
doubt worried that if details of the case became public they would
show him in a bad light, such as Du Paty's conversation with Dreyfus
and the contested handwriting evidence. Both he and Casimir-Périer
also had diplomatic complications in mind, since the press reports
gave uncomfortably accurate accounts of the finding of the *bordereau*
and clearly implicated the embassy of the German Empire in espionage against France.

Since the beginning of the case of the *bordereau* Foreign Minister
Hanotaux had sought to prevent any damage to his plans for Franco-
German *rapprochement*. Indeed the very day that Casimir-Périer questioned Lebrun-Renault about the confession story the president had
a meeting scheduled with Ambassador Münster to hear another
protest against the treatment accorded the empire and its diplomats
by the French press. After Dreyfus's conviction for giving documents
to an unspecified foreign power, Kaiser Wilhelm II formally requested
that the French government state publicly what was in fact the truth,
that the German embassy had not had anything to do with Dreyfus.
This put the French government in a difficult situation: since all of
France believed Germany to be involved such a statement would
appear to call the verdict into question, and would certainly open the
government to intense criticism for bowing to the emperor's demands.

The confession story thus came at a particularly disagreeable moment. Casimir-Périer adroitly turned aside Ambassador Münster's immediate concerns, but it still took several long days of negotiations before the two countries could agree on a statement that assuaged the Kaiser's pride and still left room for Dreyfus to be guilty.

These international problems clouded an already difficult domestic scene for the government of Prime Minister Dupuy. Charges of corruption and mismanagement relating to government railway subsidies, divisions within the cabinet, and the ambitions of several ministers led Dupuy to resign after the Chamber refused him a vote of confidence. President Casimir-Périer also resigned, tired of holding an office that bestowed much trouble but little power. On 17 January 1895 a joint meeting of the Chamber and Senate elected Félix Faure as his replacement. Mercier had let his name be placed in nomination as 'the one who had brought the traitor Dreyfus before the Court Martial', but he received only three votes. Like many presidents of the Third Republic, Faure was a somewhat mediocre personality whose main political gift was an imposing exterior. 'The poor gentleman is not a president', cracked the radical-socialist deputy Alexander Millerand, 'but a ballet dancer.' After much wrangling Alexander Ribot then formed his third government, a conservative republican cabinet composed of the usual suspects. The violent press rhetoric and diplomatic complications arising from the case of the *bordereau* had little role in these events, but the change in government did remove Mercier from the Ministry of War, in favour of General Emile Zurlinden. Nationalist critics of the new regime called this 'the revenge of Dreyfus', accusing the government of selling out to the Jews by striking at Mercier and conniving at Dreyfus's escape.

Rather than coddling Dreyfus, prison authorities subjected him to treatment that at times threatened his life. On 17 January 1895 he was dispatched by convict train to La Rochelle, his point of departure for exile. At the station a large crowd, informed of his presence, surged past the police escort and attacked Dreyfus with fists and canes, spitting upon him and shouting 'Death to the traitor! Death to the Jew!' Dreyfus remained at the ancient Saint-Martin de Ré fortress for just over a month, and Lucie had permission to visit him twice a week. She described her husband at their first meeting there as a 'harrowing vision', looking aged and bent by his ordeal, his hair and beard wildly overgrown since he was not allowed a razor.[24] On 27 February, without prior warning of his departure or destination, Dreyfus was bundled on to the convict ship *Ville Saint Nazaire*; Lucie learned of her husband's departure from the newspaper. Aboard the ship Dreyfus was caged like an animal in a steel mesh box, open at first to freezing wind and rain, then after two weeks of travel, exposed to the tropical sun. Only from chance remarks did he learn his final place of imprisonment was to be Devil's Island, seven miles off the coast of French Guiana in South America. New Caledonia was the usual place of exile, but the climate of the Pacific was deemed too mild for the traitor, and escape there too easy. One of Mercier's last acts as minister of war had been to propose a special law sending the traitor to the 'dry guillotine', as Victor Hugo had called Dreyfus's new home.

Devil's Island is a low, rocky fragment of land only a few hundred metres wide and perhaps three times as long. Until shortly before his arrival it had been a leper colony, while two nearby islands housed a prison for the most dangerous convicts and an asylum for the insane. Dreyfus was considered a worse menace than they; he was to be the only inmate in a purpose-built compound on his own island. Preparations were not complete when Dreyfus arrived, so he was locked in a seclusion cell at the prison on the Ile Royale for over a month without being allowed out to exercise or take the air. All the while, and throughout his years of imprisonment, the guards had strict orders not to speak to the traitor lest he try to win their confidence. When transferred at last to Devil's Island Dreyfus was so weak from inactivity and intestinal parasites that he had to be helped to walk.

His new prison was a four-metre square stone building, divided from a small guard room by iron bars. In this way he could be watched day and night by guards who rotated duty every two hours. At first he was allowed to move about freely on part of the island, but was always followed by an armed guard. It was a strange solitary confinement, constrained to silence yet always watched, isolated in his agony yet never alone. And it was illegal, for the families of deportees had the right to join their loved one; Lucie's requests were simply ignored. She somehow prevented their two children from learning the truth about their father's absence on his 'long voyage'. The couple's letters received the closest scrutiny, arriving only after months of delay, and they were forbidden to write of anything but family matters. Throughout his years on the island Dreyfus had no idea that his case had become an Affair.

Suicide no longer haunted Dreyfus so much as fear of losing his mind from the merciless heat, the multitude of insects, the constant surveillance, and the unbroken monotony of the island. He filled his days reading and writing, even reconstructing from memory the principles of calculus. Eventually he assembled a small library, and avidly read and reread the books, journals, and letters that sometimes arrived on the monthly steamer. Still, his unjust arrest and conviction played upon his mind, and he occasionally fell victim to the same fits of outrage and despair that had struck him since his arrest. For long hours he would compulsively draw the same abstract design over and over, as if filling the pages was a way to at least momentarily reassert control over his stolen life. There is an obsessive quality to his diary and letters, too, expressing a near monomania for honour and vindication. Yet when describing his love for his wife this rationalist often achieved a kind of late Victorian eloquence. 'In happiness we do not begin to perceive all the depth, all the powerful tenderness that the deep recesses of the heart hold for the beloved', he once wrote, 'We need misfortune, the sense of suffering endured by those for whom we would give our last drop of blood, to understand its force, to grasp the tremendous power of it.' As the years passed disease and malnutrition rotted his teeth and bent his frame, dissipating his early hopes for rehabilitation, but never fully conquering his spirit.

Dreyfus considered the original cause of his imprisonment a judicial error or an act of idiocy, but he came to emphasize intent more than accident in explaining the gratuitous cruelty of his treatment. 'All my belief in human justice, honesty, and righteousness has completely forsaken me', he confided to Lucie, and he complained of 'human nature, with its passions and hatreds'. Perhaps because he knew his letters were censored, he never wrote about whether he believed his case was influenced by anti-Semitism. He and his family considered him a martyr, but he never identified himself with causes other than abstract justice and regaining his honour. His only flashes of high anger came at the thought of the real perpetrator of the treason, for whom he imagined elaborate tortures similar to those invented for him by the anti-Semitic press at the time of his trial and degradation. Indeed, the lack of a clear enemy, of an understandable reason for his plight, wore him down as much as the dysentery ravaging his body or the spiders that crawled over his skin as he slept.

It was perhaps merciful that Dreyfus did not know of the illegalities perpetrated to assure his conviction, since over the long years on Devil's Island the weight of the iniquity may well have deranged his embattled sanity. And it may have been fortunate, too, that he did

not know that the lack of progress in his judicial rehabilitation was
due to more than want of evidence. Already there had been a subtle
escalation in the level of irregularities the investigators into the case
of the *bordereau* had been willing to contemplate. Up to Dreyfus's
arrest the investigation had encompassed only errors and bad faith
exacerbated by the irrational impulses of prejudice; Mercier's

unlawful orders to Forzinetti regarding Dreyfus's treatment after his
arrest were the most clear-cut, if relatively minor, breach of recognized procedures. After the case had gone public the need to gain a
conviction inspired more serious offences: falsification of the Guénée
Val-Carlos reports, perjury by Major Henry, and finally the premedi-
tated violation of codified legal rights when Minister of War Mercier
himself sent the secret dossier to the trial judges. The next phase will
encompass an even more startling spectacle: French officers framing
a comrade and protecting the real author of the *bordereau* to assure
that an illegally convicted officer remained imprisoned under the most
hellish conditions that the European mind of the late nineteenth
century could devise.

3

THE *PETIT BLEU* (1896–1897)

General Gonse: 'What is it to you if this Jew stays on Devil's Island?'
Lieutenant-Colonel Picquart: 'I will not take this secret to the grave.'[1]

The *bordereau* sent Dreyfus to Devil's Island; a second mysterious document freed him. In March 1896, more than a year after Dreyfus's trial and imprisonment, the 'ordinary path' for pilfering Schwartz-koppen's wastebasket produced another dramatic revelation. It was a note written on the lightweight blue paper Parisians used for sending messages through pneumatic tubes between post offices for hand-delivery to the final address. This *petit bleu* stated, 'Sir, I await above all a more detailed explanation than the one you gave me the other day on the question at issue. Consequently, I ask you to give it to me in writing so I may judge whether I should continue my relations with the firm of R. or not. C.' The officers of the Statistical Section immediately suspected that this was evidence of further betrayal, which brought to mind the traitor Dreyfus. 'It's horrifying', said Captain Lauth, 'is there yet another?' But unlike the *bordereau* this new discovery provided the name of the presumed traitor, for it was addressed to 'Commandant Esterhazy, 27, rue de la Bienfaisance'.

The new chief of the Statistical Section, Lieutenant-Colonel Georges Picquart, who had replaced the terminally ill Sandherr the year before, looked upon the new find with a sceptical eye. For some time the wastebasket of the German military attaché had brought no impor-tant papers, although it was known that French secrets were still being compromised. Picquart suspected that Schwartzkoppen knew his rubbish was being searched; could the *petit bleu* have been planted in order to sow confusion in French counter-intelligence by implicating an innocent officer in treason? The note was not in Schwartzkoppen's hand and bore no return address, which would allow him to deny any knowledge of it if questioned. Indeed, the author of the *petit bleu* has never been discovered, although Schwartzkoppen later acknowledged that it originated in his office. Fearing a trap, and because he believed the investigation of the *bordereau* had been badly mishandled, Picquart proceeded with extreme prudence when making his first inquiries into this evidently new case of treason. A cultivated, intelligent, and somewhat proud man, Picquart was one of the most promising officers on the General Staff. He had passed fifth out of Saint-Cyr and second out of the Ecole d'Etat Major, then served with distinction in Africa, Tonkin, and China. Already Picquart and Dreyfus had crossed paths: Picquart had been one of Dreyfus's professors at the Ecole de Guerre, where he had given him only mediocre marks, and he had observed Dreyfus's trial on behalf of Minister of War Mercier. Ironically, the *petit bleu*, which would lead to Picquart's imprisonment and near ruin, appeared the same month that he became at forty-two the youngest lieutenant-colonel in the French army.

When Picquart became head of the Statistical Section in July 1895, Chief of Staff Boisdeffre had encouraged him to continue inquiring into the treason revealed by the *bordereau*. According to Picquart the general warned that 'it's always possible that the Jews will mount an offensive' to free Dreyfus, and he urged Picquart to 'feed' the dossier of the case with whatever evidence could be had about Dreyfus's motive. In a search for accomplices Picquart maintained the surveillance of Mathieu and others in Dreyfus's family, and ordered agent Guénée to continue looking into the allegations of Alfred's gambling and womanizing, with no results. Over the year since the trial con men, women of the *demi-monde*, and other shady characters had also offered the Statistical Section details of Dreyfus's alleged espionage, none of which was discovered to have any foundation. Picquart remained convinced of Dreyfus's guilt not so much on the basis of evidence known to him, but because he had been told the secret dossier communicated to the trial judges, an act he had encouraged, contained incontrovertible proofs.[2] Thus when the *petit bleu* arrived in the offices of the Statistical Section Picquart had long been immersed in the case of the *bordereau*, but had no reason to link the two seemingly unrelated documents.

In determining whether the *petit bleu* was new evidence of treason or just a trap, Picquart first inquired as discreetly as possible into Commandant Esterhazy's character and lifestyle. An agent set to watching Esterhazy reported that the suspect was in constant need of money to pay for gambling and stock-market losses, and to keep up a mistress, whom he visited nearly every evening before returning to his wife and children. Esterhazy's commanding officer, Curé, who happened to be a friend of Picquart's and could be relied upon to keep silent, reported that Esterhazy had been particularly inquisitive about artillery matters, had copied many documents, and was in general a rogue and an unfit officer. Such information, which in Dreyfus's case had turned out to be false, along with the affirmation of the amateur graphologist Du Paty, had been enough to arrest Dreyfus. Yet Picquart hesitated, even though the *petit bleu* provided clear evidence of Esterhazy's relations with the German military attaché. Certainly Picquart worried that the *petit bleu* might not be authentic, although this fear subsided as other evidence against Esterhazy mounted. And certainly Picquart was a far more prudent and thoughtful investigator than Mercier, Sandherr, or Du Paty. Still, this careful treatment of Esterhazy reveals again the powerful role of anti-Semitism in prompting the many errors and assumptions of the original case against Dreyfus. Not only was Esterhazy not a Jew, he also had well-placed friends, one of whom was the Jewish officer Maurice Weil, whose wife was generally held to be the mistress of Military Governor Saussier. Weil and Saussier were close friends, and Weil was often seen about the general's headquarters. Curé may have been referring to this when he warned Picquart, 'be careful, be prudent. These matters require proofs, and you are dealing with something stronger than you.'[3] Dreyfus had no mentor in the army; Esterhazy could seemingly call upon the highest-ranking officer in France. While all of Picquart's actions in the next several years would prove his dedication to following the truth no matter where it led, he was not foolish, and did not need Curé's warning to know he could act only upon absolute proof. In 1894, after a panicked and slipshod inquiry lasting just two weeks, Mercier had told his ministerial colleagues that he knew who wrote the *bordereau*; in 1896, working patiently and discreetly, Picquart did not even inform his superiors about the *petit bleu* for nearly four months.

While Picquart pursued the new mystery, Alfred's brother and wife sought to resolve the old problem of the *bordereau*. No matter how

much Mathieu and Lucie might point to the insufficiency of the
evidence in the trial, according to French law the only avenue for retrial was to uncover new facts bearing on the case. Mathieu therefore
continued to employ agents and personally looked into many leads.
A variety of odd characters and improbable stories kept Mathieu busy:
a Mme Bernard promised to expose the officer; a retired major
offered his help, for a price; spurious documents arrived in the mail
or were pressed upon Lucie's servants. Mathieu was convinced that
much of this was the work of police trying to entrap the family into
some indiscretion. The continued investigation produced little information, and was marred by a few missteps, such as appealing for aid
from the German Emperor and from Schwartzkoppen, which the
Statistical Section took to be marks of Mathieu's complicity in treason.
In a more inventive moment Mathieu had Schwartzkoppen introduced to a lovely and willing actress, who would presumably pry
secrets from the military attaché at an unguarded moment; a dinner
was arranged, but with no results.[4]

Desperate to make progress, Mathieu even turned to paranormal
intervention, and achieved a remarkable success. Early in 1895 he
made contact with a Dr Gibert, who was conducting experiments in
hypnotism upon a particularly susceptible peasant woman called
Léonie. Under hypnosis Léonie described Alfred, then awaiting trans-
portation to Devil's Island, as wearing glasses. Mathieu believed this
could not be true, since his brother always wore a pince-nez instead.
Yet Lucie soon confirmed that Alfred had requested glasses from the
prison infirmary. At another meeting Léonie said that documents had
been shown to the trial judges without the knowledge of the defence.
Dr Gibert then visited his good friend President Felix Faure, after-
ward telling Mathieu that the president had confirmed the story of
the secret dossier. Mathieu was so impressed by Léonie that he
brought her back to live in his household in Paris, consulting her
daily for specific information and emotional support. Léonie's revelation about the secret dossier – clearly inspired by inside information – was later confirmed by Attorney Demange's colleagues at the
Palais de Justice, where it was widely rumoured that a document referring to 'that scoundrel D' had been shown to the judges in the deliberation room. Whatever the outrage of the Dreyfus family at this
illegal procedure, it was impossible to mount a successful appeal on
such vague evidence, and throughout 1895 and into 1896 Mathieu
continued searching for more definite information.

Mathieu found few supporters in these first months of the campaign for revision of the original verdict. Auguste Scheurer-Kestner, the respected vice-president of the Senate, met with Mathieu but declared he was confident of Alfred's guilt. Others refused even to give Mathieu a hearing. Hoping to keep the case in the public eye, Mathieu also tried to pay for and otherwise encourage newspaper stories about his brother's trial and conditions of imprisonment. As part of this effort he was introduced to an anarchist journalist and Jew, Bernard Lazare, who had written a well-received book on anti-Semitism. Lazare was at first indifferent, declaring that Dreyfus was so wealthy that he needed no help. But he later agreed to write several articles, soon becoming one of the most important voices in the Dreyfusard cause. He and Mathieu disagreed strongly over tactics, however. While the anarchist Lazare wanted to launch a frontal assault against the General Staff and anti-Semitism in French society generally, the moderate Mathieu sought to limit the issue strictly to the particular iniquities of the case. Lazare denounced this traditional prudence among Jews as a 'deplorable habit learned from old persecutions... of not protesting... of waiting for the storm to pass, and of playing dead so as not to attract the lightning'.[5] Indeed, at this time the French Jewish community in large measure stood aside from Mathieu's early efforts to help his brother, either from belief he was guilty or to avoid lending credibility to the anti-Semitic accusation that Jews really were a nation within the nation, loyal to themselves and not France. Grand Rabbi Zadoc Khan convened a secret Defence Committee Against Anti-Semitism in December 1895 in response to the violent rhetoric accompanying Dreyfus's trial, but it was not at first a Dreyfusard committee.[6]

Even aside from the case of Dreyfus, certain politicians, nationalists, and the anti-Semitic press kept up their relentless campaign against Jews and the Republic that protected them. In February 1895 a deputy had proposed a law excluding naturalized citizens, Jews, and the spouses of Jews from public office. In November, *La France* denounced a 'triple alliance' of Jews, Protestants, and Freemasons 'under foreign command which spies upon us in our weakness in order to strike at the first sign of our failure'. And in April 1896 *La France Catholique* encouraged all Catholics to see a 'splendid' painting depicting a ritual murder, in which Jews sacrificed a victim to their blood-lust. In May 1896 the novelist Emile Zola, acting from the hatred of injustice and prejudice that would later make him a leading Dreyfusard, responded with an article in *Le Figaro* entitled 'Pour les

Juifs' in which he scoffed at these primitive anti-Semitic impulses. 'Let
us return then to the depth of the forests', he contemptuously wrote,
'let us begin again the savage war of species against species; let us
devour each other because we do not share the same shout and our
hair is implanted differently.'[7] Lazare also took up the challenge,
metaphorically by a series of articles attacking Catholics for using anti-
Semitism as a weapon in their age-old struggle against reason, and
literally by fighting a duel with Edouard Drumont in June 1896.

However much Mathieu deplored this agitation, he took advantage of it to redirect the public's attention to his brother's plight.
Since no paper was yet willing to publish articles openly advocating
Alfred's innocence, Mathieu had recourse to a subterfuge, paying an
English journalist to publish a story in *The Daily Chronicle* on 3
September 1896 that Dreyfus had escaped. The French government
quickly confirmed by cable from Guiana that Dreyfus was still imprisoned, but the article had several important consequences. The first
was that the Ministry of Colonies ordered a double stockade built
around Dreyfus's hut, which Alfred was forbidden to leave for the
six weeks of the stockade's construction. Worse, each of those nights
the guards clamped his legs to the wooden bed, so that his limbs
bled from chafing against the iron. This was perhaps the most
desperate time in Alfred's entire imprisonment; he felt lost and
without hope, imprisoned despite his innocence and subjected to
almost medieval tortures despite his pleas. When the prison director
complained of this treatment he was replaced by a warden without
such humanitarian scruples. In September 1896 Dreyfus in despair
left off writing in his journal and sent it to President Faure, with a
letter declaring his punishment was 'the most horrendous that has
ever struck a human being'. Yet he regained strength, writing shortly
thereafter to Lucie that 'the terrible sharpness of our suffering must
not denature our hearts'. They must remain the same as they were
before 'this horrible adventure'.[8]

The second consequence of the false escape story planted by
Mathieu was far more salutary, as it did indeed revive the case in the
press. A former minister of colonies found himself under press attack
for having once dared to contemplate allowing Lucie to join Alfred,
as was her right. Drumont's *La Libre Parole* rebutted the charge that
Alfred was badly treated by depicting him living in ease, passing his
time as he pleased. But some articles recalled the ambiguous evidence
against Dreyfus, and *Le Figaro* published an almost sympathetic article,

depicting this 'unhappy man that was thought to be forgotten, gone, lost', writing constantly to his family of his innocence. The nationalist deputy Paul de Cassagnac went so far as to declare in a celebrated article that the incompetence of the government raised the question 'if there were not, over there, on Devil's Island, someone who suffers from a superhuman punishment and who may be innocent! This doubt, alone, is terrifying.' Mathieu's hopes were crowned by success when this article inspired a rejoinder entitled 'The Traitor' in *L'Eclair* on 14 September 1896. It publicly revealed for the first time that the Schwartzkoppen letter referring to 'that scoundrel D' had been secretly shown to the judges. Although incorrect on several details – the 'scoundrel D' phrase was rendered as 'that animal Dreyfus' – the article could only have been written by someone with inside knowledge of the 1894 investigation and trial, as it fully described the original evidence, the dictation scene arranged by Du Paty, and the use of the secret dossier. Most likely Du Paty, Henry, Bertillon, or some lesser player had leaked the information to allay doubts about Dreyfus's guilt; instead it provided the basis for Lucie to petition the Chamber of Deputies to order a new inquiry. Two years after Alfred's arrest the case of the *bordereau* had flared up once again.

   This renewed public discussion came at a critical moment in Picquart's investigation of the new treason revealed by the *petit bleu*. By early August 1896 a double agent had described a traitor passing secrets to the Germans that could easily be Esterhazy, finally giving Picquart the confidence to inform his superiors and recommend an arrest. However, he brought his news directly to Chief of Staff Boisdeffre, rather than his immediate commander Vice-Chief Gonse, since he believed Gonse had lost his head and acted imprudently during the case of the *bordereau*. In addition, Gonse had just written a mildly critical report on Picquart over an unrelated incident in which Picquart had not shown sufficient deference to the general's views. To minimize any suspicion of further insubordination for not having more quickly informed Boisdeffre of the new traitor, Picquart told the chief of staff that he had just uncovered the *petit bleu* and asked that legal proceedings be undertaken against Esterhazy. But Boisdeffre, like Picquart, had learned prudence from the case of the *bordereau*, and simply told Picquart to continue his investigation. Later he explained, 'I don't want a new Dreyfus Affair. We'll retire him, send him on his way; he must be removed without scandal.' That had been Military Governor Saussier's advice in 1894 regarding Dreyfus; iron-

ically, it would be put into effect in 1896 not against Esterhazy, but
against Picquart. Soon after his meeting with Boisdeffre, Picquart
discovered that with the support of Maurice Weil and others, Esterhazy was attempting to be posted to the Ministry of War, and perhaps
even to the Statistical Section itself. The presumed spy certainly did
not lack nerve. Warned of Picquart's suspicions, the new Minister of
War, General Jean-Baptiste Billot, forwarded to him several of Esterhazy's letters of candidacy, and when they arrived Picquart read them
in shock. There, before his eyes, was the same writing he had come
to know so well in the *bordereau*.

Comparing a photograph of the *bordereau* to Esterhazy's letters only
confirmed Picquart's first impression, but to be sure he consulted Du
Paty and Bertillon. He had Captain Lauth take photographs of the
letters, carefully suppressing any indication of their date or author.
Upon examination Du Paty declared, 'it's Mathieu Dreyfus', for he
still believed in Bertillon's bizarre theory that Alfred had forged his
own handwriting in the *bordereau* using his brother's writing as a
model. When put to the same test Bertillon exclaimed, 'it's the handwriting of the *bordereau*!' Told that the letters were written recently,
and thus could not have been by Dreyfus, Bertillon promptly
explained that 'the Jews' must have paid someone to imitate his handwriting. All three, then, recognized in Esterhazy's writing the same
traits as found in the *bordereau*. It then occurred to Picquart that even
if Dreyfus did not write the *bordereau*, he may have been Esterhazy's
accomplice, for there was still the evidence of the secret dossier to be
taken into account. Opening it for the first time on 1 September 1896
Picquart was astonished at its lack of substance; none of the documents proved anything against Dreyfus. But if Dreyfus was innocent,
who indeed was this Commandant Esterhazy who had so boldly
offered his services to Schwartzkoppen in the *bordereau* of 1894, and
now sought a post in the Ministry of War itself?

Marie Charles Ferdinand Walsin-Esterhazy was a most disreputable
character from a most illustrious family. Aged forty-nine in 1896, he
was the son and nephew of French generals; his grandfather was an
illegitimate offspring of the French branch of a Hungarian noble
family. Raised upon visions of his aristocratic forebears, Esterhazy
found himself at eighteen an orphan of modest means and high
expectations. Law school was too expensive, and he failed the Saint-
Cyr entrance exam, foreclosing a career as an officer unless he first
spent long years in the ranks. He turned instead to an alternate path,

joining the Pope's 'Roman Legion' protecting the Papal States from the newly united Italian nation. After six months he became an officer, then transferred to the French Foreign Legion with his rank intact. He was made a lieutenant during the Franco-Prussian War and saw action at Coulmiers, but in the general revision of ranks after the war was reduced to sub-lieutenant, a wound to his pride which appears never to have healed. Still, in the mid-1870s he inherited a small fortune from a grandmother and was able for a time to live the high life of a young, ambitious officer from an aristocratic family, even inflating his name to Monsieur le Compte d'Esterhazy. The intervention of an actress brought him a post at the Statistical Section for three years in the late 1870s. In one of those odd coincidences of which there are perhaps too many in the Dreyfus Affair, he worked there with then-Captain Henry, the same who would play such a spectacular role at Dreyfus's trial and throughout the first years of the Dreyfus Affair. Moreover, it was at the Statistical Section that Esterhazy met Maurice Weil. Most early Dreyfusards believed that Esterhazy and Henry remained close friends and later became partners in treason. But as Reinach himself admitted, there is no material evidence for these assertions.[9] Imagining Henry as co-conspirator explains a few mysteries of the Affair, yet is refuted by powerful evidence and opens up many more problems, not the least of which is that Esterhazy continued his contacts with Schwartzkoppen even after Henry presumably would have warned him of Picquart's investigation.

By the mid-1880s Esterhazy had squandered his inheritance in gambling and dissipation. His officer's pay could not cover his expenses, so for a time he made do with money from a mistress and relative, Gabrielle de Boulancy, but the affair ended badly when she sued him for repayment of loans amounting to 36,000 francs. He calmly countersued, claiming never to have received a sou from her. In 1886, to escape such difficulties, he married Anne de Nettancourt, aged twenty-two to his thirty-nine, the daughter of an aristocratic family who brought a 200,000 franc dowry, most of it inaccessible to him. By the mid-1890s Esterhazy, always in need of money, grew increasingly desperate. Not only was he responsible for the needs of a spendthrift wife, two young daughters, and a small provincial estate, but his mistress, Marguérite Pays, required clothes and an apartment. He had even taken to speculating in the Parisian financial markets. Earlier petty scams such as denying his signature on bills now esca-

lated to large-scale swindles. He bought an apartment building with
loans secured by his wife's dowry, paying far too much in return for
an illegal kick back that only covered his most pressing debts. Yet
whatever Esterhazy's difficulties he had undeniable assets: his warrior
lineage, a facility with words, and his proven attractiveness to women.
He was able to supplement his income with articles on military matters
for several journals and newspapers, notably *La Libre Parole*, and could
call upon supporters of both sexes when in need of protection or
favours in high places. In 1892 an unmerited reputation with a sword,
and perhaps his friendship with Maurice Weil, led him to second the
Jewish Captain Crémieux-Foa in a duel sparked by Drumont's attacks
on Jews in the army. This later gave Esterhazy the pretext to seek
loans from the Rothschilds while at the same time contributing to
France's leading anti-Semitic paper.

What finally prompted Esterhazy to walk into the German embassy
on 20 July 1894 to offer his services will never be known. He was
already accustomed to selling his knowledge to newspapers, to selling
himself to women who could provide money or favours, and to crimes
both large and small. He was in desperate need of money, resented
and despised the army for various petty grievances, and thought
himself entitled to a better fate than the one he had created for
himself; Esterhazy was the victim of a distinguished lineage and a
defective character. According to Schwartzkoppen's memoirs, Esterhazy
at their first meeting told him that dire financial need drove him to
a contemptible proposal: he would supply the German attaché with
French secrets in return for 2,000 francs a month. Fearing some trick
of French intelligence, Schwartzkoppen hesitated, telling the would-be
traitor that he only paid on a per-item basis.[10] He then cabled Berlin
for instructions, and even made a brief trip to see his superiors about
the matter. The Statistical Section intercepted Schwartzkoppen's
encrypted cable, but was only able to decipher several phrases. Known
as the 'doubt... proof' cable, it was later rightly included in the 1894
secret dossier of materials relating to the *bordereau*, but was incorrectly
thought to refer to Dreyfus. Upon Berlin's approval Schwartzkoppen
presented Esterhazy with a set of topics of particular interest to the
German military. Sometime in August 1894 Esterhazy responded to
this request, listing the documents provided in a covering memo.
Schwartzkoppen evidently threw it away as being of little interest,
although he always denied such culpable incompetence. It was this
bordereau that sent Dreyfus to Devil's Island.

Esterhazy appears to have not suspected that another man had been convicted for his crimes, and would not have cared in any case. For his part, during Dreyfus's trial Schwartzkoppen was genuinely perplexed by news reports that the accused had betrayed secrets to Germany, but over the next two years kept up sporadic contacts with Esterhazy. The only surviving note passed by Esterhazy is a rambling account of naval affairs based upon close attention to newspapers and the dinner conversation of other officers.[11] Those investigating the *bordereau* were simply wrong to assume that it must have been the work of an officer on the General Staff with access to highly important secrets, another of the long series of errors that contributed to Dreyfus's conviction. By the early spring of 1896 Schwartzkoppen had decided to break with Esterhazy, as the information he provided did not merit the risk of exposure. Indeed, along with the *petit bleu*, in which Schwartzkoppen asked Esterhazy for further information, another draft of a note was recovered from the embassy wastebasket telling Esterhazy that the cost of their relations was out of proportion to the benefits.[12] The *petit bleu* was never sent, but evidently the final version of this second note was. Ironically, the *petit bleu* unmasked Esterhazy at the very moment Schwartzkoppen was breaking off their association, which explains why Picquart's agents found no further evidence of treason. And doubly ironic is the fact that Esterhazy's letters soliciting a post at the Ministry of War – no doubt in order to gain access to more important secrets so he could renew his contacts with Schwartzkoppen – provided the handwriting evidence proving Esterhazy had written the original *bordereau*.

In early September 1896 Picquart informed his superiors that Esterhazy and not Dreyfus had written the *bordereau*. From that moment on Chief of Staff Boisdeffre and Vice-Chief Gonse stonewalled his investigation. Citing the threat of leaks and the possibility of casting suspicion upon an innocent man, objections never heard in 1894, they refused to allow Picquart to have Esterhazy's letters, the *petit bleu*, and the *bordereau* examined by handwriting experts. Picquart suggested laying a trap by sending a message to Esterhazy at his country house couched in terms similar to the *petit bleu* and demanding that he return to Paris at once; permission denied. Yet the generals would not authorize arresting or questioning Esterhazy without further proofs. 'Keep the two affairs separate', Gonse told Picquart, a nonsensical request since the *petit bleu* and the *bordereau* so clearly related to Esterhazy. It may be that the generals

truly believed the evidence against Esterhazy was inconclusive, just
as they believed Dreyfus to be guilty, but there were also other considerations in play. 'It's a matter that can't be reopened; General
Mercier, General Saussier are involved', Gonse told Picquart in mid-
September, 'what does it matter to you if this Jew stays on Devil's
Island?... If you don't tell anyone, no one will know.' Picquart claims
to have been dumbfounded by this attitude, replying, 'General, what
you have said is abominable; I don't know what I will do, but I will
not take this secret to the grave'.[13] Gonse evidently hoped to avoid
the scandal that would erupt if Mercier's illegal usage of the secret
dossier were confirmed, and if Saussier's connections with the suspicious Maurice Weil, friend and perhaps accomplice of Esterhazy,
became public knowledge. For Boisdeffre, too, the secret dossier was
apparently the crucial problem, because when Picquart mentioned
reading it, Boisdeffre blurted out, 'why wasn't it burned as we had
agreed?' Yet he and Gonse were also protecting themselves, for they
had fully participated in the iniquitous trial of 1894. More than the
honour of other officers, more than the honour of the army itself
was at stake; their own careers could be endangered.

Picquart's stubborn campaign to re-examine the case of the
bordereau began just days before the *L'Eclair* article of 14 September
1896 publicly revealed the illegal usage of the secret dossier. This
conjuncture is vital for understanding the actions of Boisdeffre and
Gonse, for they suspected that Picquart had leaked the article, having
fallen victim to a well-orchestrated Jewish plot to free Dreyfus.
Officers of the Statistical Section and the General Staff knew of
Mathieu's tireless efforts to find evidence and supporters to help his
brother. They had long believed that the Dreyfus family, allegedly
aided by a vast network of Jewish supporters, was attempting to
subvert justice. Archivist Gribelin of the Statistical Section later testified that as early as June 1896 he suspected that Picquart wanted to
substitute Esterhazy for Dreyfus.[14] The staff of the Statistical Section,
convinced of Dreyfus's guilt, could only see this as the result of folly
or corruption, and spoke among themselves of Picquart's obsession
with the *bordereau* and the *petit bleu*. Two of them later testified under
oath that Picquart had said in a moment of frustration that 'those on
high' were not listening to him, 'but if they don't want to move, I
know very well how to force their hand', words vehemently denied
by Picquart. And just before the *L'Eclair* article appeared Picquart
had warned his superiors that Mathieu was preparing some new

public scandal, and advised that the army ought to take the initiative in divulging the truth. It was, then, perhaps understandable that Boisdeffre and Gonse suspected Picquart. To prevent useless and possibly embarrassing questions about how the verdict of 1894 had been obtained, and to avoid potentially damaging revelations about their own role, Boisdeffre and Gonse sought to silence an officer they believed had been suborned by either forgery or bribery. This is why the case of the *bordereau* did not end in the autumn of 1896 when Picquart concluded that Esterhazy was guilty. Instead, it mushroomed over the next three years into the Third Republic's most serious political crisis.

In addition to the prompting of self-interest, Boisdeffre and Gonse may well have been convinced in good faith that Picquart had been duped into helping Dreyfus. For beyond the generals, and probably unknown to them, Major Henry of the Statistical Section, and perhaps others, was working very hard in the autumn of 1896 to shore up the verdict of 1894. Picquart's announcement to his superiors that Esterhazy had written the *bordereau* unleashed a bewildering torrent of forgeries, press leaks, and anonymous letters. For example, at this very moment the Ministry of Colonies found a message written in invisible ink between the lines of a letter addressed to Dreyfus and signed illegibly 'Weyler' or 'Weiss'. 'Impossible to decode last communication; resume former procedure for response', it read, 'indicate exactly where are the documents concerned and the combination for the strongbox. Actor ready to move at once.' The message was so maladroitly hidden that it was clearly intended to be discovered, but Picquart was alarmed that Mathieu may have bribed someone – the 'actor' – into posing as the author of the *bordereau*. He had Bertillon make an exact copy excluding the hidden writing and sent it to Dreyfus to see if the prisoner tried to heat the letter to activate the invisible ink. Dreyfus was simply puzzled by this letter from an unknown person and put it away with his other correspondence. Another letter of October 1895, just after Dreyfus had appealed to the president of the Republic for justice, also contained an invisible message, but it was not discovered until 1899. Both messages referred to difficulties in communication and to documents, and were evidently the work of someone who hoped to show that the prisoner was indeed a traitor. Henry is the prime suspect, but it may have been Guénée or some other minor player with a stake in the case.

Certainly it was Henry who changed a note from Schwartzkoppen to Panizzardi collected by 'the ordinary path' that said 'Dubois has brought me many interesting things', to read 'D. has brought me many interesting things', providing yet another brick in the edifice of Dreyfus's guilt. Then came the leaks to *L'Eclair* in September 1896 about the 'scoundrel D' letter and other details of the 1894 trial. Based upon a report by Guénée, Picquart believed that this was another of Mathieu's gambits, but the fact that the article changed the initial for Dreyfus's full name and other inaccurate but damning details in the article suggests instead that Henry or someone else sought to incite public opinion against the condemned man. Years later an investigation into whether Du Paty wrote the article brought no indictment. Generals Boisdeffre and Gonse, perhaps prompted by Henry, suspected Picquart.

Nor was Picquart obeying Gonse's injunction to 'keep the two affairs separate'. Boisdeffre, who respected and admired Picquart, tried to bring him around by hints and suggestions. The two went riding in the middle of October 1896, and Boisdeffre again argued that the *bordereau* had nothing to do with the *petit bleu*. Indeed, Boisdeffre apparently believed the *petit bleu* to be a forgery, perpetrated by Dreyfusards in order to implicate an innocent officer. But Picquart answered every point, making it clear that he still thought Dreyfus innocent and Esterhazy guilty. Later that month Guénée reported to Gonse that Picquart was investigating Du Paty's commentary of 1894 on the secret dossier. Picquart had also asked probing questions about Guénée's (falsified) 1894 account of Val-Carlos's denunciation of a traitor on the General Staff, which had been the basis for Henry's spectacular accusation during Dreyfus's trial. Picquart was evidently determined to continue his inquiries, and was beginning to question every aspect of Dreyfus's conviction.

Having failed to discourage Picquart's curiosity, Boisdeffre simply applied to Picquart a version of the strategy he had originally suggested for Esterhazy: on 27 October 1896 Picquart was told that he would soon be sent to inspect intelligence operations on the eastern frontiers. 'I knew immediately that it was done to keep me at a distance', Picquart later said. General Boisdeffre argued, and seemed genuinely to believe, that sending Picquart away was in the best interest of his misguided friend, that Picquart was too wrapped up in the case to see the issues clearly. Henry tried to warn off Picquart, telling him the story of an officer who justly accused the son of a colonel of theft; the officer was broken, the thief went free. In other words, causing trouble for such well-connected persons as Esterhazy and Weil might not be wise. Soon, however, Henry came to believe that Picquart had been won over by Mathieu's money and had become, not a mistaken officer, but a dangerous enemy. Henry grew increasingly certain that he had never received the pieces of the *petit bleu* from the cleaning woman of the German embassy; how, then, had it come to Picquart, unless he had forged this odd document that gave not only the name, but the address of an alleged traitor? Seeing Picquart talking with agents while the secret dossier lay unopened upon his desk, he thought Picquart was divulging secrets, and although he was Picquart's inferior in rank, he asked Gonse to retrieve the secret dossier from Picquart.

Determined to provide further proofs for his troubled superiors, no doubt convinced that the *petit bleu* was a forgery, Henry once again decided to fight fire with fire. On 1 November 1896 he rearranged the pieces of some letters from Panizzardi to Schwartzkoppen collected by 'the ordinary path', forging parts where necessary, to create a note stating, 'I have read that a deputy is going to raise questions about Dreyfus. If Rome is asked for further explanations I will say that I never had contact with the Jew. It is understood. If you are asked, just say that, because it must never to anyone be known what happened with him. Alexandrine.' The forgery, known as the 'false Henry', was carefully constructed; Henry had even included an ungrammatical phrase, as if it were written by the Italian military attaché. But the bull-chested, bull-headed soldier had made an error that when discovered two years later would literally be fatal for him, and would do more to bring about a revision of the case than any act of the most enthusiastic Dreyfusard. He had mixed pieces of two types of paper, one with very faint blue-grey lines, the other with similarly faint reddish-purple lines, and what is more, the line spacing was not the same. These differences were only discovered in 1898, and in the meantime the 'false Henry' constituted a powerful new weapon in the campaign to defend the verdict of 1894.

Bypassing his superior Picquart, Henry brought his creation directly to Gonse and Boisdeffre. They then went to Minister of War Billot, not with the original 'false Henry', but with a somewhat fuzzy photograph authenticated in writing by Henry, Lauth, Gribelin, and Gonse. All agreed to withhold the new find from Picquart because he was already under suspicion of colluding with Mathieu. This unusual

procedure has suggested to some that the entire Statistical Section
knew of the forgery, but it is more likely that Henry was simply able
to convince his colleagues that a document of such importance
required special handling.[15] If everyone at the Statistical Section knew
of the forgery, why did they not simply destroy or 'lose' the original,
something virtually impossible for Henry to do on his own? Had this
been done, Dreyfus would never have left Devil's Island. The
discovery of the *petit bleu* in 1896 had set in motion a momentarily
successful defence of Dreyfus's conviction, but when the 'false Henry'
was revealed to be a forgery in 1898 the edifice constructed to maintain the verdict of 1894 collapsed.

Mathieu Dreyfus knew nothing of these events behind the scenes
in the army, but was well satisfied with the continuing public rever-
berations of his false story of Alfred's escape. Not only had the *L'Eclair*
article of 14 September 1896 provided the basis for Lucie's petition
for revision, but the renewed press interest in Dreyfus prompted the
nationalist deputy André Castelin to announce his intention of questioning the government's lax handling of the traitor and his apologists once the Chamber reconvened in late October. The 'false Henry'
was a direct response to this threat, intended to bolster Minister of
War Billot's confidence in the verdict of 1894. Yet Mathieu was as
careful as Henry in timing his manoeuvres. Indeed, in the four years
after the 1894 trial the two were locked in a kind of asymmetrical
duel, for while agents of the Statistical Section knew of Mathieu's every
move, Mathieu was acting almost wholly blind.

Coinciding with Castelin's interpellation, in early November
Mathieu had 3,000 copies of a pamphlet by Bernard Lazare, *A Judicial Error: the Truth about the Dreyfus Affair*, distributed to nearly every
French newspaper and politician, as well as many army officers,
professors, and other notables. Lazare had written the pamphlet
earlier, but hurriedly rewrote it to respond to the inaccuracies and
accusations in the *L'Eclair* article. Bowing to Mathieu's wishes, Lazare
did not denounce anti-Semitism so much as the injustice of Dreyfus's
trial. *A Judicial Error* gave the exact wording of the *bordereau*, which
had been incorrectly rendered in the *L'Eclair* article, and also
correctly noted that the 'scoundrel D' document, publicly divulged
for the first time in that article, did not give Dreyfus's full name, but
only an initial that could apply to anyone. Otherwise, Lazare pointed
out, why had the army not arrested Dreyfus when that document
was intercepted, rather than waiting several months until the

bordereau came to light? Drawing upon Alfred's copy of his indictment, procured through warden Forzinetti, Lazare demonstrated
that the *bordereau* was the only document presented during the trial,
and that the five handwriting experts were nearly evenly divided on
the question of whether Alfred wrote it. Lazare then denounced
Mercier's usage of the secret dossier, concluding, 'Captain Dreyfus is
innocent and his condemnation was obtained by illegal means: the
trial must be re-opened'.

Most of the press ignored Lazare's pamphlet as an apology for a
traitor, but on 10 November 1896 *Le Matin* responded with an article
that even while affirming Dreyfus's guilt, provided another piece of
evidence for Mathieu's campaign for vindication. To bolster its claims
to accuracy, *Le Matin* published for the first time an exact copy of the
bordereau, based upon a photograph obtained from one of the experts
at the 1894 trial. Mathieu then reproduced the *bordereau* in poster
form, hoping that someone would recognize the writing and
denounce the real culprit. Several people did in fact recognize Esterhazy's writing, but none stepped forward at the time. Ironically, one
was the son of Grand Rabbi Khan, who was working for a lawyer
trying to collect a debt from Esterhazy. When he brought a copy of
the *bordereau* and several of Esterhazy's letters to his father, Rabbi
Khan did not see any similarity, and admonished his son for
suspecting the man who helped Jews in their duels with Drumont:
'There is no officer more deserving of sympathy and respect than
Commandant Esterhazy!'[16]

At just this moment, on the eve of Castelin's intervention in the
Chamber, someone – possibly Henry – thought it best to put Weil and
Esterhazy on their guard. On 13 November Weil received a note signed
'Pierre' and addressed from Paris, stating 'A friend informs you that
M. Castelin, in his interpellation, is going to accuse Esterhazy and you
of being Dreyfus's accomplices'.[17] Henry seemed convinced at this time
that Castelin was working covertly with Mathieu, and may have
thought Weil and Esterhazy, whom he had known when they were
posted to the Statistical Section, ought to be prepared for any inconvenient questions about their ties to General Saussier. In any event,
the publication of the *bordereau*, and the warning to Weil (who sent
the note to Minister of War Billot), constituted the last straw for Vice-
Chief Gonse. He suspected that Picquart had leaked the photograph
of the *bordereau* to *Le Matin*, so he presented Billot with an ultimatum:
either Picquart must go, or Gonse would resign. Fortified by the 'false

Henry' and convinced that Picquart had become a loose cannon, Billot
sided with Gonse. On 14 November Billot called Picquart to his office,
showed him the 'Pierre' note and upbraided him for allowing his
inquiry to be compromised. Billot feigned shock that Picquart had
opened Weil's letters, a common practice in the Statistical Section, but
his indignation may indicate a particular concern with protecting
General Saussier's personal life from scrutiny. He then summarily
ordered Picquart, still officially head of the Statistical Section, to leave
Paris within forty-eight hours for his delayed inspection of intelligence
operations on the French borders. Gonse intended to have him
dismissed at an appropriate moment.

Castelin's interpellation in the Chamber need not have worried
Minister of War Billot. Far from being Mathieu's accomplice, Castelin
on 18 November 1896 denounced Jewish attempts to buy Dreyfus's
freedom and criticized the government for not bringing charges
against Lazare for publishing confidential documents. Neither Billot
nor Prime Minister Méline wanted to pursue Lazare, who publicly
dared the government to indict him, as this would inevitably reopen
the case of 1894. Just over a year later Emile Zola would adopt the
same strategy as Lazare, with far more consequential results. The
government parried Castelin's request by supporting a vague resolution declaring it would look into the matter. Billot for his part declared
that the 1894 verdict conformed to the rules of military justice,
although he must have known this to be a lie. Castelin's intervention
and Billot's declaration momentarily ended interest in the case of the
bordereau; two weeks later the Chamber's commission on pardons
rejected Lucie's appeal for revision. With the Chamber satisfied,
Picquart at a safe distance, and the press quiet, by late 1896 Billot,
Gonse, and Henry – each in his own way – appeared to have resolved
the complications unleashed by the discovery of the *petit bleu* the
previous spring.

It would be almost another year before the case of the *bordereau*
again agitated the press and public. Over the course of 1897, however,
developments along several relatively independent tracks finally
converged to reveal Esterhazy's name to the small band of early Dreyfusards led by Mathieu. It was his public denunciation of the traitor
in November 1897 that constituted the real beginning of the grand
Affaire that shook France to its core. The first track was Mathieu's
undaunted struggle on behalf of his brother, which threatened at any
time to unlock secrets that could destroy careers, undermine confi-

dence in the army, or even destabilize the governing coalition. The second was the continuing campaign within the General Staff and Statistical Section against Picquart, provoking him to defend himself with the truth about who really authored the *bordereau*. Picquart's measures for self-protection then combined with Mathieu's efforts to convince a powerful politician, Vice-President of the Senate Auguste Scheurer-Kestner, of Dreyfus's innocence, opening an avenue for revision at the highest levels of the government. The final track for reopening the case of the *bordereau* was the behaviour of the traitor Esterhazy himself, whose attempts at self-preservation only further enmeshed him in a web of his own weaving.

The brash Esterhazy does not appear to have been worried by the *L'Eclair* article of September 1896 publishing the text of the *bordereau*, but the *Le Matin* article of November providing a facsimile of the incriminating document had a very different effect. 'I don't know what's wrong with him; he's wild [*vert*]', reported an agent of the Statistical Section after watching Esterhazy fly madly about Paris, from his bank, to newspaper offices, to Weil's apartment, and back again. At just this time Weil received the 'Pierre' letter warning that Castelin was going to denounce him and Esterhazy in the Chamber. When Esterhazy saw the note he grew tremendously agitated and told Weil that they must stop Castelin at all costs, but offered no explanation. Esterhazy reportedly admitted to his friends at *La Libre Parole* that 'there was a terrifying resemblance between my writing and that of the *bordereau*', concluding in his melodramatic way that when he saw the facsimile, 'I thought I was lost.'[18] But Esterhazy soon regained heart, for he had not been arrested and aside from the 'Pierre' letter there was no reason to believe he was even suspected. Thus the impoverished adventurer, apprentice con man, and one-time spy boldly maintained his search for a place in the Ministry of War or Statistical Section. Oddly, Military Attaché Schwartzkoppen seems to have had more scruples for the plight of the prisoner on Devil's Island, for he later wrote of the pain he felt upon realizing that Dreyfus had been convicted for the crimes of his former agent. Schwartzkoppen's duty and self-interest forbade doing anything more than confiding in his partner Panizzardi, although the two once again let it be known among diplomatic circles that they had never had any dealings with Dreyfus.

Even though Esterhazy was not arrested, the scrutiny of his personal life occasioned by Picquart's inquiry further undermined

Esterhazy's precarious position. Already facing bankruptcy and ruin, his career now deteriorated and collapsed, leading the high-strung officer to indulge in opium to calm his nerves when he needed to sleep. In the autumn of 1896 he resorted to stealing thousands of francs from his nephew Christian under the pretext of investing it at a guaranteed 20 per cent interest rate with his alleged friends, the Rothschilds. In late 1896 and early 1897 Esterhazy spent much time and energy trying to find the twenty-year-old a rich wife, who very likely was intended to be the beneficiary of similar financial services. Esterhazy bought a partnership in a brothel with Christian's money, supplying in addition the names of some 1,500 potential clients. These activities were not unknown to the General Staff. When a deputy approached Minister of War Billot for a post on Esterhazy's behalf, Billot told him flatly that he should not concern himself with a man of such scandalous habits. Even Weil broke with him in early 1897, perhaps because he suspected him of writing the *bordereau*, but it is more likely that Saussier had informed him of Esterhazy's swindles or that he had grown tired of soliciting favours on his behalf.

In March 1897 Esterhazy's commanding officer, prompted by Billot, bluntly told Esterhazy that he should resign from the service. Esterhazy, who suffered from tuberculosis, was given medical leave until August, when he finally resigned his commission. By this time Esterhazy had realized that Minister of War Billot was behind his difficulties, and believed that Major Henry had connived at his disgrace. In the spring of 1897 he orchestrated a press campaign with the anti-Semite Drumont of *La Libre Parole*, the acerbic Rochefort of *L'Intransigeant*, and the nationalist Cassagnac of *L'Autorité* against Billot and the allegedly incompetent senior officers of the army more generally. An article in *L'Intransigeant* that may well have been written by Esterhazy denounced Saussier as a worthless old man, Boisdeffre for being 'ignorant as a carp', and Henry, acting head of the Statistical Section, for not knowing a word of any foreign language. Cassagnac reproached the Republic for naming generals who were either 'imbeciles or simply courtesans'.[19]

These attacks could only add to the desire of the General Staff to prevent Picquart from raising a scandal over the *petit bleu* and Dreyfus's conviction. While Picquart was sent wandering from Chalons-sur-Marne to Besançon, to Dijon, to Grenoble, and then to Marseilles, Henry continued the surveillance of Esterhazy and Weil, but also began compiling a dossier on Picquart. He was, after all, suspected of leakages to the press, and in the eyes of Gonse and Henry must have fabricated the *petit bleu*, which Henry now denied ever receiving from the cleaning woman who emptied the German embassy's wastebasket. Henry was genuinely mistaken, but his conviction that Picquart was dangerous evidently led him to ever more fabrications, and this time not just to support the 1894 verdict against Alfred Dreyfus, but to undermine his superior. He began by scratching out part of Esterhazy's name on the *petit bleu*, then recopying it, to make it appear that Picquart had written Esterhazy's name on the document. To his later discomfort, Henry forgot that the unretouched *petit bleu* had been photographed.

In November 1896 Henry intercepted a letter to Picquart – for his mail was now being read for evidence of complicity with the Dreyfus family – from a friend named Ducasse who was a sometime agent for the Statistical Section. Ducasse had a taste for elliptical phrases and odd nicknames, and his letter, written partly in Spanish, partly in French, read in part, 'The great work is complete; Cagliostro has become again Robert Houdin', and 'The demi-god asks the countess every day when he can see the good Lord J'. Henry might reasonably have been alarmed at this odd message, but his actions suggest he well knew that the first phrase referred to work done for the Statistical Section, while the second sentence referred to acquaintances at a salon frequented by Picquart and Ducasse. For rather than using the note against Picquart, or investigating Ducasse, the letter became the basis for a forgery much more damning to Picquart. Signed 'Speranza', this latest forgery read in part, 'our friends are filled with consternation, your unfortunate departure has altered everything. Hasten your return, quickly, quickly! The holidays being very favourable for our cause, we are counting on you for the 20th. *She* is ready, but *she* cannot and will not act until after having spoken with you. The demi-god having spoken, we will move.' The similarities between this almost laughably cryptic wording and the phrase 'Actor ready to move at once' found in the 'Weyler' note in invisible ink sent to Dreyfus just six weeks before – which in turn appears connected to the message in invisible ink sent to Dreyfus in October 1895 – suggests that Henry was behind the earlier fabrications as well as this one. Henry showed Gonse the 'Speranza' letter on 15 December, and upon Billot's approval Picquart was immediately ordered to Tunisia, ever further from Paris.

Given the implications of the 'Speranza' forgery, it is unclear why Billot, Boisdeffre, and Gonse did not take further measures against Picquart. Perhaps they were unsure about the authenticity of the letter, or sought to accumulate more evidence against Picquart, or simply hoped to stifle the whole matter quietly because doing otherwise would force re-examination of the 1894 trial. Alternatively, Gonse for one may have known the letter was a fraud, and may have only wanted to use it to neutralize Picquart without provoking the outright struggle and scandal consequent to an arrest or interrogation. And it is not impossible that Henry was himself duped by someone who sent the 'Speranza' note in order to protect the 1894 verdict and strike at Picquart, who was not universally liked in the Statistical Section. Guénée, for example, is known to have been producing other false documents at about this time. In late November 1896 he wrote several reports alleging that Picquart had shown his friend and lawyer Louis Leblois the *petit bleu*, which Picquart later vehemently denied. These reports made their way into Henry's dossier on Picquart. Yet all indications are that Henry himself perpetrated the 'Speranza' fraud, and it is certain that transferring Picquart to Tunisia corresponded to his interests. As long as Picquart remained away, Henry would run the Statistical Section. If Picquart were officially dismissed, however, another officer might be brought in, since Henry's lack of formal education and ignorance of foreign languages rendered him unsuitable to formally hold such an exalted post.

Although Gonse and Henry continued writing friendly letters to Picquart, as winter gave way to spring he grew increasingly resentful of his treatment and the only half-hidden surprise of officers when they found the head of the Statistical Section personally looking into matters of minor importance. At first he felt merely humiliated, but in April 1897, after a brief visit to Paris, this coldly rational man dramatically appended a codicil to his will, writing on the envelope that in the event of his death it was to be delivered to the president of the Republic 'who alone is to know about it'. Picquart outlined his inquiry into the *petit bleu* proving that Esterhazy, 'and perhaps his friend Weil', was the real German agent. If Picquart had earlier thought Billot, Boisdeffre, and Gonse misguided in their refusal to believe him, his testament demonstrates that as of spring 1897, at least, he thought they knew the truth and simply wanted to avoid responsibility for the 1894 trial, 'conducted with an unheard of carelessness, with a preconceived idea that Dreyfus was guilty, and with contempt for legal forms'. He even described the contents of the 1894 secret dossier, affirming 'it is this dossier, *not communicated* to the accused and his lawyer, that led to Dreyfus's condemnation'. Like Bernard Lazare's pamphlet of November 1896, Picquart's testament already contained some of the high rhetoric and elevated sentiments that would characterize Dreyfusard discourse at the height of the Affair, stating that he wrote 'in the interest of truth and justice'. Certainly Picquart sought truth and justice, but the timing and manner of his subsequent acts suggest as well that he was at least equally concerned with protecting himself from the manoeuvres of his colleagues in the Statistical Section.

In May 1897 Picquart's sense of humiliation at his position finally overcame his stoic dignity. Tired of the charade that he still ran the Statistical Section, Picquart sent back one of the reports Henry still forwarded to him with the notation, 'Let it at last be known that I have been relieved of my duties, or that I am no longer in office. I have no reason to be ashamed by that. What I am ashamed of are the lies and mysteries that my true situation has led to over the last six months.' This prideful reference to 'lies and mysteries' by a man suspected of complicity with treason seems to have touched a nerve in Paris, for after consulting Gonse, Henry responded with a letter of menacing formality. 'As the result of an investigation conducted here', Henry wrote, 'the word "mystery" may be applied to the facts related below', each of which had the unmistakable air of an accusation against Picquart.[20] First was 'the opening of letters unrelated to the Service for reasons no one here has understood', a reference to Picquart's interception of both Esterhazy and Weil's correspondence. Second, Henry charged that a proposition had been made (meaning, by Picquart) to induce two unnamed members of the Statistical Section (Lauth and Gribelin) to state that 'a classified document' (the *petit bleu*), had been seized in the mail, presumably in hopes of providing the suspicious document with a spurious authenticity. Picquart denied ever making this suggestion, although in their distrust of Picquart, Lauth and Gribelin may well have honestly misinterpreted one of Picquart's comments about the *petit bleu*. Finally, Henry rebuked Picquart for examining 'a secret file' about which 'certain transgressions then transpired', referring to the articles divulging the contents of the *bordereau* only a month after Picquart had first read the 1894 secret dossier. 'As for the word "lies", which is also contained in the aforementioned note', Henry mockingly concluded, 'our inquiry has

not yet been able to determine where, how, and to whom the word
should be applied.'

Picquart knew this assault could only have been launched with the
consent of his superiors. He also knew that a phrase in Henry's note,
'the material proof of these facts exists here' could only mean the
Statistical Section had compiled a dossier of alleged evidence against
him, similar to that used against Dreyfus. After several days' reflection he realized that passivity would be taken as admission and
surrender, so he applied for leave to visit Paris and on 10 June 1897
cabled Henry a terse note protesting against his insinuations. Picquart
spent just over a week in Paris at the end of June consulting with
his friend and lawyer Leblois about how best to defend himself,
revealing everything except the content of the *petit bleu* and the fact
that Mercier had sent the secret dossier to Dreyfus's judges. Before
returning to Tunisia Picquart gave Leblois complete freedom to act
as he saw fit, except that he was in no way to contact the Dreyfus
family, which would open Picquart to the charge of complicity with
treason. The gloves had come off in the struggle between the Statistical Section and Picquart, and both he and Leblois knew their best
weapon was the truth about the *petit bleu* and the *bordereau*. Picquart's
irritated but otherwise insignificant note about the 'lies and mysteries'
surrounding his own position had precipitated a crisis that would
soon sweep over France.

Leblois did not have to search far to find allies in his quest to
save Picquart. By the summer of 1897 Mathieu had commissioned
nearly a dozen handwriting experts from across Europe to examine
the facsimile of the *bordereau* published by *Le Matin* the previous
November, all of whom concluded that it had not been written by
Alfred. Bernard Lazare was also indefatigable, his crusading spirit
and taste for drama contrasting so greatly with Mathieu's prudence.
In addition to writing *A Judicial Error*, Lazare personally lobbied his
friends and acquaintances in the worlds of politics, journalism, and
academia. Often these new adherents then convinced others,
enlarging the Dreyfusard cause. For example, Lazare converted the
philosophy professor Lucien Lévy-Brühl, who then won over Lucien
Herr, a socialist and librarian at the Ecole Normale Supérieure, who
in turn convinced a number of *normaliens*, including Léon Blum,
future prime minister during the Popular Front of the 1930s. A few
other academics like the Protestant historian Gabriel Monod also
supported revision of Dreyfus's trial. A very small number of politi-

cians, such as the Radical senator Arthur Ranc, the more conservative Jewish deputy Joseph Reinach, and the former justice minister
Ludovic Trarieux, had already joined the cause. These Dreyfusards
were not a compact group, nor were they yet a brotherhood of
adversity, but rather a floating network of sympathizers and
supporters, moving among various Parisian literary, political, and
journalistic circles.

Ranc and Reinach placed particular hopes in Auguste Scheurer-
Kestner, vice-president of the Senate. He was one of the founding
figures of the Third Republic, having gained particular esteem for his
long efforts on behalf of refugees from Alsace, his home before its
annexation by Germany. Like nearly everyone, Scheurer-Kestner had
thought Dreyfus guilty, but from his contacts in the region he knew
that the Dreyfus family was rich and respected, leading him to question a seemingly motiveless crime. Thus when Ranc and Reinach laid
siege to the senator he did not reject their arguments out of hand.
Troubled by the thought of an injustice, especially one concerning a
fellow Alsatian, in the spring and summer of 1897 Scheurer-Kestner
undertook his own investigation, questioning the handwriting experts
from the 1894 trial and interviewing Dreyfus's attorney Demange,
who confirmed that a secret file had been illegally sent to Dreyfus's
judges. Finally, Scheurer-Kestner visited his old friend Minister of War
Billot, who told him that in November 1896, at the time of Castelin's
interpellation, new proof of Dreyfus's guilt had arrived at the ministry.
Billot then summarized the 'false Henry' for Scheurer-Kestner,
emphasizing that it indeed contained Dreyfus's name. Although not
fully convinced of Dreyfus's guilt, Scheurer-Kestner told Reinach that
he would give up his inquiry if by mid-July he had not found out
anything conclusive.

Leblois entered the scene at this very moment. In early July, just
days after Picquart had returned to Tunisia, Leblois heard Scheurer-
Kestner at a dinner party voice doubts about the 1894 verdict and
decided to seek the help of the influential politician in protecting
Picquart. At a meeting on 13 July 1897 he swore Scheurer-Kestner
to silence, then recounted Picquart's story of the *bordereau*, the *petit
bleu*, Esterhazy, and the General Staff's attempt to quash the investigation. He showed Scheurer-Kestner letters by Gonse and Henry to
Picquart that seemed to confirm the tale. Had Mathieu not kept up
a relentless campaign for his brother, had others such as Lazare and
Reinach not prepared the ground, then it is questionable whether the

presentation by Leblois could have overcome Scheurer-Kestner's natural scepticism. But Scheurer-Kestner was convinced. The next day, at the Bastille Day military review at the Longchamps racecourse, Scheurer-Kestner told the leaders of the Senate that he believed Dreyfus to be innocent. Within days the news had spread far and wide that one of the Republic's most prestigious figures had declared his faith in a convicted traitor.

It still took several months before Picquart's investigation within the army, which was the basis of Scheurer-Kestner's certitude, finally converged with Mathieu's public campaign. Although Scheurer-Kestner allowed Reinach to tell Mathieu and Lucie that he believed in Alfred's innocence, he and Leblois still hoped to protect Picquart and so would not reveal either Picquart's existence or the name of the actual traitor. Only in November 1897 did Mathieu discover who wrote the *bordereau*, and through an unexpected source. Strolling along the *quais* of the Seine, a stockbroker paused to look over one of the posters of the *bordereau*. He noticed the writing looked familiar, and returned home to compare the poster with the letters of a former client whom he knew to be irresponsible and dishonourable. This seeming chance explains how Mathieu learned from a stranger that his brother had been convicted for the crimes of an officer named Esterhazy. Yet just as in the case of Scheurer-Kestner's conversion by Leblois, here too Mathieu's efforts had prepared the way, by keeping the case before the public and by distributing copies of the *bordereau* and Alfred's writings to prove their dissimilarity. But afterwards it occurred to Mathieu that Esterhazy might not be the person suspected by Scheurer-Kestner. He rushed to Scheurer-Kestner's home and told him he knew Esterhazy was the culprit; both were immensely relieved that their two paths had led to the same person.

Like a spark arcing across a void, Mathieu's meeting with Scheurer-Kestner closed the gap between the public and covert sides of the campaigns to exonerate Dreyfus and protect Picquart. On 12 November 1897, the day after Mathieu met with Scheurer-Kestner, the key Dreyfusard leaders met in a veritable war council to consider their next step: Mathieu, Scheurer-Kestner, Leblois, Demange, and a new ally, Emmanuel Arène, the editor of *Le Figaro*. They decided upon a carefully calibrated series of press revelations, culminating in a public denunciation of Esterhazy as the real author of the *bordereau*. From this point on the General Staff of the army faced a kind of general staff of Dreyfusards, each side planning attacks on several fronts: in the courts, in legislative assemblies, in the newspapers, in public meetings, in the streets. The Dreyfusard leadership was optimistic in the autumn of 1897 that the plan to denounce Esterhazy publicly would quickly liberate Dreyfus. However, the officers of the army General Staff would not give up so easily, and already had begun a counter-offensive to protect the 1894 verdict. The Dreyfus Affair was about to begin.

4

A SUCCESSFUL COLLUSION
(AUTUMN 1897)

I am Colonel Du Paty de Clam of the staff of the army, and you have only to do what I tell you to do.[1]

Some three years after Dreyfus had been arrested, his brother and the small group of Dreyfusards launched what they hoped would be the final campaign for revision of the case of the *bordereau*. 'Mr Minister', Mathieu wrote to Billot in an open letter of 16 November 1897,

> The only basis for the accusation against my unfortunate brother in 1894 was an unsigned, undated letter stating that confidential military documents had been given to a foreign power. I have the honour of informing you that the author of that letter is Count Walsin-Esterhazy, Infantry Commandant... I cannot doubt that knowing the author of the treason for which my brother was condemned you will quickly have justice done.

Rather than investigate Mathieu's allegation against Esterhazy, however, officers of the Statistical Section and the General Staff resorted to collusion with the accused man and other illegal devices to protect themselves and the verdict of 1894, confusing their own interests with the honour of the army. Not only was justice not quickly done, but during the next two years France would be wracked by every form of public turmoil, including riots, duels, attempted assassinations, and a botched *coup d'état*. The case of the *bordereau* would

continue in the courts, but Mathieu's public denunciation of Esterhazy marked the beginning of the Dreyfus Affair.

Mathieu's allegation came as no surprise to the highest authorities
of the Republic and the army. Some such dramatic revelation had
been expected since the previous summer, when vice-president of the
Senate Scheurer-Kestner had stated that he believed Dreyfus to be
innocent. The long months between Scheurer-Kestener's announcement and Mathieu's accusation had, however, allowed Major Henry
and others to erect new defences against revision. Henry's task was
all the more urgent because even officers of the army and members
of the government could not be counted upon to maintain a firm attitude. Minister of War Billot was particularly worrisome, since he was
considered by some in the army to be a 'political general', a staunch
republican who was unimpressed by the continued anti-Semitic
campaign against the government and Dreyfus. Chief of Staff Boisdeffre had convinced Billot to send Picquart on his spurious mission
to Tunisia, but the minister of war was still uneasy when he learned
that his old friend Scheurer-Kestner said he had evidence exonerating Dreyfus. Several times in September 1897 Billot had subordi-
nates discreetly approach Scheurer-Kestner and other Dreyfusards,
including Mathieu himself, to ascertain what material evidence lay
behind their belief in Alfred's innocence. Since Mathieu as yet had
no knowledge of Esterhazy, and Picquart's lawyer Leblois had
forbidden Scheurer-Kestner to reveal what he knew, these inquiries
produced no concrete result. Scheurer-Kestner was in a particularly
difficult position, since he could not in honour produce any evidence
for his conversion, yet the press continually reported that he claimed
to have some decisive document. Scheurer-Kestner even left Paris
rather than meet with President of the Republic Faure because he
could offer no proofs for his position. Still, the senator continued to
proclaim that Dreyfus was innocent, in mid-October telling one of
Billot's emissaries that, 'I know everything'.

This affirmation, however imprecise, appears to have spurred the
officers concerned with the case to further action. Since the autumn
of 1896, Henry, Boisdeffre and Vice-Chief Gonse had suspected that
a mistaken or suborned Picquart was working to substitute Esterhazy
for Dreyfus. The officers knew that Picquart had conferred with
Leblois and that Leblois and Scheurer-Kestner were in frequent
contact. They suspected that Picquart had illegally passed on to the
Dreyfusards the content of the secret dossier and also that he had

perhaps forged the *petit bleu*, in which Schwartzkoppen named Esterhazy as his informer. They knew Esterhazy to be an impetuous, reck-
less, disreputable character, and apparently feared that if publicly
named as the traitor he would commit suicide or flee in a panic, or
perhaps otherwise muddy the case against Dreyfus. And so they
decided that Esterhazy must become part of the campaign to prevent
revision, step by step becoming more deeply involved in protecting
the man who turned out to be the real traitor. Once this collusion
was revealed, most Dreyfusards – including Reinach, Alfred and
Mathieu – believed it proved Henry to have been Esterhazy's accomplice from the beginning. One of the finest recent historians of the
Affair, while denying this allegation, has written that the army officers' behaviour 'took the indisputable form of treason'.[2]

Yet if one grants that the officers were absolutely convinced of
Dreyfus's guilt, a belief that none of the key officers expressed doubts
about even years after the Affair, then the collusion takes on a more
understandable aspect. Esterhazy had been watched first by Picquart
and then by Henry until October 1897, and during that year and a
half no evidence surfaced against him except the *petit bleu* that had
started Picquart's inquiry. Faced with what they believed to be an
unscrupulous and well-financed conspiracy to free a traitor and
imprison an innocent, if unsavoury, officer; faced with the possible ruin
of careers and reputations from former Minister of War General
Mercier through the highest officers of the army to the entire staff of
the intelligence service; faced with the prospect of dishonouring the
army and undermining its moral authority; faced with this powerful
intersection of personal and national interests, the defence of the original verdict appeared to require that Esterhazy, the weak link in the
chain binding Dreyfus to the *bordereau*, had to be shielded. Just as
saving Dreyfus was for Picquart the only way he could save himself,
so the officers calculated that shielding Esterhazy was the surest way
of protecting themselves. The larger goal of the officers was not,
however, to save Esterhazy, but to prevent an inquiry into the case of
the *bordereau*, a crucial difference. If the Dreyfusards forced a new
investigation by bribery and forging evidence then the illegal tactics
used in the trial and subsequent defence of the verdict would be
exposed. Dreyfus the traitor might well have to be freed, but even if
he remained in prison an inquiry would likely destroy nearly everyone
associated with the case and perhaps irreparably damage the army, the
nation's only defence against the looming German menace.

To handle the delicate task of alerting Esterhazy, Gonse once again called upon Boisdeffre's cousin and loyal servant Du Paty de Clam, who had been specially commissioned to arrest Dreyfus in 1894. Throughout the collusion between Esterhazy and officers of the General Staff, Boisdeffre and Gonse remained in the background, later denying any knowledge of it, but it was Vice-Chief Gonse who according to Du Paty said on 16 October 1897 that Esterhazy must be warned of 'the campaign undertaken to substitute Esterhazy for Dreyfus'. Gonse assured Du Paty that the long inquiry had produced no evidence against Esterhazy, and he even invoked a non-existent court martial which had supposedly declared him innocent. 'If Commandant Esterhazy, not being warned, resorted to some reproachable act', Gonse told Du Paty, 'there could result the greatest harm for the country and for certain army chiefs.'[3] As always in the Affair, the salvation of individual officers was equated with the salvation of the army.

Du Paty's collaboration was not long in bearing fruit. On 19 October 1897, minister of war Billot received an anonymous note declaring that the Dreyfusards were preparing to accuse an officer named Esterhazy of Dreyfus's crime. Probably the work of Henry, this letter no doubt was intended to both warn Billot and force him to take decisive measures to protect Esterhazy. When Gonse asked Billot for permission to contact Esterhazy, however, the minister of war flatly refused. Gonse and Henry resolved this difficulty by simply disobeying the minister. They made a great show to Du Paty of the minister's refusal to send an anonymous note to Esterhazy, but indicated with a wink and a nudge that that was exactly what they expected of him. In the event it was probably Mme Henry who wrote the letter, modelled on the note received by Billot, that arrived at Esterhazy's country house soon thereafter. 'Your name is going to be subject to a great scandal', it read in part, 'the Dreffus [sic] family is going to accuse you publicly as being the author of the document that was the basis for the Dreffus trial... A colonel who was at the ministry last year, M. Picart [sic] has given the documents to the Dreffus family.' It was signed 'Esperance', an echo of the 'Speranza' note of December 1896 which had been sent – probably by Henry – to incriminate Picquart in a Dreyfusard conspiracy. This attempt to prevent Esterhazy from taking precipitous action very nearly had the opposite effect. As soon as Esterhazy received the Esperance note he rushed to Paris and began preparing a dramatic suicide. In a mad scramble he arranged to have the lease on the apartment in which he had installed his mistress, Marguérite Pays, transferred to her name, so that the furnishings would not be part of the probate of his estate. He then hesitated for days, all the while declaring to Pays that he was determined to kill himself. He managed only to conjure up enough courage to respond to the assertion in the Esperance note that the Dreyfus family was conspiring against him by anonymously writing a threatening letter to Dreyfus's father-in-law.

While Esterhazy hesitated, Henry continued to prop up the case against Dreyfus. On 20 October he and Gonse called in Lebrun-Renault, the guard at Dreyfus's ceremonial degradation who was reported in January 1895 to have heard Dreyfus confess, and had him sign a statement recounting this fictional incident. At about this time Henry also falsified more documents against Dreyfus, notably a message from Panizzardi to Schwartzkoppen stating that 'P. had brought me many interesting things', in which he changed the P to a D. Finally, on 22 October Henry and Du Paty sent Gribelin, the archivist of the Statistical Section, suitably disguised in dark blue glasses, to arrange a meeting with Esterhazy at the Park Montsouris. Before going to the rendezvous Esterhazy visited Schwartzkoppen, where he waved about a revolver and threatened to kill the military attaché and then himself right there inside the German embassy if Schwartzkoppen refused to denounce Dreyfus as the traitor. Schwartzkoppen calmly replied that he would have covered Esterhazy were it not that an innocent man was 'over there', and showed Esterhazy the door.[4]

At the Parc Montsouris that evening Esterhazy was met by Gribelin, still in his blue glasses, and Du Paty, who sported a false black beard and glasses for the occasion. Henry watched from a nearby carriage. Esterhazy still carried his revolver, for he feared a trap, but Du Paty assured him that they were there to protect him from 'monstrous manoeuvres' by the Dreyfusards. Du Paty then spoke of Picquart's accusations, but assured Esterhazy that he had powerful protectors. Not yet knowing who his saviours were, Esterhazy at one point declared that he had often worked confidentially for Sandherr, the former head of the Statistical Section, but Gribelin vehemently denied this tale and Esterhazy did not insist. Already, then, Esterhazy had devised the cover story that would later become his last line of defence: instead of a traitor, he was a secret agent who had written the *bordereau* upon Sandherr's order as part of an elaborate scheme to misinform the Germans.[5]

Since the whole point of the collusion for Henry and Du Paty was to neutralize whatever information Picquart may have given Scheurer-Kestner, their instructions to Esterhazy mirrored the senator's campaign point by point. Du Paty and Henry knew that Scheurer-Kestner was urging Billot to open a new inquiry into the *bordereau*, so they had Esterhazy write to Billot protesting his innocence and claiming that Dreyfus had copied his handwriting. To explain this they alleged that Dreyfus had stolen an example of Esterhazy's writing expressly for this purpose. They knew, also, that on 29 October Scheurer-Kestner was to have an interview with President Faure, so they had Esterhazy demand protection from the president in a letter timed to arrive that morning. 'If I have to undergo the painful experience of not being listened to by the chief of my country', Esterhazy impudently wrote, 'then I reserve the right to call upon the chief of my house, the suzerain of the family Esterhazy, upon the German Emperor. He himself is a soldier, and he will know how to place the honour of a soldier, even if he is an enemy, above the mean and suspicious intrigues of politicians.'[6] Esterhazy evidently hoped that this threat would assure the protection of the French army and government out of fear of foreign complications. There need have been no concern about Faure, however, as when he met with Scheurer-Kestner his only response was to manufacture excuses as to why he could not become involved in the case.

On 30 October 1897 Scheurer-Kestner finally met with Minister of War Billot. The senator urged the general to reopen the case of the *bordereau*, but presented no new evidence since he still hoped to protect Picquart. To prove Dreyfus's guilt Billot cited the 'false Henry', constructed by Henry a year earlier, in which Panizzardi was made to say that he and Schwartzkoppen had had dealings with Dreyfus. Scheurer-Kestner ridiculed it as an obvious forgery. At the end of the difficult interview Scheurer-Kestner gave Billot two weeks to undertake an inquiry, and the two agreed to say nothing to the press of their discussion. The next day, however, accounts of the meeting appeared in several papers stating that Scheurer-Kestner had been unable to provide proofs for his assertions, convincing Scheurer-Kestner that his old friend had deceived him. He nonetheless wrote to Billot reiterating his request for an inquiry, putting his finger on the key point of careers and reputations when he argued 'in what way would it hurt the army if in good faith the generals themselves recognized that perhaps there had been a judicial error? They would

be strengthened, General Mercier and the others. Public opinion
would be with them, be sure of it.'[7]

The press reports of the meeting were only part of a larger newspaper campaign against Scheurer-Kestner and other Dreyfusards. At
the end of October and into the first weeks of November, Nationalist,
Catholic, and anti-Semitic newspapers recounted Scheurer-Kestner's
efforts on behalf of the alleged traitor, heaping ridicule and hatred
upon the senator: Reinach was a 'lipomatose gorilla'; Scheurer-
Kestner a paid German agent. Henry, Du Paty, and Esterhazy fed
these papers a constant stream of invective and information in the
hopes of undermining Scheurer-Kestner's credibility and defusing any
Dreyfusard revelations. In addition to coordinating a public press
campaign, Henry and Du Paty continued their collusion with Esterhazy, who needed no goading to defend his besmirched honour in
the most outrageous manner. On the recommendation of the officers
Esterhazy asserted his innocence in meetings with the highest officers
in the army, including Military Governor Saussier and Minister of War
Billot himself. On 31 October, just before Scheurer-Kestner was to
meet – to no effect – with Prime Minister Méline, Esterhazy wrote a
second letter to President Faure, keeping his claims before the highest
political circles of France. Esterhazy reiterated his threat to unleash
diplomatic complications with Germany if he were not protected,
referring for the first time to 'a generous lady' who had alerted Esterhazy to the Dreyfusard plot against him. Later this non-existent
personage would become famous as a 'veiled lady', and in this second
letter to Faure Esterhazy suggested that she had stolen from Picquart
the photograph of a document 'highly compromising for certain
diplomatic personages'. 'If I am to obtain neither support nor justice,
and if my name is made public, this photograph, which is now in a
safe place, will be published immediately.' Esterhazy did try to soften
this threat with the apology that he had 'taken recourse to means so
little in keeping with my character' only because he was defending
the honour of his family.

In a third letter to Faure soon thereafter Esterhazy wrote that the
document 'proved the scoundrelry' of Dreyfus, using the French word
canaillerie, an echo of the 'canaille de D' letter passed illegally to
Dreyfus's judges in 1894. Evidently this allusion was intended to
convince those in the know that Esterhazy really did possess a secret
document. And this third letter also raised the stakes: the document
was not only 'compromising', its publication would 'force France to

humiliate herself or go to war'. Thus the collusion had reached the point that Esterhazy, and indirectly, Henry and Du Paty, was now blackmailing the president of the Republic with the threat of an international conflagration. This time Esterhazy had gone too far, and he was questioned by General Saussier about having secret documents; there was some question of a court martial, but Saussier had no desire to become mired in a scandal that could only cause complications. To end the episode Henry brought a copy of the 'scoundrel D' letter to Billot, pretending it had come from Esterhazy, who probably never had it in his possession. For his part Faure took Esterhazy's absurd letters seriously enough to have Picquart questioned in Tunisia about any documents he may have taken home, where presumably the 'generous lady', perhaps a jilted lover, could have obtained them.

Picquart was surprised by the Statistical Section's new machination against him, but had even stranger events to ponder. On 10 November he had received a telegram reading, 'Stop the demi-god; all is discovered; very serious matter'. Not only did the telegram repeat the reference to a 'demi-god' found in the note of December 1896 sent by Henry to tie Picquart to the Dreyfusard syndicate, but it had the same signature, 'Speranza'. Esterhazy's mistress later admitted writing it at the behest of the collusionists. Fearing that the telegram was incorrectly addressed, the inept conspirators sent another telegram to Picquart: 'There is proof the *petit bleu* was forged by Georges. – Blanche.' This second telegram, like the first, was intended to constitute more evidence against the colonel, whose first name was indeed Georges, and whose friend Blanche Comminges had already been implicated in the first Speranza letter in 1896. Esterhazy also sent Picquart a letter which he signed demanding an explanation for Picquart's accusations against him. Picquart did not reply, but asked his superiors to open an inquiry into these various messages, whose authors he well knew.

Thus when Mathieu issued his public denunciation of Esterhazy on 15 November 1897 the main themes of the Dreyfus Affair were already in place. The emerging Dreyfusard circle contended that to secure Alfred's conviction the highest officers of the French army had resorted to illegalities, and to prevent public disclosure they had compounded their crime by fabricating evidence to protect themselves and the real traitor. The outline of this argument appeared publicly in *Le Figaro* on 14 November, in an article signed merely 'Vidi', but which represented the views of the most active Dreyfusards. 'Vidi' even described the contents of the 'false Henry', upsetting Henry so greatly that Du Paty thought the officer had gone mad. The officers retaliated by publishing the next day a piece by 'Dixi' alleging that an unnamed officer of the General Staff (Picquart) had been suborned into creating false evidence (the *petit bleu*) against an unnamed fellow officer (Esterhazy). This became the constant refrain of the interested officers of the army, from the Ministry of War to the Statistical Section, until the end of the Affair.

Gradually a wider circle of partisans gathered around the rival groups, enlarging the issues bound up in the controversy. The narrow case concerning who had written the *bordereau* had sprouted shoots that would eventually penetrate into virtually every political and social question facing France. The first stage of this process had begun with the original trial, when anti-Semites, nationalists, and some Catholics used the conviction of a Jew for treason as evidence in their indictment of the corrupt Republic. By November 1897 a second phase had begun, however, in which the campaign for revision, as small and weak as it was initially, finally found a few supporters of influence or high office. The first Dreyfusards were almost invariably people who had known Alfred or had some other connection to him: his wife and brother; his lawyer; well-wishers from Alsace (Scheurer-Kestner), or from the Jewish community (Lazare; Reinach). Yet then there came to the cause a larger circle of those drawn to the crusade not only by a thirst for justice, but also to a certain extent by the realization that the case offered possibilities for advancing other issues.

First among these crusaders, as early as 1895, had been Lazare, who always sought to widen the campaign for Dreyfus into an attack on anti-Semitism. In November 1897 he issued a second edition of his pamphlet *A Judicial Error* that included evidence by handwriting experts showing that Alfred did not write the *bordereau*, and that sharpened his attack on anti-Semitism as the root of the injustice: 'It was because he was a Jew that he was arrested, it was because he was a Jew that he was tried, it was because he was a Jew that he was found guilty, and it is because he is a Jew that the voice of truth and justice is not allowed to speak out on his behalf.'[8] Such language prompted Scheurer-Kestner's remark that 'we must take great care to ensure that the Dreyfus question does not remain within the Jewish domain. It is too much there already. The question is one of justice.'[9] The Protestant senator certainly had the interests of justice foremost in mind, but this coexisted with his desire to root out clericalism from the Republic and Jesuitism from the military, which for him were the most powerful forces for injustice in France. Picquart and his lawyer Leblois also had several motives for their advocacy. They were tortured by the thought that Dreyfus was innocent, but had acted only when the colonel's interests seemed to demand it.

The two most important additions to the Dreyfusard camp at this time exemplify this double motivation of humanitarianism and interest, Georges Clemenceau and Emile Zola. Clemenceau later led France to victory in the First World War, but in 1897 he appeared to be have left his best days behind. As a radical deputy in the 1870s and 1880s he was so dismayed by the flabbiness and corruption of the 'Opportunist' Republic that for a time he encouraged and supported General Boulanger, who some hoped would overthrow the Republic and establish a more assertive regime. Clemenceau's sharp rhetoric in the Chamber made him a wrecker of governments, but he was too pugnacious to inspire much backing for his own ambitions. Compromised in the Panama scandals of the early 1890s, in part on forged evidence, he was defeated for re-election and retired from elective politics, turning instead to journalism. Initially Clemenceau did not doubt Dreyfus's guilt, but in the autumn of 1897 Scheurer-Kestner and Ranc convinced him that the trial had been a travesty. Instinctively sensing an opportunity to undermine the government as well as disgusted with the injustice of Dreyfus's conviction, in November Clemenceau began a series of revisionist articles in L'Aurore, eventually becoming one of Mathieu's closest collaborators. The Dreyfus Affair was Clemenceau's first step in his return to political prominence, a turning point that set him on the path to the most powerful office in the French state.

If political calculation explains much of Clemenceau's initial engagement, it was the drama of the emerging Affair that first inspired Zola's participation. More read than admired, infamous for novels depicting the degradation of the lower classes, the ravages of alcoholism, and the *demi-monde* of actresses and prostitutes, Zola saw the emerging Affair as a vast drama, with heroes, villains, and startling plot twists. Lazare had tried to interest Zola in Dreyfus's plight in 1896, but it was only in November 1897, after Scheurer-Kestner told him of Esterhazy's role, that he threw himself into the fray. His first public intervention was a powerful defence of the senator in the 25 November *Le Figaro* that portrayed Scheurer-Kestner as a man 'conquered little by little by an insatiable need for truth. Nothing is more elevated,

nothing is more noble, and what happened to this man is an extraordinary spectacle that fills me with enthusiasm – me, whose vocation
is to weigh upon consciences. There is no more heroic struggle than
the advocacy of truth for justice.' In concluding the article Zola found
a phrase that became a slogan among Dreyfusards: 'Truth is on the
march, and nothing will stop it'.

Over the next weeks and months Zola's was the most prominent
voice in the revisionist campaign, earning him the particular enmity
of anti-revisionist journalists, cartoonists, and politicians. It had taken
just under three years, but Mathieu had finally inspired and provoked
a small but vociferous group of supporters. Several newspapers were
now willing to give space to the Dreyfusard cause, a contrast to
previous moments when the case of the *bordereau* had been in the
public eye – during the 1894 trial, and in the autumn of 1896 after
Mathieu's false story that Alfred had escaped. First among the Dreyfusard papers was *Le Figaro*, directed by the deputy Arène, but by
autumn 1897 *L'Aurore*, *Le Siècle*, *Le Radical* and other papers welcomed
revisionist articles.

Dreyfus himself knew nothing of the growing uproar over his case.
Since the autumn of 1896 when he had been manacled each night to
his cot he had stopped keeping a journal, a sign of a some despair,
but he generally maintained a stoic demeanour, promising Lucie in
May 1897 that 'discouragement would never once enter into my soul'.
The thought that his wife would lose heart seemed to torture him,
so he – the victim of truly inhuman treatment – felt it necessary to
sustain her, pledging 'I will write to animate you with my indomitable
will' and ending his letter, 'courage, courage, and will!'[10] Only very
infrequently did his nerve break, when he again descended into
suicidal anguish. As always, he cherished and often spoke to the three
photographs of his wife and children, just as Lucie treasured her
pictures of Alfred. 'Sometimes I have such a need to confide in you,
to tell you my hopes, and to lean on you that I embrace your photograph', she once wrote, 'I hold it with all my strength, I speak to it
and I want to bring it to life. I search in that image for your look,
so kind, so gentle, and then I am seized by sadness and I return to
painful reality.'[11]

Dreyfus received only copies of Lucie's letters to prevent secret
communication, and even then many letters were extensively censored
or not even delivered. She tried to surreptitiously inform her husband
that prominent men such as Scheurer-Kestner were investigating his

case, but generally the censor allowed only the most banal messages. In September 1897 Dreyfus did receive a letter from Lucie stating that 'we have made a giant step towards the truth', an allusion to the senator's public support, but Alfred later noted that these messages remained an enigma to him. By this time Dreyfus had been moved to a somewhat larger compound; the previous one with its high wooden walls close to the cabin had been so airless, hot, and humid that the prison doctor, concerned for Dreyfus's life, had ordered the construction of new quarters. A wooden wall nearly three metres high still enclosed his new hut, however, and in the rainy season several centimetres of water often pooled in his shack. As before, insects, spiders and parasites crawled over his furniture, food and body. One new feature was a guard tower mounted with a rapid-firing 'Hotchkiss gun' to destroy any ships that should violate the five-kilometre security zone around the island. Thirteen guards watched in turn over the presumed traitor through an iron grill, and Dreyfus later wrote that of all his torments the worst was 'having two eyes always aimed at me, day and night, every moment, in every situation, without a minute's respite'.

While Dreyfus endured the beginning of another sub-equatorial summer of searing heat and drenching thunderstorms, November 1897 in France brought the first crack in the iron wall of denials and forgeries that protected the original verdict. The renewed controversy in the press and Scheurer-Kestner's public support for a convicted traitor led several nationalist deputies to state that they intended to question the government about its dealings with the senator. In preparation, on 9 November the cabinet discussed the emerging Affair. Hoping no doubt to prevent awkward questions, Méline and Billot said nothing of the *petit bleu* and Picquart's investigation, and the cabinet simply voted to issue a statement that Dreyfus had been 'normally and legally condemned'. Not only the prestige of the army but that of the government was becoming bound ever more closely to the original verdict. With elections in less than six months the campaign season had begun, and few deputies and no minister wanted to draw the ire of the nationalists and anti-Semites. Thus Mathieu's public letter of 15 November accusing Esterhazy of writing the *bordereau* left the government little choice but to open a new investigation, since the nationalists had framed his statement as an attack on the honour of the army and an officer. On 16 November Billot stated in the Chamber that justice demanded 'the author of the

denunciation produce his justification', thereby in effect turning the
inquiry upon Mathieu rather than upon Esterhazy.[12] Still, after nearly
three years Mathieu's long efforts had finally brought a new inquiry
into the case of the *bordereau*.

Although the partnership between the General Staff and Esterhazy
had failed in its original goal of preventing an investigation, the collusion continued with even greater urgency with the beginning of the
new inquiry by General Georges de Pellieux. The point now was quite
clearly to shield Esterhazy at all costs, since he was in a position to
deeply compromise the General Staff. Gonse forbade Du Paty and
Henry to have further dealings with Esterhazy since he was the subject
of an official investigation, but Du Paty, at least, always believed that
Gonse authorized indirect contact, and such was the typical procedure in the Statistical Section, where credible denial was a fine art.
For this task Du Paty and Henry recruited Esterhazy's mistress and
his nephew Christian, whose matrimonial fortunes had been of so
much interest to Esterhazy. While de Pellieux heard witnesses and
assembled documents, Du Paty met daily with Christian to coordinate
Esterhazy's defence, telling Esterhazy what to say and when to remain
silent, meeting in out of the way places like public lavatories where
they read and wrote messages by match-light.[13] With each step Henry
and Du Paty perpetrated new outrages to add to the iniquities of the
original trial. By this time they were engaged in covering up the
cover-up, miring themselves ever deeper in contradictions, inconsis-
tencies, and complications made sustainable only by more blatant forgeries and lies.

A violent public campaign of vilification matched the secret
campaign of obstruction and entrapment. After Mathieu's public accusation of Esterhazy, Henry worked assiduously to ensure publicity for
the army's case, and Boisdeffre had to punish his own chief of staff
for passing information to the anti-revisionist press. Esterhazy regaled
an enthralled press with tales of the veiled lady who had warned him
of the Dreyfusard plots, while journalists and ordinary citizens outdid
themselves in guessing her identity; indeed, several women came
forward to claim that they were the mysterious personage. Mathieu,
Reinach, Zola, and Scheurer-Kestner were splattered with the most
vile insults as members of a Jewish syndicate ready at any moment
to deliver France to her enemies. One insightful observer has noted
that it was at this time that the contending sides developed their 'clan
languages', with their own vocabularies of abuse and particular appeal

to elevated values.[14] Reinach and Scheurer-Kestner believed the Jesuits pulled the strings upon which the General Staff and the anti-revisionist press danced; they denounced the clericalist conspiracy almost as forcefully as the anti-Semites derided the Jewish syndicate. Less convinced of a conspiracy, Zola nonetheless agreed that the Roman Catholic church in France was using anti-Semitism to bring the straying flock back to the fold. He believed Catholic and anti-Semitic fanatics hoped to unleash a religious war, to crush the Rights of Man gained with such difficulty in 1789. 'You are going back to the past', he wrote 'the past filled with intolerance and theocracy that your illustrious forebears struggled with and believed they had slain through the sacrifice of their intelligence and blood.'

Drumont and Rochefort abused all who spoke up for Dreyfus, including for example warden Forzinetti, who in November 1897 wrote heart-rendingly of Dreyfus's days at the Cherche-Midi prison and of Du Paty's efforts to force a confession. Rochefort's invective prompted Forzinetti to ask for satisfaction on the field of honour, but the journalist refused to duel. In addition, Scheurer-Kestner's former friend Juliette Lamber, better known by her pen name Edmond Adam, wrote a scathing article accusing the senator of being in the pay of the Germans. On the other hand, sentiment abroad favoured Dreyfus, and Scheurer-Kestner recounted in his memoirs numerous messages of support and even endearing notes from nineteen-year-old women, which seemed to particularly affect the elderly statesman. Nationalists and other anti-revisionists saw the overwhelming inter-national support for Dreyfus as proof of the conspiracy against France, but to Dreyfusards it proved only that the French were too mesmer-ized by their respect for the army to see the truth. Many crowned heads were drawn to the 'strange and horrible beauty of the drama', as Reinach put it, most being sympathetic to the condemned man. But from London the Orleanist pretender to the throne hoped to gain some advantage from the agitation, stating that in contrast to the current regime he at least would know how to preserve the honour of the army.[15]

As public opinion – or the newspaper tumult that passed for it – flared to new heights, the governments of Germany and Italy again protested against the daily assaults on their nations in the French press. German ambassador Münster once more categorically asserted that Schwartzkoppen had had no dealings, direct or indirect, with Dreyfus. It was at just this moment, when Esterhazy's name was first

made public, that Schwartzkoppen returned to Germany. According
to Berlin he had been promoted to serve in the Emperor's Guard;
the Dreyfusards said he had been recalled because his agent Esterhazy had been unmasked. Panizzardi wrote to Foreign Minister Hanotaux that he, too, had never dealt with Dreyfus. Hanotaux, who in
1894 had attempted to dissuade Mercier from arresting Dreyfus,
apprised the cabinet of these *démarches*, and the government issued a
deceptively worded statement that it was not true, as some had
reported, that Kaiser Wilhelm had written a letter of protest to President Faure. It was a classic, and effective, manoeuvre, denying the
most extravagant exaggerations of one's opponents so as to imply that
their entire argument is without foundation.

Against this backdrop General de Pellieux on 17 November 1897
officially opened his inquiry into Mathieu's charges against Esterhazy.
Mathieu provided copies of the *bordereau* and Esterhazy's writing for
comparison, but was astonished when de Pellieux said that he had
no intention of submitting them to expert scrutiny. The general
argued that doing so would constitute retrying the original case,
which he was not authorized to do. When Panizzardi, who had been
a full partner in Schwarztkoppen's undertakings, offered to testify
that he had had no dealings with Dreyfus, Boisdeffre refused to allow
de Pellieux to hear him, alleging that it would be intruding on a
domestic matter. Convinced of Dreyfus's guilt by the 'false Henry',
de Pellieux was, however, more than willing to look into Picquart's
activities, and upon reading the spurious Speranza and Blanche telegrams concluded that Picquart was implicated in a wide-ranging
conspiracy against Esterhazy. Picquart's apartment in Paris was
searched, while that of Esterhazy, the official subject of the investigation, remained inviolate. De Pellieux did not even want to call
Picquart as a witness, but Scheurer-Kestner threatened to bring the
matter before the Senate and the general capitulated. A second, trun-
cated inquiry was then necessary to hear Picquart, brought back
expressly from Tunisia, but his testimony did nothing to shake de
Pellieux. On 3 December he reported that there were no grounds
for suspecting Esterhazy. Instead, de Pellieux recommended that
charges be brought against Picquart for divulging secrets to his lawyer
Leblois (which Picquart and Leblois always denied); indeed, the
general had suspicions that Picquart had concocted the *petit bleu*.
Throughout his two investigations the honest but naïve de Pellieux
was in constant contact with the officers of the Statistical Section and

with Esterhazy, and it is therefore no wonder that his findings conformed to the line laid out by so much forgery and perjury. It was about this time that Henry, in recompense for such effective service, was promoted to lieutenant-colonel.

Seeking to press his advantage, Esterhazy on 2 December asserted his right to a court martial to end the slanders against him. Esterhazy was perhaps encouraged by an episode that had originally appeared highly damaging. In late November, as de Pellieux was finishing his second investigation, Mme de Boulancy, the cousin and former mistress of Esterhazy, brought to Scheurer-Kestner several letters written by the prodigal rascal fifteen years before. Having failed to recover money he owed her, the aggrieved de Boulancy now took her revenge. On 28 November *Le Figaro* published the most scandalous missive, in which Esterhazy noted that the French 'are not worth the cartridges necessary to kill them... if someone said to me today that I would be killed tomorrow as an Uhlan Captain while stabbing Frenchmen to death, I would be completely happy... I would not hurt a dog, but I would with pleasure have a hundred thousand Frenchmen put to death'. Esterhazy ended the so-called 'Uhlan letter' with an apocalyptic scene of Paris under the blood-red sun of battle 'taken by assault, and abandoned to the pillaging of a hundred thousand drunken soldiers. That is an occasion about which I dream.'[16] When the letter first appeared Esterhazy again seemed ready to commit suicide or flee; Mme Esterhazy, disgusted with her husband, sought a divorce but was persuaded to put off deserting her husband in his time of need. Eventually Du Paty calmed Esterhazy and the story was put out that the Jews had paid tens of thousands of francs for this supposed forgery. Still, the Uhlan letter caused more than one observer to doubt the character of an officer who was being hailed in much of the press as a maligned hero. That many were willing to believe this in the face of Esterhazy's letters suggests the depth of feeling against Dreyfus, guilty by judgement of a court martial, but doubly guilty by virtue of his heritage.

By early December 1897 a third inquiry had been undertaken by Commandant Ravary in preparation for Esterhazy's trial on the same charge of writing the *bordereau* which de Pellieux had found groundless. The Ravary inquiry lasted the entire month of December and essentially replicated the work of de Pellieux; if anything, Ravary worked even more closely with the General Staff, meeting with Gonse whenever he was puzzled by the complexities of the case.

Unlike de Pellieux, however, Ravary did order a comparison of the *bordereau* and Esterhazy's handwriting. To the amazement and consternation of the Dreyfusards the three consultants concluded that Esterhazy did not write the *bordereau*. They explained the many similarities between Esterhazy's writing and that of the *bordereau* by arguing that the author had used Esterhazy's script as the model for a habile forgery. Furthermore the consultants reasoned that if Esterhazy had indeed written the *bordereau* he would certainly have disguised his handwriting. Or as Reinach put it, 'since the writing in the *bordereau* is Esterhazy's, Esterhazy is not the author of the *bordereau*'.[17] No one seemed to realize that if the *bordereau* was such an elaborate fabrication it would be impossible to say who wrote it, including Dreyfus. The experts even cast doubt on the authenticity of Esterhazy's Uhlan letter; but their findings are perhaps more easily understood when it is realized that the experts worked in common under Ravary's direct supervision. Unsurprisingly, on 31 December Ravary issued a public statement concluding that there was no credible evidence against Esterhazy. With such a favourable report the General Staff pushed ahead for a trial, scheduled for 10 January 1898, intended to definitively exonerate Esterhazy and close the case of the *bordereau* once and for all.

Meanwhile the clamour in the press for the first time created serious political difficulties for the government. The Affair was having a peculiar effect on the coalition politics of the Chamber, cutting across party lines and uniting the rightists and nationalists with some socialists in opposition to the government. For the hard right the government was too lenient with the apologists of a convicted traitor; for the socialists, many of whom identified Jews with capitalists, the government wasted too much time on the rich bourgeois Dreyfus, ignoring the larger injustice of economic exploitation. Méline's government rested upon a centre-right coalition which appeared solid for the moment, but like all governments of the Third Republic might fracture unexpectedly. Indeed, most of the few Dreyfusard sympathizers came from republican ranks, weakening the majority against the attacks of the far left and right. Thus on 4 December Méline, armed with de Pellieux's exoneration of Esterhazy, had hoped to quash discussion in the Chamber by a declaration that was repeated ironically ever after, 'I will say right away what will be the last word of this debate: There is no Dreyfus Affair. There is none at present and there will be no Dreyfus Affair.'

Of course Méline did not have the last word, and Count Albert de Mun, a respected conservative Catholic, immediately raised the question of the Jewish syndicate, demanding that the government explain 'if there is in this nation a mysterious and hidden power strong enough to cast suspicion at will upon the commanders of our Army'.[18] The socialist Alexandre Millerand then castigated Reinach for seeking to save Dreyfus when he should have been looking to rehabilitate his own family. Reinach responded to this reference to the Panama scandal by sending his seconds to challenge Millerand to a duel. As in 1896 at the time of the Castelin interpellation, Billot calmed the Chamber by declaring unequivocally that he believed Dreyfus had been justly judged and legally condemned, adding furthermore that he was personally convinced that Dreyfus was guilty. That both Méline and Billot were prejudging the outcome of an official investigation did not seem to bother either of them. Eventually seven different motions vied for a majority, chaotically fragmenting the assembly, as each deputy sought to prove his patriotism by proposing stronger language than the last. The final text declared that the Chamber respected the verdict of 1894 and scorned the 'ringleaders of the odious campaign to trouble the public mind'.[19]

The government had much less trouble deflecting Scheurer-Kestner's long-awaited intervention in the Senate on 7 December. Although he felt personally insulted by the Chamber's admonishment of Dreyfusard 'ringleaders', Scheurer-Kestner as always avoided directly attacking the government and members of the General Staff, caught as he was between his hope for justice, his respect for the army, and his fear of weakening the Republic. At the last minute Leblois retracted permission to publicly cite some letters from Gonse to Picquart which proved that Picquart had investigated Esterhazy with the approval of the General Staff. Scheurer-Kestner's interpellation of the government was much anticipated. French and foreign spectators packed the galleries, and many deputies sat in as well. But lacking some new revelation, unwilling to scandalmonger, Scheurer-Kestner's speech fell flat; as he descended the podium before the silent assembly hopes faded for revision through political channels. As the most prominent Dreyfusard, Scheurer-Kestner continued to be the favoured target of anti-revisionists, who began organizing demonstrations of students outside the senator's home. Zola called upon them to rally for justice and truth rather than for the bigotry of anti-Semitism, writing, 'does it not cover you with shame that it is not you,

but the old men, the men of the past generation, who, full of enthusiasm which should be yours, are performing your work today?'[20]
Zola's appeal had to appear in pamphlet form, however, as *Le Figaro*,
suffering from falling subscriptions, retreated into neutrality. Indeed,
in late December Scheurer-Kestner himself, ill from cancer, weary of
the fight, and disgusted with the public agitation provoked by both
sides, retired from active participation in the struggle.

Still, on the eve of Esterhazy's trial the Dreyfusards could convince
themselves that events were moving in their direction. On 15
December the first public meeting in favour of Dreyfus opened a
new terrain for combat. It was organized by the anarchists Sébas-
tian Faure and Louise Michel, who saw in the Dreyfusard campaign
a weapon against militarism and the abuse of authority. The newly
founded feminist journal *La Fronde* also declared its support for the
prisoner on Devil's Island.[21] Intellectuals continued to join the
cause, notably the Catholic poet Charles Péguy. Mathieu had even
won a victory in court when a suit brought by the General Staff
against him for allegedly attempting to bribe Colonel Sandherr in
1894 was dismissed as groundless. Finally, just days before Esterhazy's trial, Reinach and Mathieu arranged the publication of the
1894 indictment, proving incontrovertibly that the *bordereau* had
been the only evidence admitted into court against Dreyfus. This
set the stage for the first full confrontation in court between the
growing band of Dreyfusards and the beribboned ranks of the
General Staff.

Esterhazy's court martial for allegedly writing the *bordereau* began
on 10 January 1898 in the same room in which Dreyfus had been
convicted. While waiting for the proceedings to begin the witnesses
passed the time in their own manner: Henry, hearty and loud, talking
with the other witnesses from the Statistical Section; Du Paty, pacing
somewhat nervously; Gonse, maintaining a correct aloofness. To
Scheurer-Kestner, Esterhazy perfectly fitted the role of a rogue, with
his dark moustache and deeply wrinkled face. Picquart, independent
and proud, remained aloof from his former colleagues. That day he
first met Mathieu and Scheurer-Kestner, and he told the senator that
he was determined to reveal all, even though his enemies were capable
of having him imprisoned for years, 'who can say, with adversaries
like them!'[22] Even Lucie attended, so overwhelmed with her sorrows
that she appeared ill to Scheurer-Kestner. The crowd filled the courtroom and spilled on to the street outside, supporters of Esterhazy for

the most part, but also some Dreyfusards who had called out encouragement as Mathieu or Scheurer-Kestner entered the building.

As at Alfred's trial, the first question was whether the trial would be public. The court took a seemingly reasoned position, allowing the civilians to testify in public, but emptying the room once the officers began to be heard in order to protect state secrets – all of which had filled the pages of the newspapers for weeks. This had the effect, however, of publicly silencing Picquart, whose testimony would be vital. One by one the witnesses told their tales. Esterhazy regaled the court with the veiled lady who had alerted him to the Dreyfusard plot. Mathieu calmly showed that Esterhazy disposed of all the information in the *bordereau*, and proudly asserted his right to defend his brother, even if he spent money doing so. Henry and Grebelin testified that Picquart had revealed secrets to Leblois, and the fact that Leblois was not even in Paris at the time they indicated seemed to make no impression on the court. Scheurer-Kestner told of his inquiry but could offer no proofs. Picquart's was the most important testimony; he was heard for two sessions of the court. As he described the *petit bleu* and the later machinations against him he was questioned with such hostility by several of the officers on the tribunal that one of the other judges remarked 'I see that Colonel Picquart is the real accused'.[23] In the end, Esterhazy's lawyer pleaded for five hours on behalf of the accused, but he need hardly have bothered. The panel of officers deliberated less than five minutes, for the central question of whether Esterhazy had written the *bordereau* was quite simple. The experts were unanimous, and so were the judges: Esterhazy was innocent. The assertions of Dreyfus's guilt by the minister of war and the prime minister in both the Chamber and the Senate may only have played a modest role in this result. Upon the announcement the courtroom erupted with cries of 'Long live France! Down with the Syndicate!' Mathieu found it difficult to pass through the hostile crowd outside; Esterhazy was received like a hero.

The following two days brought the nadir of Dreyfusard fortunes. Esterhazy's acquittal meant he could never be convicted of writing the *bordereau*, seeming to forestall possibilities of legal recourse. Billot had Picquart arrested early on the morning of 12 January, charged with passing secrets to Leblois, thus silencing the person who most threatened the General Staff. And Scheurer-Kestner, habitually reelected vice-president of the Senate, was defeated on 13 January 1898, neutralizing the most powerful Dreyfusard politician. Two months earlier Mathieu had denounced publicly the real traitor and the end of the nightmare seemed within reach; now Esterhazy was untouchable and all avenues for revision seemed blocked. The concerted action of the General Staff with Esterhazy and their allies in the government and press had effectively countered Mathieu's gambit. Discouraged and pessimistic, the Dreyfusards did not know even where to begin to take up the struggle after so many grievous blows to the cause. Yet already the tide of despair was turning: Zola had spoken.

5

THE GRAND *AFFAIRE* (1898)

The Dreyfus Affair is now a religion, the religion of justice and truth.[1]

There have been moments when one individual has reshaped destiny's patterns. In mid-January 1898 the case of the *bordereau* was over. Dreyfus had been convicted and Esterhazy acquitted. Picquart was arrested, Scheurer-Kestner defeated. Then Zola – that deeply flawed egotist with his novelist's sense of the dramatic – transformed the landscape. 'Mr President', he wrote to Faure in *L'Aurore* on 13 January,

I accuse Lieutenant-Colonel du Paty de Clam of having been the diabolical agent of a judicial error...
I accuse General Mercier of having made himself an accomplice...
I accuse General Billot of having had in his hands absolute proof that Dreyfus was innocent and of having suppressed it...
I accuse General Boisdeffre and General Gonse of making themselves accomplices to the same crime...
I accuse General de Pellieux and Commandant Ravary of having conducted a villainous inquiry...
I accuse the Ministry of War of having led an abominable press campaign...
I accuse, finally, the first court martial of having violated the law by condemning a suspect on the basis of a document unknown to him, and I accuse the second court of having covered up this illegality under orders by committing in its turn the judicial crime of knowingly acquitting a guilty man.

This article was perhaps the most sensational media event of the newspaper age in France. Within hours *J'accuse* sold 200,000 copies; within days riots and demonstrations broke out in dozens of cities and towns; within months Colonel Henry's edifice of forgeries collapsed in the blood of his self-inflicted wounds; within a year France suffered from a fever of rage and hate; but in two years Alfred Dreyfus walked freely in the land that he loved. And it was Zola who had unleashed the avalanche.

From the beginning of the Esterhazy trial Zola had believed that the army would arrange for an acquittal. When the verdict was announced he had already decided that a direct and impassioned appeal to public opinion was the only remaining path to revision of the 1894 court martial. But Scheurer-Kestner and some others disagreed, fearing that the ensuing upheaval might endanger the Republic that was his life's work. Zola calculated that if he could force the government to prosecute him for libel he could bring out facts in a civil court that the army had been able to suppress in the two courts martial. Thus, in addition to recounting the entire history of the case of the *bordereau*, *J'accuse* also taunted the government and General Staff, 'Let them dare to summon me before a court of law! Let the inquiry be held in the light of day! I await.' Bernard Lazare had played the same gambit when he first published *A Judicial Error* in November 1896, but the government had not risen to the bait. Now, with the 'veiled lady', and spurious telegrams filling the press there was indeed no choice. On 13 January Prime Minister Méline, who had so audaciously proclaimed that there was no Dreyfus Affair, found himself repeatedly questioned before an indignant Chamber about whether Zola's outrageous insults aimed at the highest officers of the army would go unpunished. With only months before parliamentary elections the radicals in particular sensed an opportunity to overthrow the cabinet, which they castigated as too timid in defending the army. Méline explained to the assembly that Zola sought prosecution only in order to continue the struggle for Dreyfus, but then he capitulated, announcing from the podium that the author of 'these abominable attacks' would be brought to justice. Zola thus used the very passion of the anti-revisionists to compel continued action in the case, when their calm enjoyment of victory would have buried Dreyfus for ever on Devil's Island.

Yet even Zola had not foreseen the violence of the popular reaction to his *coup d'audace*. Riots and demonstrations immediately broke out

in dozens of French towns and cities, outbursts of anger at Zola and
at the Jews who allegedly had paid for his attack on the army. Most
of the incidents were spontaneous and relatively short lived, with little
damage and no injuries, involving no more than crowds of youths
shouting in the streets. In thirty cases the crowds attacked Jewish
shops, revealing popular discontent with such merchants who were
said to gouge patrons or refuse to extend credit. In seven towns mobs
surrounded and stoned synagogues or the residences of rabbis. Some
of the 69 incidents over the following weeks and months were even
more serious, with injuries or property damage spread over several
days of violence, leading to 61 arrests at Lyon, 103 at Bordeaux, 108
at Marseilles, and over 200 in Paris.[2] Algeria, a unique case with its
volatile mixture of resentful indigenous peoples, a large Jewish population, and small French colonial presence, witnessed the most violent
episodes. Rioters burned entire streets in the Jewish quarter of Algiers,
2 Jews were killed, and 500 persons arrested. Demonstrations were
contagious, often triggering violence in other towns, but most resulted
from an inflammatory poster, public speech, or newspaper article. In
14 cases Catholic or anti-Semitic groups appear to have fomented the
trouble, while Drumont's *Libre Parole* and the Assumptionist journal *La
Croix* openly encouraged violence. As far as can be known students
formed the largest group among the participants, being 29 of 83
known rioters in Paris, for example, and 25 of 60 in Lyon. The
remainder appear to have been the sorts typical in urban crowds of
the day: some artisanal and industrial workers, a few clerks and other
low-level white-collar workers. The 'intelligent' classes were content to
incite violence by speech and press rather than participate.

Paris and other cities were the centres of both revisionism and anti-
revisionism, so much so that a distinguished historian has called the
Affair 'a storm in an urban teacup'. For most of France, 'the Affair
was never more than a distant irritant, irrelevant and abstract',
another has concluded.[3] Yet at crisis moments the agitation did
encompass peasant France, notably during these riots, even if most
of the population did not closely follow the bewildering events of the
Affair. Those areas that did experience sustained agitation or acute
outbursts of violence often had a substantial Jewish population. In
other cases, incidents spread from a town along a railway line, like
sparks shooting down a wire from a dynamo. When the Affair did
reach the provinces its symbols and episodes were appropriated and
redefined for local usage, as when peasants burned effigies of Zola

during the traditional Lenten celebrations.[4] It was common, too, to nickname chamber pots 'Zolas'. In the department of Isère, the anti-Dreyfusard *La Croix* doubled its circulation in 1897–98, and the wide distribution of anti-Dreyfusard postcards, games, fans, toys and songs throughout France testifies to the impact of the Affair. The poison of anti-Semitism had already infected the body politic, so where the Affair did resonate in provincial France its effect was to exacerbate a traditional prejudice and prepare the ground for still greater tragedies during the Second World War.

Nor does the number of riots adequately reflect the fear and apprehension of Jews and Dreyfusards when faced with this incipient pogrom. Many Jews went into hiding for a time, or walked uncertainly in the streets of their home towns, acutely aware that some of their neighbours considered them dangerous aliens. Most Jews and educated French knew that violence against Jews was a part of life in parts of eastern Europe and Russia, indeed, an increasing number of Jews had fled to France from those areas. But that street violence should occur against a religious and cultural minority in a land that considered itself the centre of European civilization shocked many French, and not just Dreyfusards.

For his part, Reinach wondered why a nation so proud of its defence of liberties did not rise up in favour of Dreyfus, speculating that perhaps alcohol had brutalized and numbed the popular classes. He was more accurate in suggesting that few cared to help a rich bourgeois, who moreover was a Jew. Popular resentment against supposedly rich Jews transposed easily into resentment against the rich generally, so there was an element of class warfare in the demonstrations as well as anti-Semitism. The riots also expressed the fear of many that traditional France was threatened by Jews and their Protestant, Republican, or German allies. Books and newspaper articles about French decadence and decline, evident in the low birth-rate and poor condition of army recruits, fuelled anxieties about national survival in a Darwinian world. Lashing out at some internal enemy, at conspirators and corrupters who sow division and discontent, is a common reaction in such circumstances, a temptation from which few nations have been immune.

The politicians reflected and inflamed this street violence. On 22 January deputies came to blows on the floor of the Chamber when discussing the charges the government had lodged against Zola. Fearful of reopening the entire case of the *bordereau*, Méline and Billot had framed the accusation as narrowly as possible, charging Zola and his editor with libel only for having asserted that the judges in the Esterhazy trial had been ordered to vote for acquittal. The socialist Jaurès thundered from the podium that the government was lying and cowardly for its 'incomplete pursuit' of Zola. Just days before he and other socialist leaders had declared that the Affair was a bourgeois civil war between clericalists and anti-clericalists, and that the working classes should stand aside; there was no difference between Reinach the Jewish Dreyfusard and de Mun the Catholic conservative. Still, the government's weak response to *J'accuse* presented a fine opportunity to castigate the government, and as Jaurès railed the Compte de Bernis, a royalist deputy, shouted that Jaurès himself was part of the syndicate. 'You are a wretch and a coward', Jaurès shot back. The count rushed towards the podium and several socialists struck him, although he managed to graze Jaurès with his fist. This set off a general mêlée that continued in the corridors of the building long after the presiding officer had adjourned the meeting and guards had cleared the hall.[5]

Violence in the streets, in the Chamber and in the press drew enormous attention to Zola's impending trial. In preparation the army brought Picquart before a board of inquiry to decide whether he should be forced from the service for having allegedly shown his lawyer the secret dossier from the 1894 trial. Officers of the Statistical Section, including Henry, Lauth and Grebelin, testified that they had seen Picquart conferring with Leblois over the open dossier. Lauth also testified that Picquart had asked him to verify fraudulently the authenticity of the *petit bleu*. Given such powerful testimony the verdict was not in doubt, and Picquart could only ask ironically if the court really believed that he should be 'driven from the army while commandant Esterhazy parades about with his cross [of the Legion of Honour] and his rank'. The board recommended expulsion, discrediting Picquart's expected testimony in the Zola trial, but Billot postponed official action in order to maintain Picquart under military discipline.[6]

The Dreyfusards, too, were preparing for the looming struggle. On the legal front, Reinach formally requested that the Ministry of Justice annul Dreyfus's conviction on the grounds that documents shown to the judges had not been given to the defence. His request was simply ignored, although it was widely known that Mercier had breached the rules of evidence. Reinach also successfully brought

Rochefort to court for defamation of character. On the public relations front, in late January Alfred's wrenching letters to Lucie began
appearing in the press under the title *Lettres d'un innocent*. Sympathizers read the letters with tear-filled eyes, others thought the publication a cynical ruse.

Poignant as they were, Dreyfus's letters did not reveal the worst
excesses he suffered on Devil's Island, for he held back the most
painful details from his wife and family. As much as he treasured
them, even Lucie's letters added to his ordeal, for he would alter-
nately gain hope from her hints of new developments and then
succumb to disappointment when no decisive news arrived. 'For three
years I have been the play-thing of so many events over which I
have no control', he wrote in November 1897, 'that, despite my
wishes, the bitterness rises from my heart to my lips, anger takes me
by the throat, and cries of grief escape me.' Although ignorant of
events in France, Dreyfus spoke the same language found in all revisionist texts. In a letter of February 1898 to the president of the
Republic he urged continuing the search for the real traitor without
regard for reasons of state. 'To act otherwise would be to return to
the darkest centuries of our history, when truth was suppressed, when
light was suppressed.' As he later noted with bitter irony, 'these letters
arrived [in France] at the very moment when the author of the crime
was glorified, while ignorant of everything that happened in France
I was nailed to my rock, shouting my innocence to the public authorities'. He may have gleaned some information from his guards,
although they seemed to observe religiously their orders not to speak
to him, for according to an official report he had said that 'the guilty
one must be at the Ministry of War, and has designated me as the
victim to hide his infamous crimes'.[7] Fearing for Alfred's mental and
physical state, at about this time Lucie again asked that her right to
join her husband be respected, but again to no effect.

Meanwhile a third trial of the case of the *bordereau*, this time against
the author of *J'accuse*, was getting under way in France. Zola arrived
at the Palais de Justice on 7 February 1898 by the still sensational
conveyance of an automobile. He was accompanied by his lawyer,
Fernand Labori, who had represented Lucie Dreyfus at Esterhazy's
court martial and was known for his passionate eloquence. The
inevitable crowd greeted them upon arrival, some hostile, a few
supportive, but most simply curious. Inside waited nearly every figure
of importance in the Affair, except Billot, excused from testifying by

the Ministry of Justice, and Mathieu, who did not want to provoke hostile outbursts. On that first day the unfortunate Esterhazy, snubbed by both sets of witnesses, paced furiously in the limbo between the two camps. Esterhazy complained to Commandant Ravary, and two days later all the officers dutifully shook his hand in a show of support for the man who might have written the Uhlan letter, but after all had been acquitted of treason.

Lucie Dreyfus, in mourning black, was the first witness called. Zola hoped that the wife of the condemned man would arouse sympathy from the court, preparing the way for the more than 200 witnesses the defence intended to call. While Zola planned to expose every aspect of the case of the *bordereau* to public scrutiny, the presiding judge, Delagorgue, was legally bound to limit the trial to the question of whether Esterhazy's judges had been ordered to acquit. This led to a prolonged duel between the defence and Delagorgue, as Labori and Zola sought to introduce discussion of the 1894 trial at every opportunity, and Delagorgue sought to head off every diversion. In the event, Delagorgue did not allow Lucie to respond when asked if she thought Zola's article was in good faith, a key point under libel law, interjecting that 'the question will not be posed', a phrase rendered famous by its repetition in the days ahead. Indeed, Delagorgue decided that Lucie would not be heard at all, prompting Zola to demand the right of even accused murderers to call witnesses in their defence. When he was cited chapter and verse in support of Delagorgue's decision, Zola peevishly cried 'I don't know the law and I don't want to know the law!' making a bad impression even on his supporters. Although Zola botched that encounter, over time Delagorgue's repeated refrain that 'the question will not be posed', forbidding discussion of the central issues agitating France, contrasted poorly with Zola's motto that 'the truth is on the march, and nothing will stop it'.[8]

Delagorgue did allow Picquart's lawyer Leblois to detail the collusion between Esterhazy and the General Staff, since this directly spoke to the issue of whether the traitor was being protected by the army. This developed into a retrial of the Esterhazy court martial, with its veiled women and forged telegrams from 'Blanche' and 'Speranza'. As the days passed Boisdeffre, Gonse, Lauth and other officers testified at length, Delagorgue allowing them wide latitude when it came to affirming their conviction that the 1894 verdict was just, or that absolute proofs existed that Dreyfus was a traitor. Du

Paty and Henry wisely chose instead to say little, the former by simply
refusing to answer questions, the latter by alleging to be sick. 'I have
eighteen campaigns behind me', he pleaded, 'and I have every right
to have a touch of fever.' Both Labori and Albert Clemenceau,
George's brother and the lawyer for Zola's editor, missed a chance
to conclusively demonstrate the illegality of the 1894 verdict when
questioning General Mercier. Labori misquoted the 'scoundrel D'
letter that had been part of the secret dossier, allowing Mercier to
deny all knowledge of the document referred to. It may not have
mattered since Mercier was willing to perjure himself anyway,
affirming 'Dreyfus was a traitor who had been justly and legally
condemned'. Zola's quick temper and large ego betrayed him yet
again during the testimony of General de Pellieux, who boasted that
he was proud to have helped acquit Esterhazy. 'There are several
ways to serve France', Zola burst out, 'General de Pellieux has, no
doubt, won great victories, I have won mine as well. Through my
works the French language has travelled the world around. I have
my victories! I leave posterity the name of General de Pellieux and
that of Emile Zola: it will decide between us!'

At the end of each day the witnesses had to run a gauntlet of jeering
or cheering spectators, who sometimes jostled and pursued the Dreyfusards. When supporters of the General Staff shouted 'Long Live
the Army!' the revisionists answered, 'Long Live the Republic!' As
during the first trial, the same vicious cries of 'Death to the Yids'
echoed in the streets of Paris. The most violent were the young toughs
who made up the Anti-Semitic League, led by the anti-Semitic journalist and agitator Jules-Napoléon Guérin, ominously foreshadowing
the uniformed thugs of the interwar era. *La Libre Parole* and *La Croix*
continued their campaigns of vile invective, while sporadic demonstrations and riots flared in Paris and other cities. The nationalist and
anti-Semitic press published the addresses of the jurors to assure that
they would feel the full weight of public opinion. On 11 February a
crowd very nearly sacked the Dreyfus residence in Paris, although by
then Lucie had taken the two children to a country retreat. Occasionally the witnesses themselves came to blows, as when warden
Forzinetti assaulted Lebrun-Renault, who had testified that Dreyfus
had confessed.

Once the testimony of the officers had ended the tide began to
turn in Zola's favour. A former minister of justice pointed out how
suspicious it was that Mercier refused to deny that he had sent docu-

ments to the 1894 judges. Delagorgue shouted down another witness who was ready to testify about the secret dossier, and he refused to allow any questioning of Dreyfus's judges. Such frantic stonewalling seemed proof to the Dreyfusards, at least, that illegalities had occurred. Then Picquart took the stand. This was the first time he was heard in public, and the courtroom listened avidly to his version of the inquiry into the *petit bleu* that led to his belief in Dreyfus's innocence. His calm recitation left some cold, but his officer's bearing and obvious resolution made a strong impression on others. Yet there is a mystery at the heart of his testimony, for he never explicitly stated that the 1894 verdict had been procured by illegal means. Perhaps he thought Dreyfus could be freed simply by showing that Esterhazy was guilty, in which case it would not be necessary to dredge up the damaging illegalities of 1894 that could end so many careers. Perhaps some peculiar conception of honour or military discipline prevented him from revealing the crimes of his superiors. In 1894 Picquart had agreed that the secret dossier should be shown to the judges, and it is just possible that this may have been one reason he passed over the whole issue in silence. After all, he had only confided in Leblois when his own defence had demanded it; his quest for justice and truth had always been tinged with an element of self-interest.

Picquart's reserve broke only momentarily, when Henry confronted him. The large soldiers' soldier maintained his story that Picquart had shown Leblois the secret dossier, and when Picquart proved this was impossible Henry boldly called him a liar. Trembling with rage Picquart explained to the jury that 'Henry, Grebelin, helped by Du Paty and under the supervision of Gonse, had been the principal artisans of the other affair', adding 'tomorrow perhaps I will be driven from this army that I have loved and to which I have given twenty-five years of my life!' Some days later he and Henry fought a duel that ended with Henry wounded lightly on the arm. Picquart's honest indignation won over some, but the quiet testimony of Demange was perhaps even more effective. He seemed at first to criticize Zola, perhaps lulling Delagorgue into inattentiveness. 'Didn't a judge of the court martial affirm the existence of a secret dossier?', Albert Clemenceau asked, and Demange quickly responded, 'mais oui, par bleu!' Although Delagorgue cut off further discussion, the damage had been done. There was now sworn testimony that the 1894 verdict was tainted.

The high tide of fortune for Zola, and indirectly for Dreyfus,
occurred during the testimony of the five handwriting consultants
from the Dreyfus court martial. Since none of the five had changed
his opinion they still split two to three, but the testimony of
Bertillon, who believed Dreyfus guilty, turned into a triumph for
the defence. His explanation of how Dreyfus had copied his own
writing using the script of several relatives as models had reached
a pitch of such insane complexity that even the army officers and
anti-Dreyfusards laughed him off the witness stand. 'There you have
the accusation of 1894', Labori summed up as Bertillon hurried
away, 'there is one charge: the *bordereau*; and there you have the
expert, the principal expert!' The three consultants from the Esterhazy court martial who had collectively agreed that Esterhazy did
not write the *bordereau* refused to testify, and for good reason: the
contradictions between their system of explanation and Bertillon's
would have called into question the outcome of both trials. When a
series of defence consultants convincingly testified that the *bordereau*
was not by Dreyfus, but by Esterhazy, the case seemed nearly won;
reports reaching the Ministry of War indicated the jury was leaning
towards acquittal.

By 17 February 1898, then, the Zola trial had reached the same
crucial moment as had been attained in the original trial of Dreyfus,
when Picquart and other official observers had thought the case lost.
As in the earlier trial an authoritative witness now asked to be
recalled to the stand. In 1894 it had been Henry who had fraudulently but dramatically pointed to Dreyfus as the traitor named by
an anonymous, respected source – Val-Carlos. In 1898 de Pellieux
took it upon himself to similarly evoke a decisive document not in
evidence. Honestly convinced of Dreyfus's guilt, he had watched the
parade of witnesses with mounting horror and frustration, not
understanding why the other officers did not bring forth the 'false
Henry'. 'You want the truth, well here goes', he began, repeating a
phrase associated with Henry, and he recounted how in November
1896, at the time of Castelin's interpellation of the government, 'an
absolute proof' arrived in the Statistical Section. He then recited
from memory Henry's forgery in which Panizzardi supposedly told
Schwartzkoppen to reveal nothing of their relations with 'the Jew'.
And like the judge in 1894, Delagorgue allowed the testimony to be
heard, ignoring the repeated pleas of the defence that the documents be produced in court.

Gonse then rose to repair the damage done by the over-zealous de Pellieux, saying, 'these proofs, which exist, which are real, which are absolute, cannot be brought forth publicly here'. It is not clear whether he hoped to prevent examination of the 'false Henry' because he knew it to be a forgery or, as he always stated, because he feared the diplomatic consequences of publicly citing a secret document. Yet de Pellieux wanted more vigorous support than Gonse provided, and even though Delagorgue said he would call Boisdeffre the next day, de Pellieux ordered an aide to summon the chief of staff immediately. A small incident perhaps, but highly illuminating of the mentality of even honest officers like de Pellieux, who when faced with an obstacle did not hesitate to trample judicial authority, issuing orders as if they were upon a battlefield rather than in a court of law. By the time Boisdeffre arrived Delagorgue had adjourned the court, leading to tremendous confusion as rumours flew that Zola and his Jewish paymasters had insulted the army in their desire to lead France to war and destruction. The halls of the Palais de Justice rang with angry threats, and the evening editions of the anti-Semitic press called openly for a new St Bartholomew's Day of reckoning. If the Jews bring on a war, one article read, 'the next day not a single Jew would be alive in France'.[9]

With a night for reflection Boisdeffre had prepared an exquisitely powerful statement. 'I will be brief', he told the court. 'I confirm every point of General de Pellieux's deposition as to its exactitude and authenticity', he said, 'I don't have a word more to say; I don't have the right.' He then repeated with quiet emphasis, 'I don't have the right', signalling to the feverish courtroom and the city beyond that it was a question of war or peace for France. Then Boisdeffre landed his own blow for conviction, telling the jury, 'you are the nation. If the nation does not have confidence in the leaders of its army, in those who are responsible for the national defence, they are ready to leave to others that heavy task. You have only to say the word.' Violating legal procedure, Delagorgue refused to allow Labori or Albert Clemenceau to question Boisdeffre. Having told the jury as clearly as was possible to convict Zola – and symbolically, Dreyfus – or face the resignation of the entire General Staff at a moment of national danger, Boisdeffre simply left the stand. Nobody noted that the penal code defined hindering legal proceedings by the threat of resignation to be a crime. For Dreyfusards, Boisdeffre's statement was a shocking affirmation that Zola had spoken truly: the army was

indeed in the habit of commanding the outcome of trials. For anti-
revisionists Boisdeffre spoke as a dignified warrior defending his
honour and that of the French army.

The double blow by de Pellieux and Boisdeffre seemed decisive to
many observers, but in fact the defence had presented no evidence
that the army had ordered Esterhazy's court martial to acquit. Even
the merciless cross-examination of Esterhazy by Labori and Albert
Clemenceau did not affect the outcome. For an hour he sat pale with
anger and frustration, refusing to respond – for to do so might open
him to charges of perjury – while the lawyers exposed his every tawdry
trespass and criminal violation. He was the last major witness. On 23
February 1898 the jury announced that Zola and his editor had
indeed libelled Esterhazy's judges. Zola was given the maximum
sentence of a year in prison and a 3,000 franc fine. Celebrations
greeted the news across France, and much of the press hailed this
third symbolic conviction of Dreyfus. Yet unlike after the Esterhazy
court martial, Dreyfusards did not lose heart. Their numbers had
grown dramatically since the publication of *J'accuse*, and they believed
Zola's trial had revealed to all who were not blinded by prejudice or
misguided patriotism that grave questions, at least, remained about
the legality of the 1894 trial.

Despite Zola's conviction, the Dreyfusard cause continued to gain
strength. Since Mathieu's denunciation of Esterhazy in November, a
steadily growing list of writers, artists and academics had joined the
fight. The sociologist Emile Durkheim, who was among their number,
explained that the educated classes supported Dreyfus because they
were relatively immune to the 'enthusiasms of the crowd', and the
'prestige of authority'.[10] Anti-revisionists referred to them derisively
as 'intellectuals', suggesting they were only addled aesthetes without
common sense. At the time of the Esterhazy trial some 1,200 such
Dreyfusards had signed a petition for revision and Georges
Clemenceau had called it the 'manifesto of the intellectuals', initiating
the modern definition of intellectuals as a politically committed
literary, scholarly or artistic elite. With some significant exceptions
most Dreyfusard intellectuals were 'marginals' – relatively young,
unknown and unestablished, although many became prominent
during or after the Affair.[11] Those with a position or reputation
tended to oppose revision, making the Affair for intellectuals a case
of 'ins' versus 'outs'. For each well-known writer or academic who
worked for revision, such as Léon Blum, Gabriel Monod, Stéphane

Mallarmé, Charles Péguy, or Anatole France, there were three or four others who were opposed, including Maurice Barrès, Charles Maurras, François Coppée, Jules Clartie, and J. M. Huysmans. Among artists, Monet, Pissarro, Luce, Signac and Cassatt showed sympathy for the prisoner on Devil's Island, while Cézanne, Rodin, Renoir and Degas were hostile.

Similarly, in many other groups those who eventually opted for Dreyfusism tended to be in some sense outsiders. While Protestant Dreyfusards like Scheurer-Kestner, Edmond de Pressensé, and Senator Trarieux might be notables, most Protestant organizations remained anti-revisionist. So too, many Jews rallied to the cause, but the largest and most influential Jewish organizations remained aloof. As the Zola trial was ending the lack of organized support prompted Trarieux and others to found the Ligue des Droits de l'Homme, intended to fight for justice wherever it was violated. The Ligue is the most enduring concrete legacy of the Affair, for it still works for civil rights around the world. Within a year it had attracted more than 22,000 members, but its rival, the Ligue de la Patrie Française, counted 100,000, including over half the members of the prestigious Académie Française.

It became commonplace to remark that the Affair had divided France into two camps, as Maurras said, 'one shouting *Truth! Justice!* and producing nothing but fables and insults; the other: *Fatherland, Honour, Flag*, without proposing any practical or rational answers'. According to Reinach, 'there were in fact two justices, two conceptions of rights and of honour, two mentalities, two Frances'. François Goguel formulated the division as between a 'party of order' and a 'party of movement', while others found that the Affair divided believers in French particularism from the adherents of universal values.[12] Moreover, Paris was relatively more Dreyfusard than the provinces, adding yet another line of demarcation.

The Affair seemed to satisfy a need to affirm an unshakeable principle – whether for or against – in a world in which rapid changes were eroding traditional beliefs of all kinds. On every side much of the energy behind the polemics arose from the search for personal redemption or validation through a grand cause or noble movement. Reinach referred to Scheurer-Kestner once as 'mon cher Arouet', identifying them both with Voltaire's crusade for justice in the eighteenth century.[13] Similarly, some anti-revisionists believed their cause alone embodied France. The facts of the Affair were so confusing that people of good will could honestly differ, and the absence of proof left the door open to the clarity of faith. As Monod put it, 'the Dreyfus Affair is now a religion, the religion of justice and truth'. An anti-Dreyfusard expressed the same sentiment somewhat more cynically, 'why does one need proof, when one has one's convictions?' Even the pervasive anti-Semitic rhetoric was driven in part by a misguided yearning for the promised land of a pure and noble France. Both sides, however, sullied their cause with violent rhetoric and dishonest demagoguery although the anti-revisionists were by far the more egregious offenders.[14]

After the Zola trial the details of the case of the *bordereau* receded in importance as larger and more divisive questions emerged: loyalty to which ideals, which version of France, which institutions. Some tried to bridge the widening chasm: Barrès and Zola maintained the tradition of literary salons by having three dinners in November and December of 1897, but Barrès attended only on condition that the Affair was off limits. Indeed, the most famous cartoon of the era depicted a large bourgeois family serenely sitting down to dinner with the *père de famille* saying, 'above all, no talk of the Dreyfus Affair'; in the next frame the room is in disarray, everyone – including the pets and servants – clawing, striking, or scratching each other, with the simple caption, 'they did'.

Internationally the Affair was also a sensation, not because opinion was divided, but because there was near-universal wonderment at the ferment in France. The Chicago *Tribune* called the Zola trial a 'perversion of justice', the London *Times* said Zola would be honoured 'wherever men have souls that are free', while the *Daily News* noted that France was 'virtually in the hands of a military government'. The *Berliner Tageblatt* made the most cutting comment, writing after the Zola verdict that, 'yesterday the French army won its first victory since its defeat in 1870'. Supporters of Zola and Dreyfus organized demonstrations and marches as far away as Australia. In the wake of Zola's trial the German and Italian governments again denied that Dreyfus was their agent, with the same incredulous response as before.

Prime Minister Méline believed that the trial had finally put an end to the whole Affair. While he mildly criticized Boisdeffre and de Pellieux for crossing the line in their justifiable outrage at having their word questioned, he reserved most of his wrath for the Dreyfusards. On 24 February he announced to the Chamber of Deputies that there was no longer a Zola trial nor a Dreyfus trial, then threatened 'those who would continue the struggle' with legal repression. Since the anarchist bombings of the early 1890s the government had wide powers to arrest and try persons suspected of undermining the security of the state. The Dreyfusards were evidently a greater threat, for Méline pointedly added, 'if the weapons in our hands are not sufficient, we will ask for others'. The government began the campaign of repression by officially dismissing Picquart from the army, revoking Leblois as vice mayor in the seventh district of Paris, and firing a professor who had testified on behalf of Zola. Several months later Lebois's colleagues in the legal profession suspended him from prac tising law for six months.

Yet in the months after Zola's trial the fortress erected by the government and General Staff to protect the 1894 verdict began to collapse under its own weight. As if acting under the impulse of a premonition, Minister of War Billot decided that with elections approaching the time had come to put some order into the Dreyfus dossier at the Statistical Section. Throughout March and April 1898 Gonse meticulously annotated and numbered about 1,500 documents and notes that bore some relation to the case, not hesitating to change a few dates or leave out certain inconvenient information. Upon finishing he proudly wrote that some had the temerity to accuse officers of falsifying evidence, but 'you can't fabricate 1,500 documents!' Impressive as it looked, the new dossier collected all the evidence of Henry's crimes in a single place, considerably aiding later investigators. Furthermore, despite Gonse's confidence in the dossier, the solid front presented by the General Staff began to crumble from within. Du Paty began the disintegration by privately raising doubts about the authenticity of the 'false Henry' even before the end of the Zola trial. By his own account he went so far as to tell Henry that he thought the document might be a Dreyfusard trap. From this point on Du Paty was viewed with increasing suspicion within the Statistical Section and General Staff.

A more serious breach of the ramparts against revision occurred in late April 1898, and fittingly it arose from Esterhazy's own tortured machinations. Christian Esterhazy, who had helped in the collusion with the General Staff out of genuine belief in his uncle's innocence, began in March and April to ask for an accounting of the tens of thousands of francs he had given Esterhazy to invest for him. In his impudence Esterhazy insulted the young man, eventually threatening to denounce him as an unregistered money-lender. Far from being intimidated, Christian seems to have finally realized what a scoundrel his uncle really was. He consulted Zola's lawyer Labori, and then met with Trarieux. The new evidence he provided of the complicity among Esterhazy, Du Paty, and Henry came at a propitious moment, for a certain Judge Bertulus was doggedly pursuing the case of the false telegrams sent to Picquart in Tunisia. Christian did not as yet give evidence directly to Bertulus, but a new avenue for attacking the anti-revisionist edifice had unexpectedly opened up. Meanwhile, on 2 April an appeals court overturned Zola's conviction on the grounds that the Ministry of War, rather than the judges of the Esterhazy court martial, had filed the charges. Further legal wrangling postponed the retrial for several months.

The May 1898 elections unexpectedly catalysed these developments, creating a turning point in Dreyfusard fortunes. The elections themselves were a disaster for Dreyfusards. Nearly every candidate sympathetic to revision was defeated, while perhaps thirty anti-Semitic candidates, including Drumont and Rochefort, entered the Chamber. Reinach lost the seat he had held for nearly a decade, and Jaurès was also defeated, although the Affair had not played an important part in his campaign. The composition of the Chamber changed little, but the nationalists and Radicals had grown increasingly restive under the supple Méline. Led by Henri Brisson, the Radicals wanted more resolute anti-clericalist legislation, all the while clamouring almost as loudly as the nationalists against the Dreyfusards. Some, like Godefroy Cavaignac, frightened traditional conservatives by advocating an income tax, even if he sought harsh measures against the Dreyfusards. In mid-June Brisson narrowly managed to overthrow Méline, then formed a government dominated by Radicals.

None of this political manoeuvring would necessarily have affected the Affair, except that in trading ministries for votes Prime Minister Brisson appointed Cavaignac as minister of war, ending Billot's two-year period in office. The confident Cavaignac, son of the legendary republican general who had suppressed the June Days insurrection of 1848, believed he was just the man to finally bring an end to the tumultuous Affair. In anticipation of yet another interpellation about the Affair the new minister of war examined the massive dossier compiled by Gonse, finding it utterly convincing. He then brought Brisson and the minister of justice to the war offices to show them a selection of documents and gain their assent to refer to several of them in the Chamber. Like de Pellieux at the Zola trial, Cavaignac hoped to strike the decisive blow for justice, but both ultimately found that it was a far different form of justice than they had anticipated.

Standing masterfully at the podium on 7 July 1898 to confront questions about the Affair, Cavaignac first dispensed with Esterhazy: he was a dishonoured soldier who would be punished by an upcoming court martial. Although he did not say so, Cavaignac believed Esterhazy and Dreyfus to be accomplices in treason, so he was all the more determined to finish with the myth of Dreyfus's innocence. He read to the Chamber three documents from the huge file at the Ministry of War; unfortunately, two were forgeries, and the third had nothing to do with either Dreyfus or the *bordereau*. The first was the note from Panizzardi to Schwartzkoppen in which Henry had changed the initial 'P' to read 'D'; the second was Henry's magnificently inept forgery of 1896 giving Dreyfus's name in full; the third was the 'scoundrel D' letter. As the spurious evidence piled up, the Chamber grew ever more enthusiastic. Finally, all doubt could be banished, the troublesome Affair would be over. When Cavaignac finished the deputies rose almost as one to vote his speech the honour of being posted on the walls of each of the 35,000 town halls in France.

This public triumph only temporarily masked the disintegration of the General Staff's position. On 11 July Judge Bertulus finally heard Christian's tale of his uncle's collusion with the army. The judge's inquiry into the 'Blanche' and 'Speranza' telegrams was hindered by lack of handwriting samples for comparison, so Mathieu procured a sample of the writing of Mlle Pays by having someone write to the courtesan seeking an assignation. When Pays replied the trap was sprung: Pays had indeed written the 'Speranza' telegram. To this day no one knows who wrote the 'Blanche' telegram, but there is no doubt it too grew out of the collusion. Bertulus had been thought reliable by the General Staff, but despite Cavaignac's remonstrances he now arrested both Esterhazy and Pays on suspicion of sending the fraudulent telegrams.

Meanwhile the Dreyfusards had begun to attack Cavaignac's evidence. Jaurès for the first time proclaimed his unequivocal support for Dreyfus and launched a devastating press campaign against both Cavaignac and Brisson. The prestige and oratorical power of Jaurès eventually brought most socialists into the revisionist camp, significantly undermining left-wing anti-Semitism in France. However, the radicalism of some leftist Dreyfusards tainted the cause in the eyes of some uncommitted moderates, as when Urbain Gohier, a dedicated anarchist and pacifist, savagely attacked the French army and its General Staff. Reinach preferred to simply point out the suspicious coincidence that the 'false Henry' had appeared just when Castellin had announced his interpellation in 1896. Finally, a Dreyfusard war council that gathered Demange, Reinach, Labori and Trarieux decided that Picquart should himself denounce Cavaignac's documents as forgeries. In an open letter of 9 July Picquart stated he was willing to prove to 'any competent jurisdiction' that Cavaignac had cited forgeries to the Chamber; *Le Siècle* started a collection to pay for posting Picquart's letter next to Cavaignac's address on all the town halls of France. Outraged, Cavaignac wanted the minister of justice to bring libel charges against Picquart. When that failed, Cavaignac had Picquart re-arrested for passing secrets to his lawyer Leblois. Ironically, Picquart was sent to the same prison that had welcomed Esterhazy two days before.

Thus in the summer of 1898 the Affair became mired in complicated legal manoeuvring lasting for the next several years. Cavaignac opened his own military inquiry into the case of the false telegrams, competing with Bertulus for jurisdiction. In addition the magistrate investigating Picquart's relations with Leblois broadened his inquiry into a re-examination of virtually the entire Dreyfus Affair. Several other cases occupied protagonists on both sides, the most important of which was Zola's second trial for libelling the tribunal of Esterhazy's court martial in *J'accuse*. His lawyer Labori hoped to replay the first trial, but the assize judges made clear their determination to keep the trial narrowly focused. Under these conditions the outcome of the case was a foregone conclusion. Clemenceau and others convinced Zola that he could best serve the cause in exile rather than prison, and on the night of 18 July he left for England. Zola's flight was a blow to the Dreyfusards, but they soon regained heart because of the obvious progress of their crusade in the press and larger public.

Frustrated by the legal wrangling and obsessed with ending the Affair once and for all, Cavaignac at one point in August suggested to his ministerial colleagues that all the major Dreyfusard figures be brought before a High Court of Justice and charged with undermining the security of the state. When Prime Minister Brisson baulked, Cavaignac prepared to bring charges against Trarieux, Picquart and Labori for falsely accusing Esterhazy of treason. Although misguided, Cavaignac was at least even-handed. After Bertulus's charges against Esterhazy and Pays had been dismissed for lack of evidence the minister of war also contemplated libel charges against Christian. He then had Esterhazy cashiered from the service for his irregular relations with Pays and his thinly veiled threats to President Faure and others. Esterhazy's hearing revealed many details of the collusion, ruining Du Paty's career and ultimately driving him, too, from the service. Gonse and Boisdeffre, having stayed in the background during the hearing as during the collusion, managed to escape unscathed.

Du Paty was only the first of the General Staff casualties in the war with the Dreyfusards. Henry was the second. The intrepid officer had thus far prevented revision only by audacious forgeries and by conspiring – perhaps unknowingly – with the actual traitor. He must have been under an almost intolerable strain as the ramparts against revision crumbled. Although he was outwardly confident and gruff, his real frame of mind may be gauged by an incident of 18 July 1898 in which his careful façade appears to have momentarily cracked. Bertulus by then had discovered much of Du Paty's role in the collusion and suspected that Henry had also taken part. He and Henry had long known each other and had always got on well, so Henry was undoubtedly caught off-guard when the magistrate suddenly accused him of helping protect Esterhazy. Henry fell stupefied into a chair, and in a flash it occurred to Bertulus that Henry might even have been Esterhazy's accomplice. 'Is Esterhazy the author of the *bordereau?*', he asked the trembling officer, but Henry did not answer directly. Instead he broke into tears, crying 'The honour of the army above all! Do not insist! Do not insist!' Then Henry, evidently desperate for sympathy and beside himself with dread, leapt up and kissed the astonished magistrate full upon the mouth. Alarmed, Bertulus did not press further, for he pitied the blubbering giant and already regretted suspecting him of treason. But the episode convinced Bertulus that the General Staff knew Esterhazy was guilty, and that Henry had helped protect him.[15]

Then in August 1898 came the débâcle. Cavaignac had ordered a re-examination of the dossier at the Ministry of War, so for over a month an investigating officer had been staying late to verify the authenticity of each document. At around ten o'clock on the night of the thirteenth he finally reached the 'false Henry'. Holding it to a lamp for a closer look he discovered that the document, allegedly pieced together from Panizzardi's correspondence with Schwartzkoppen, included paper with lines of two different widths and two different colours. He informed Cavaignac of his discovery the next day.

For two weeks Cavaignac bided his time, carefully preparing his next move. On 30 August he called Henry to his office and in the presence of Boisdeffre, Gonse and General Roget began the difficult interrogation of the officer. First Cavaignac closely questioned Henry about how he had reconstituted the letter from the detritus brought to him by the cleaning woman. Having dispensed with any possibility that Henry had mistakenly mixed up several documents or otherwise made an error, Cavaignac relentlessly hammered at Henry: 'What did you do?' 'What would you have me say?' 'I want you to give me an explanation.' 'I cannot.' 'What did you do?' 'I did not fabricate the papers.' 'You aggravate your situation by these concealments.' 'What I did I did for the good of the country.' 'That is not what I asked.' Even while denying wrongdoing Henry progressively mired himself in contradictions and admissions, explaining at one point 'my superiors were anxious, and I wanted to reassure them and give their minds some peace'. Seeing that Henry would not forthrightly declare his crime, Cavaignac finally supplied the explanation: 'Tell everything... You received in 1896 an envelope with a letter inside it, a letter of no importance. You suppressed the letter and forged another instead.' Henry, cornered and exhausted, finally answered, 'Yes'.

Cavaignac sent Henry under arrest to the Mont-Valérian fortress. Along the way the distraught officer kept mumbling to himself, 'I would be prepared to do what I did all over again; it was for the good of the country and the Army... My poor wife, my poor little boy. Everything has collapsed in a second.' In some ways, Henry was replaying the tragic scene of Dreyfus's arrest, for both men had had their world crumble around them without warning. The next morning Henry asked unsuccessfully to see Gonse, and then wrote his wife a note that already constituted the beginning of a defence:

My adored Berthe, I see that except for you everyone is going to abandon me, and yet you know in whose interest I acted. My letter is a copy and contains nothing, absolutely nothing, false. It only confirms verbal information that had been given me several days before. It is known that I am absolutely innocent, and everyone will know it later; but at this moment I cannot say more.

Henry's note employed the same tactic he had used at Dreyfus's trial, basing an allegation on verbal information that was impervious to refutation. His suggestion that he was acting in the interest of another has caused much speculation. He may have been referring to a particular individual such as Saussier, Mercier or Sandherr, but most probably he simply meant to warn Cavaignac and others that his fall would necessarily lead to the ruin of other, more important, figures.

Exactly how the confidence evident in Henry's letter to his wife evaporated cannot be known. As the hot day wore on Henry appears to have drunk half a bottle of rum. At some point he began another letter to his wife, its incoherence suggestive of a rapidly degenerating sanity: 'My beloved Berthe, I'm like a madman, a horrible agony grips my brain, I am going to swim in the Seine.' When the orderly brought dinner he found Henry lying in a pool of blood, his hand still clutching the razor with which he had slit his throat.

News of Henry's confession and suicide struck Paris like a double hammer blow. Momentarily dumbfounded, the anti-revisionist press could only join in the general consternation. The overjoyed Drey-fusards were nearly as amazed; from his exile in England Zola declared he was 'mad with joy' and that 'this is the beginning. The enemy is being routed.' Up to this point Mathieu, Reinach, Picquart, Zola and most other Dreyfusards considered Du Paty to have been the prime architect of the campaign against revision. They now became convinced that Henry had been Esterhazy's partner in treason, and that he and Esterhazy had engineered Dreyfus's convic-tion. For his part, Esterhazy soon realized that his position had become precarious. He tried to pass off Henry's confession as incon-sequential, but upon hearing of his suicide Esterhazy prudently caught a train for Belgium. Several days later he left for London; so confused had become the fluctuations in the Affair that Great Britain now harboured both Zola, the most prominent voice among the Drey-fusards, and Esterhazy, their most passionate adversary.

The shock waves from Henry's confession and suicide also shat-tered the high command of the army. When Henry was sent to Mont-Valérian Boisdeffre had submitted his resignation, for he had personally vouchsafed the authenticity of the 'false Henry'. Yet aside

from acquiescing to the usage of the secret dossier in 1894 and threatening resignation to assure Zola's conviction, there is no unambiguous
evidence that Boisdeffre had committed other illegalities or improprieties during the Affair. A few months later Gonse, too, was replaced
as vice-chief of staff and put on half-pay; he could be reproached with
much more, particularly overseeing the collusion. De Pellieux
remained at his post, although he had submitted a scathing letter of
resignation stating that as 'the dupe of men without honour' he had
'lost faith in those of my superiors who set me to work on forgeries'.
Henry had sought to protect the General Staff; instead he had tainted
nearly all of his superiors.

Cavaignac was the most highly placed victim of Henry's demise.
The misguided minister refused to admit that Henry's forgery, dating
from 1896, could have any bearing upon the case of the *bordereau*.
When a member of the cabinet asserted that revision was now
inevitable, Cavaignac responded in his imperious way, 'Less than
ever, Sir!' Brisson, however, had decided that the Dreyfus case must
be reopened. Méline, and then Cavaignac, had hoped that repression would stifle the Dreyfusards; Brisson hoped to end the Affair
by finally returning to the roots of the agitation, although he rarely
receives the credit he deserves for his efforts under tremendously
difficult circumstances. Indeed, he had to overcome the opposition
of his own cabinet. In the three days after Henry's suicide the council
of ministers met nearly a dozen times to thrash out a course of action.
Cavaignac remained adamant throughout, but after some waffling
Brisson, too, held firm. Not wanting to bear the risk of initiating
revision on his own, Brisson finally sent Mathieu a note requesting
that he submit a formal request for revision. He then dispatched the
minister of justice to speak one last time to the minister of war; far
from capitulating, Cavaignac spoke again of bringing the Dreyfusards
before a High Court of Justice. Brisson even offered to step aside as
prime minister in favour of Cavaignac if only he would consent to
revision. Instead, Cavaignac resigned on 3 September, writing in a
public letter to President Faure that 'I remain convinced that Dreyfus
is guilty'. The path was now apparently clear for revision.

The year 1898 had begun with Dreyfusard fortunes at their nadir.
Esterhazy's court martial in January had been a kind of gladiatorial
spectacle, with the heavily armed General Staff dispatching the
hapless Dreyfusards before a raucous crowd. In retrospect, however,
Zola's trial has more the aspect of David versus Goliath, and that

encounter ended very differently. In this instance the fallen giant had more than symbolic existence, but was incarnate in the body of Lieutenant-Colonel Henry. Zola's audacity and Cavaignac's blind arrogance had seemingly brought Dreyfus to the verge of liberation from his aptly named prison-hell on Devil's Island. But the anti-revisionists had life in them yet; they had found their Zola, and were poised to strike back.

6

IN THE BALANCE (1898–1899)

We will overthrow this republic to replace it by a better one.[1]

Early September 1898 saw the anti-revisionists in full retreat. Even Drumont said Henry's forgery had been 'idiotic and culpable', while Rochefort's *L'Intransigeant* called it 'odious and stupid'. Henry's suicide and Esterhazy's flight led many of the undecided to support reopening the case of the *bordereau*, even if they might not be convinced that Dreyfus was innocent. When Prime Minister Brisson solicited Mathieu and Lucie to request revision of the 1894 trial the Dreyfusards could well believe their case had been won.

Yet now it was the turn of the anti-revisionists to find an unexpected champion in their hour of crisis, exactly as Zola had come forward for the Dreyfusards after Esterhazy's acquittal. Indeed, Henry's rehabilitation began remarkably early. On 2 September the widely distributed *Petit Journal* announced that Henry's forgery was merely a kind of banknote drawn against the capital of indisputable authentic evidence that Dreyfus was guilty, but which could not be made public from fear of war. On 3 September *La Croix* reported that the Jews had murdered Henry to silence him. But it was left to the young Charles Maurras to sketch out the main themes of what soon became a veritable cult of the lieutenant-colonel. Heretofore known only to a few as a defender of French culture against German romanticism, the intervention of Maurras at this point in the Affair constituted his first steps on the path to national prominence as the intellectual force behind integral nationalism and Action Française, the proto-fascist organization founded in 1899 that bedevilled French political life to the end of the Second World War.

110

In the face of mounting evidence that Dreyfus might not be guilty, Maurras and some other anti-revisionist intellectuals had developed a notion of relativist justice. 'While there are societies without justice', he asserted, 'there is no justice without society; the idea of justice is not divine but human, not absolute but relative, not individual but social, not primary but subordinate.' Barrès agreed, declaring that 'We must teach French truth, that is to say that which is useful for the nation'.[2] And for them the most useful truth, whatever the evidence, was that the Jew Dreyfus was a traitor, while the soldier Henry was a patriot. 'We wait for justice to pay Henry the public respect he deserves. Meanwhile, the French have vowed a *culte domestique* to this brave soldier, this heroic servant of the great interests of the State', Maurras wrote in the royalist journal, *La Gazette de France.* 'Henry sacrificed himself, with death before his eyes, to the task of deceiving for the public good the chiefs he loved.' Far from an odious or stupid act, Maurras transformed Henry's document into a patriotic forgery, intended to assure the punishment of a traitor while shielding France from war. 'Colonel', Maurras concluded, 'in life as in death you took the lead. Your unfortunate forgery will be counted as one of your greatest acts of war.'[3] This article gave heart to anti-revisionists, who had been badly demoralized by the reverses associated with Henry's confession.

From exile Esterhazy contributed to the adulation. For the first time he publicly pretended that under Sandherr's orders he had worked closely with the fallen hero to trick the Germans by feeding them false information, including the *bordereau.* Hoping to profit from the Affair, in November he published a book purporting to tell the entire truth of his dangerous espionage on behalf of the Statistical Section, convincing many that the discredited officer was really yet another martyr for the nation. Yet Esterhazy's story contributed to confusion in the anti-revisionist ranks, for it contradicted Cavaignac's now publicly stated assertion that Dreyfus and Esterhazy had been accomplices in treason. For this reason, and because of his admission that he and not Dreyfus had written the *bordereau,* some anti-revisionists proclaimed that Esterhazy himself had been bought by the 'syndicate' of Jews and other enemies of France. Years of lies and forgeries had by now muddied the waters to such an extent that the anti-revisionists could not even agree among themselves on a single version of events.

General Emile Zurlinden had replaced Cavaignac at the Ministry of War, and immediately opened his own inquiry into the Affair. He consulted with General Roget and others and read the dossier at the ministry, which still included many forgeries, and became convinced not only that Dreyfus was guilty, but also that Picquart had forged the *petit bleu*. This was yet another legacy of Henry's forgeries, for he had tampered with the *petit bleu* in order to suggest that Picquart had written Esterhazy's name on an innocuous document. At a meeting of the cabinet on 12 September the government divided evenly between Brisson and Zurlinden on the question of whether to seek revision of the 1894 verdict, and the issue was put off until the 17th. Realizing that he had simply exchanged one recalcitrant minister of war for another, Brisson cast about for another general to replace Zurlinden, even consulting Reinach and Mathieu to see if they knew of an officer favourable to revision. In the event, when Zurlinden, too, resigned on 17 September in order not to have to preside over revision, Brisson replaced him with General Charles Chanoine, who had agreed to do so. This ministerial comedy had taken most of September, but finally the council voted to refer Lucie's petition to a *conseil de révision* which would decide whether there were grounds for reopening the case of the *bordereau*.

Meanwhile, Zurlinden, having replaced Saussier as Military Governor of Paris, moved against Picquart. A civil court was about to release Picquart from prison since there was little evidence that he had divulged secrets to Leblois; Zurlinden, with Minister of War Chanoine's acquiescence, simply had him deferred to a military court on charges of forging the *petit bleu*. Some months before this a some-time agent of the Statistical Section named Lemercier-Picquart who had been active on the margins of the Affair had been found dead under mysterious circumstances; Henry's suicide had caused some Dreyfusards to question whether both men had been killed by the General Staff in order to keep them quiet. Now, about to be handed over again to military authorities, Picquart took the opportunity of his last public hearing to show that he believed that certain officers were indeed capable of anything. 'This is probably the last time before secret proceedings that I can speak in public', he told the court on 21 September, looking directly at Gonse and de Pellieux, who had been called as witnesses, 'I would like it to be known, if Lemercier-Picquart's noose or Henry's razor is found in my cell, that it will have been murder, for never would a man such as myself think of committing suicide.' Dreyfusards were outraged at the continued persecution of Picquart, while revisionists exulted in this evidence that the General Staff had not given up the fight.

Brisson felt deceived by his new minister of war but did nothing, for he had other worries. His ministerial crisis in September coincided with a tumultuous strike and a foreign emergency, convincing many that France was on the verge of war at a time of incipient social conflict. Thousands of construction workers who had flooded into Paris to begin work for the Paris Exhibition of 1900 had gone on strike. They were soon joined by others, particularly railway workers, whose union leaders advocated a General Strike. Paid by the Orleanist pretender to the throne, Guérin's anti-Semitic gangs incited violence against the strike breakers in order to sow confusion and undermine the Republic. In addition, the nationalist deputy Paul Déroulède chose this moment to resuscitate his Ligue des Patriotes, an organization that had been banned for its inflammatory militancy at the time of the Boulanger episode in the 1880s. Determined to show strength in the crisis, Brisson called out 60,000 soldiers to patrol the streets and operate the railways, giving Paris the aspect of an armed camp. With Guérin and Déroulède whipping up their followers and turmoil in the offices of the Ministry of War, rumours of a military coup ran rife in Paris. For a time, Mathieu among others feared that the General Staff would use the disorder as an excuse to declare martial law, enabling them to take the offensive against their Dreyfusard adversaries.

Then came news that French and British troops in Africa had stumbled upon each other at Fashoda, in the Sudan, and might well come to blows over which nation had precedence in the region. Even the moderate press rose to dizzying heights of nationalist outrage, while the British and French militaries prepared for any eventuality. Faced with 60 million Germans, however, Foreign Minister Delcassé wisely realized that France did not need more enemies, and in negotiations with the British conceded every major point with as much grace as possible. Indeed, the Fashoda crisis marks the beginning of a gradual improvement in Anglo-French relations, leading to the *Entente Cordiale* of 1905 and the alliance of the First World War. In 1898, however, Fashoda added yet more weight to Brisson's burdens.

The luckless prime minister may have thought that referring Lucie's petition to the *conseil de revision* had removed the Affair from his purview. Not a bit of it. In late September the six-member panel

proceeded to split evenly on the question of whether to refer
Dreyfus's case to a court of appeal, bouncing the decision back to
the government. Minister of War Chanoine now firmly opposed
revision, but on 26 September Brisson finally convinced a bare
majority of his colleagues on the council to recommend the case to
the Cour de Cassation, the appeals court with final authority over
the legality of judicial proceedings. It had been nearly four years
since Dreyfus's arrest.

After this defeat the anti-revisionists in the army, press, and
government carried out a stinging counter-offensive throughout the
autumn and winter of 1898–99 that several times threatened to
reverse the momentum for revision. The army undertook the investigation of Zurlinden's charges against Picquart with a zeal reminis-
cent of Du Paty's persecution of Dreyfus in 1894. Not only was
Picquart held in solitary confinement, but he was not told of the
exact charges against him or allowed to confer with counsel. The
inquiry dragged on for months, in part because the civil and military authorities differed over who had jurisdiction in the case.
Picquart had become the most prominent symbol of the Dreyfusard
cause, and crowds often gathered outside his prison to cry 'Free
Picquart!' or 'Long live Picquart!' Reinach, Clemenceau and others
castigated Brisson for allowing Chanoine to authorize this judicial
harassment, but Brisson feared the resignation of another minister
of war would bring down his government.

Minister of War Chanoine also refused to hand over the dossier
on the Affair to the Cour de Cassation, seriously hampering its investigation. The court was divided into three chambers, and the president of the Criminal Chamber directly charged with the inquiry was
an Alsatian named Louis Loew who had already angered anti-
revisionists by upholding Zola's appeal of his first verdict. The anti-
Semitic press now asserted that Loew was actually Lévy-Loew, a Jew
from Alsace like Dreyfus who was eager to do the syndicate's
bidding. It did not help matters that Loew's brother had remained
in Strasbourg after 1871 and so had become a German citizen.
Loew's choice to be the principal investigating magistrate was the
most junior member of the court, Alphonse Bard, convincing many
anti-revisionists that Loew had passed over unbiased judges in
favour of one he could control. Loew said he chose the middle-aged
Bard because he was single and so could not be intimidated by
threats from 'a certain press', against a wife or children.[4] Indeed,

Drumont's *La Libre Parole* later published the addresses of all the judges, asking menacingly, 'what precious lives are sheltered at these mysterious addresses?'[5] By the middle of October Cavaignac was arguing in the press that the case should be remanded from the Criminal Chamber to the entire Cour de Cassation to assure an untainted verdict.

The radical nationalists and anti-Semites were also at work in the streets and press. Guérin of the Ligue Antisémitique and Déroulède of the Ligue des Patriotes vied for the honour of stirring up the most trouble, sending their followers to demonstrations or to break up Dreyfusard meetings. The two leaders differed in their political solutions, however, for Déroulède advocated a kind of authoritarian Republic while Guérin accepted money from the Duc d'Orléans. In anticipation of the opening of the legislature on 25 October both leaders issued manifestos calling for rallies outside the Chamber of Deputies to cry 'Down with the Jews, Long Live the Army, Down with Traitors!' The Ligue des Droits de l'Homme warned its members against this 'perfidious rendezvous by an association of miscreants', while a coalition of anarchists and socialists advocated a counter-demonstration. Planning for all eventualities, Brisson ordered additional police protection around key government buildings.

This tension in the streets, combined with the conflict over the Cour de Cassation inquiry, set the stage for the return of the Chamber on 25 October. Foreseeing a vote of confidence, Brisson was prepared to argue that he had finally removed the Affair from politics and placed it in the hands of justice where it belonged. Most Radical deputies were willing to follow Brisson, but many moderates feared his solution to the crisis might be worse than the disease. Almost from the moment the session began the nationalists assailed the government for not defending the army and striking down the Dreyfusards. With his Ligue des Patriotes even then noisily demonstrating outside – leading to 500 arrests – Déroulède demanded that the Chamber cast out the ministry, 'even if' he concluded, 'however great our respect for the army, our vote besmirches General Chanoine'. As if acting on cue the minister of war then leapt up to speak. 'This disastrous affair that led to the resignations of my predecessors was referred to just now', Chanoine said, 'I have the right to my opinion: it is the same as theirs.' He then stunned the assembly by announcing, 'I hereby tender, from this podium, my resignation as minister of war'.

Parliamentary courtesy dictated that ministers notify the president of the council before resigning; Chanoine may have acted impetuously, but it is more likely that he had coordinated his announcement with the anti-revisionists to overturn the government. If so, the plan nearly misfired. Brisson had the presence of mind to shift the discussion to defence of the Republic, asking that the Chamber affirm the supremacy of civil authorities over the military, an indirect way of supporting Brisson against his now former minister of war. After the Chamber had unanimously so voted, however, a fractious and confused debate resulted in a vote of no-confidence against Brisson. His was the fifth ministry since the discovery of the *bordereau*. Unable to prevent the Cour de Cassation from reopening the case of the *bordereau*, the anti-revisionists had made a first step towards returning the government to sympathetic, or at least neutral, hands. Their victory came at a price, however, for some deputies now began to wonder whether the Republic itself might not be in danger from the coalition of nationalists, anti-Semites, and conservative Catholics brought together by the fight against revision.

The flexible Charles Dupuy succeeded Brisson, the same who had been prime minister when Dreyfus had been arrested and tried. For minister of war he chose Charles Freycinet, a venerable republican who had served in the same office from 1888 to 1892 and was widely respected in both the army and Chamber. Neither man had strong opinions on the question of revision, desiring only that the Affair disappear as quickly as possible. For this reason, Dreyfusard hopes in the winter of 1898–1899 focused increasingly upon the judicial sphere. For their part, the anti-revisionists fought on two fronts, the first against Picquart, the second against the Cour de Cassation. With Zurlinden still governor of Paris and Freycinet unlikely to intervene, Picquart's court martial for forging the *petit bleu* and other alleged offences would seem to be a straightforward affair. The prosecution made much of the fact that Picquart in 1896 had lied to his superiors about the date the *petit bleu* arrived in the Statistical Section. Picquart had misled Gonse so as to pursue his investigation in strictest secrecy, but prosecutors saw this as clear proof of guilt. The discovery of original photographs of the *petit bleu* proving that it had been tampered with after Picquart had been sent wandering about France and Tunisia made no impression upon the investigators. The act of indictment in preparation for a court martial argued forcefully that Picquart had forged the *petit bleu* to frame Esterhazy.

Hence the outrage of the anti-revisionist officers and public when on 8 December, just two days before the court martial was to begin, the Criminal Chamber of the Cour de Cassation stepped in to indefinitely postpone the case. The court held that the military authorities would have to await the termination of criminal proceedings against Picquart, which were in fact unlikely to ever reach a court. Picquart remained in detention, but had been spared the prospect of joining Dreyfus on Devil's Island.

Anti-revisionists denounced the magistrature as corrupt, but a more serious question is whether French judges were sufficiently insulated from administrative and political pressures to render an independent verdict. Although judges sat for life, the Ministry of Justice had powerful means of disciplining them, particularly through its control of honours and appointments. Several scholars have suggested that in cases as highly charged as that of Dreyfus judges often acted more as official agents of the government than as impartial arbiters; others, however, have found that the civil courts acquitted themselves 'with rigor and method'.[6] The record of the Cour de Cassation suggests that despite overwhelming social and political pressures, French judges could indeed find their way to verdicts that conformed to the preponderance of evidence.

Since Loew and the other judges of the Criminal Chamber were proving so obstreperous, the anti-revisionists exerted their newly resurgent political power to bypass the court. Led by Cavaignac, anti-revisionist deputies argued that given the alleged biases of the judges of the Criminal Chamber the case should be transferred to the Cour de Cassation as a whole. Throughout November and December their campaign was aided by the revelations of Judge Quesnay de Beaurepaire, president of the Civil Chamber, another of the three sections of the Cour de Cassation. Beaurepaire had an eventful past, having resigned his judicial position upon the fall of the Second Empire in 1870, but after rejoining the judiciary he had then prosecuted General Boulanger when others shrank from the task. He kept a keen eye upon the Criminal Chamber's inquiry, magnifying small incidents into mountains of iniquity. He claimed, for example, that he overheard Bard address Picquart as 'My dear Picquart', and upon another occasion he said Bard told Picquart, 'Here is Gonse's testimony. I think we've got him'.

Beaurepaire's allegations against the Criminal Chamber received tremendous attention in the press, adding to a sense of mounting crisis. In November and December 1898 Joseph Reinach and others had publicly asserted that Henry must have been Esterhazy's accomplice from the beginning. Wild speculations worthy of the anti-revisionists as to the amount of money Henry had allegedly been paid or the extent of their collusion soon filled the Dreyfusard press. In response, the anti-Semitic crusader Drumont began a fund-raising drive through *La Libre Parole* to help Henry's widow pay for a libel suit against Reinach. A giant banner hung outside the newspaper's offices declaring, 'For the widow and orphan of Colonel Henry, Against the Jew Reinach'. Within weeks Drumont collected 25,000 contributions totalling 131,000 francs.

Drumont's subscription drive provides a snapshot of the anti-revisionist movement at the height of the Affair.[7] Most prominent among the contributors were army officers, students and members of the liberal professions such as doctors and lawyers. Contrary to the over-heated rhetoric of Clemenceau and Reinach, no members of the higher clergy gave their name as contributors, although several hundred priests made offerings. Very few peasants, workers, or small merchants contributed, suggesting that they were not so exercised as the members of the political classes. The ferocity of the comments included with many contributions speaks to the depth of hatred among these committed anti-revisionists for Jews especially, but also Freemasons, intellectuals, republicans, Protestants and foreigners. 'To hang Reinach' wrote one, and others: 'To grill the gorilla; To lynch Loew; Dreyfus and Picquart to prison!; For God, His country, and to exterminate the Jews.' Many prominent intellectuals and anti-revisionist activists contributed, including Mercier, Count de Mun and Barrès, not to mention half a dozen dukes and duchesses, a pair of princes, scores of marquesses, and several hundred counts, viscounts and barons.

As Drumont's campaign continued, the anti-revisionist leagues increased their activity. Already Guérin's Ligue Antisémitique counted many thousands of members, and its paper, *L'Antijuif*, printed in runs of 40,000 copies. Déroulède's Ligue des Patriotes staged large and noisy public meetings to denounce the Jewish syndicate that had corrupted the politicians and the judiciary. In late December they were joined by the Ligue de la Patrie Française, whose leaders included Cavaignac and Maurras, among other politicians and intellectuals. The new organization's main task was to unite anti-revisionist intellectuals and respectable members of the middle class behind the

drive to remove Dreyfus's case from the jurisdiction of the Criminal
Chamber. Anti-revisionists saw this as a fight for the integrity of the
judicial system; Dreyfusards thought it a cynical perversion of justice.
Perhaps because of the league's abstract platitudes about the need
for union among all patriotic French, it quickly dwarfed the Dreyfusard Ligue des Droits de l'Homme, becoming the most prominent
vehicle of anti-revisionist sentiment.

Against this backdrop the Criminal Chamber continued its investigation into Dreyfus's first trial, stretching from November 1898
well into the new year. Its proceedings were supposedly secret, but
leaks to the press made the precaution a mockery. Among its first
witnesses were the five ministers of war who had served since 1894,
each of whom affirmed his unswerving opinion that Dreyfus was
guilty. Since the court specifically had to decide whether the 1894
trial had been just, Bard and others questioned General Mercier
closely about the 'secret dossier' of 1894: he simply refused to
answer. Cavaignac argued that Dreyfus and Esterhazy were accomplices, and that Esterhazy had copied the *bordereau* from Dreyfus's
writing, a thesis which even the inventive Bertillon could not have
concocted. In late November the court heard Picquart, then moved
on to lesser figures in December and January. Esterhazy provided
some diversion in this parade of familiar witnesses. Under cover of
immunity he returned briefly from exile to testify about his
collusion with Du Paty and Henry in the autumn of 1897. He would
say nothing of the *bordereau* or his alleged work for Sandherr.
Reinach and some others believed that the General Staff had paid
for his silence, since his story of writing the *bordereau* for Sandherr
obviously meant Dreyfus had been wrongly convicted.

While the Criminal Chamber proceeded at a stately pace, Beaurepaire's allegations were having their effect upon the Chamber of
Deputies. In January, the deputies amidst great uproar debated
whether the judges of the Criminal Chamber had shown favouritism
to Picquart by serving him a hot toddy. That vital question was laid
to rest when Minister of Justice Georges Lebret affirmed that hot
water and rum had been at the disposal of all the witnesses in the
chilly Palais de Justice. On 6 January Beaurepaire ostentatiously
resigned from his post as head of the Civil Chamber, demonstrating
that he did not wish to be associated with the alleged iniquity of the
Criminal Chamber's proceedings. To calm the furore, First President
of the Cour de Cassation Charles Mazeau, who had authority over all

three of its sections, decided that Beaurepair's allegations merited an investigation. Thus in late January 1899, as the Criminal Chamber was finishing its work, it found itself the object of a board of inquiry led by Mazeau himself. After ten days of hearings the three-judge panel concluded that there were no grounds for impugning the integrity of the Criminal Chamber, but contrary to all precedent their report nevertheless argued that Dreyfus's case should be heard by the entire Cour de Cassation. Mazeau and the others argued that the responsibility for such a momentous case should not fall only upon the Criminal Chamber, and that its judges, 'troubled by insults and outrages', would not have the 'tranquillity and moral liberty' necessary to render a just verdict. In effect, the board was arguing that the Criminal Chamber should accede to anti-revisionist demands because of the violence of the anti-revisionist press.

With Mazeau's report as cover, Prime Minister Dupuy decided to support a 'law of dispossession' to remove Dreyfus's case from the Criminal Chamber and remand it to the entire Cour de Cassation. Dupuy believed that this was the best way to terminate the Affair: a verdict by the entire court would be unquestioned, while a decision by the Criminal Chamber, whatever it might be, would leave a notable part of the political nation inflamed and embittered. Still, the law was a remarkably frank imposition of political considerations upon judicial processes. In presenting the law to the Chamber, Minister of Justice Lebret could only argue from expediency, not legal merit, saying it was a 'law of necessity and of pacification'. When the law of dispossession came to its final vote in the Chamber on 10 February 1899 Lebret made little pretence of a principled argument, telling the deputies to 'look to your districts', where anti-revisionist sentiment was overwhelming. Although denounced by Dreyfusards and many uncommitted deputies as an offence to the principle of impartial justice fundamental to the Republic, the law passed both the Chamber and Senate in late February, just days before the Criminal Chamber was to give its verdict. Now the Cour de Cassation would have to repeat the investigation into the trial of 1894, further dragging out the already interminable legal proceedings.

Anti-revisionists could well savour their success in the Chamber, but an unexpected death gave the Dreyfusards a political victory of their own. On 16 February 1899, President of the Republic Faure carried out his duties as usual, meeting for example with a German aristocrat who once again communicated the assurance of Kaiser Wilhelm II that the empire had had no dealings with Dreyfus. In the mid-afternoon he retired to his private quarters for a rendezvous of another kind with a Mme Steinheil, as again was not uncommon. Some time later piercing screams brought Faure's secretary running, only to find the hysterical lady stark naked, with the sixty-year-old president unconscious before her. The *femme fatale* was rushed out of a side door while doctors tried to revive Faure, who died that night from a brain haemorrhage. 'Félix Faure has just died', wrote Clemenceau, who blamed the president for supporting the anti-revisionist movement, 'that does not mean there is one less man in France.'

Two days later a joint session of the Chamber and Senate elected Emile Loubet to the presidency. Aged sixty, Loubet most recently had served as president of the Chamber of Deputies, the traditional stepping-stone to the presidency of the Republic. He was known as a solid republican and commonsense politician, but in the eyes of the nationalists he was a traitor. Not only had he been implicated in financial corruption during the Panama Affair in 1892, he was said to be pro-British at a time when emotions still ran high over the Fashoda incident. Indeed, a letter from the commander of the French expedition alleging that news of Dreyfusard attacks on the army had badly demoralized his troops in the field later added fury to the anti-revisionist campaign. Furthermore, Loubet reportedly favoured revision. Not content with buying justice, the nationalist press complained, the syndicate of Jews and their lap-dogs, who now were supposedly funded by the British government, had bought a Dreyfusard president. When Loubet paraded to the Elysée palace, the seat of the presidency, Déroulède and Guérin set their followers to chanting 'Resign! Panama!', adding 'Oh Yes!' in English, which passed for a typical Britishism. Déroulède then convened many of his followers beneath a statue of Joan of Arc and declared that Loubet was 'elected by the Jews' as an act of defiance against France. 'Thursday' – the day of Faure's funeral – 'let us gather and I will do my duty; we will chase this newly elected man who for me is not the head of the French nation. We will overthrow this republic to replace it by a better one.'

Having announced a coup, Déroulède set about organizing it. First he alerted his Ligue des Patriotes and other groups, sending thousands of telegrams and postcards under the pretext of organizing a wreath-laying ceremony at Faure's grave. Guérin of the Ligue Antisémitique and the royalists cooperated, although jealous rivalry divided the three groups; Déroulède even declared that if the Duc d'Orléans appeared he would have him arrested. Next, Déroulède attempted to enlist the aid of a general, and may have believed that he had won over de Pellieux, who was to command part of Faure's honour guard. Police reports indicated that many officers and generals frequented royalist salons and 'talked seriously about a *coup d'état*'.[8] Reinach and other Dreyfusards, at least, thought de Pellieux had given his half-hearted consent. De Pellieux may indeed have been tempted, for at about this time his hatred for the Dreyfusards had led him to write to his mother that 'this race [the Jews], which brought us the cult of the golden calf, seeks to push demoralisation and dishonour to the farthest extreme'. Pressured by alarmed republicans, Dupuy forbade Déroulède's gathering, prompting him to issue a poster denouncing a government that repressed patriots while giving 'the country-less', meaning Jews, and 'insulters of the army' a place of respect.

Déroulède had hoped that thousands would heed his call, but perhaps because of Dupuy's prohibition, when Thursday, 23 February arrived only several hundred showed up for the demonstration. Worse yet for the ill-starred deputy, de Pellieux had begged off his duty. Instead, General Roget commanded the detachment Déroulède had chosen as his instrument to cleanse France of the corrupt parliament. Still, Déroulède made a valiant effort. As the troops returned from the funeral, Déroulède grabbed Roget's horse by the reins and shouted, 'Follow us, my General, have pity on the Nation, save France and the Republic. Follow us to the Bastille, to the Hôtel de Ville. To the Elysée, General!' Roget, who was hard of hearing, seemed to be completely bewildered by the gesticulating figure. Mastering his startled horse with difficulty, rather than leading an assault upon the presidential palace he simply pointed with his sabre the way back to barracks. Déroulède and his followers then attempted to block the way, but the column brushed them aside, in the process pushing Déroulède and a few others into the barracks. Fearful of trespassing upon parliamentary immunity – for Déroulède ostentatiously sported his official sash – instead of arresting the invaders, Roget tried to convince them to leave the barracks. Yet Déroulède obstinately declared himself a prisoner of the army, hoping to salvage what he could from the ignoble débâcle. After hours of consultation, Prime Minister Dupuy had Déroulède arrested for refusing to leave a military installation. Déroulède insisted upon adding to the police report that he had attempted to 'seduce the troops to an insurrectionary movement and overthrow the parliamentary Republic'. Seeing the coup turn badly, an agent of the Duc d'Orléans telegraphed the anxious prince in Brussels that he need not cross the frontier. Three months later Déroulède and several others went to trial. It was an odd affair, for the accused attempted to aggravate their offences into acts of high rebellion, while the prosecution – hoping to avoid creating martyrs – argued only that it was a case of provocation against state security. To Déroulède's chagrin and the government's delight, he and his co-defendants were acquitted.

Déroulède's comic-opera coup appears ludicrous in hindsight, but for Dreyfusards and many other republicans the conjunction within the anti-revisionist movement of powerful groups hostile to the current system constituted a serious threat to the Republic. Bowing to pressure from the left and centre of the Chamber, Dupuy ordered prosecution of the leagues as unauthorized organizations, but to appear even-handed he prosecuted the Dreyfusard organizations as well as those which had sponsored the coup. All were fined a derisory amount, and continued to function as before.

Meanwhile, in early March the entire Cour de Cassation began its inquiry into the 1894 trial. It was conducted by Alexis Ballot-Beaupré, Beaurepaire's replacement as president of the Civil Chamber of the Cour de Cassation, an austere jurist who suffered some ridicule from the fact that he still lived with his mother. Aside from his long judicial experience, he had the great merit of never having pronounced an opinion about the Affair. By the end of the month the Cour de Cassation requested and finally received the dossier on the Affair from the Ministry of War; one judge was so puzzled by the dossier's lack of evidence against Dreyfus that he asked whether it was indeed the entire file. The court meticulously detailed nearly every aspect of the 1894 trial. Oddly, however, it refused to hear testimony from the 1894 judges about whether they had received documents outside the courtroom, finding that this would suggest some misdeed on the part of the judges. One of the judges did testify that the *bordereau* was the only document admitted as evidence in the trial, implying that other documents known to the judges had indeed been communicated illegally. Another decisive point came when one of the three 1894 handwriting consultants who had found that Dreyfus wrote the *bordereau* testified that after seeing Esterhazy's writing he had changed his opinion. Thus the five original consultants now split for, rather than against, Dreyfus.

Since the investigation by the whole Cour de Cassation, like that of its Criminal Chamber, proceeded in secret, the door was wide open for distortions and rumours in the press. Indeed, an entire cottage industry arose devoted to speculation about the likely vote of the forty-six judges. To combat the lies of Rochefort and Drumont, Mathieu Dreyfus and the Dreyfusard general staff decided to publish the Criminal Chamber's minutes, even though this was illegal. They arranged an elaborate ruse to cover their tracks: Labori, Zola's lawyer, had his secretaries copy the records at Mornard's residence, who as Lucie and Mathieu's lawyer had legitimate access to them; Bernard Lazare then recruited several Jewish Russian immigrants to copy this copy, since the Dreyfusards were sensitive to the danger of handwriting analysis; finally, this copy was delivered anonymously to Le Figaro for publication. When the material first appeared at the newspaper Mathieu was asked to examine it, since he had access to the originals, putting him in the strange position of authenticating his own leak. Throughout April 1899 the newspaper published the records, for the first time placing most of the facts about the 1894 trial before the public.

While the press tumult continued, another political imbroglio roiled the Chamber. A professor at the army's prestigious Ecole Polytechnique had been heckled by students after he had written that the army should avoid linking its fortunes to the disreputable Esterhazy. Annoyed by the professor's oblique criticism, and perhaps fearful of Drumont's wrath, Minister of War Freycinet had suspended the unruly academic, only to meet a storm of criticism from many deputies. Just a few months before, anti-revisionism had seemed the prudent choice for timorous deputies. Now, Déroulède's botched coup and the revelations in Le Figaro of the Criminal Chamber's findings had emboldened many Radicals, in particular, to edge towards greater assertiveness in support of Dreyfus. But on 5 May 1899 Freycinet resigned, stating that without the confidence of the Chamber he could no longer serve. Dupuy chose another civilian to replace him, the Minister of Public Works Camille Krantz. He was the fifth minister of war in less than a year, all four of his predecessors having fallen victim of the Affair. Krantz immediately reinstated the professor, and for good measure suspended an officer who had admitted funnelling information to the anti-revisionist press.

Throughout these months of legal and political battles Dreyfus continued his monotonous life on Devil's Island. Henry's confession and suicide were unknown to him; Picquart's imprisonment, the fall of Brisson, and the game of musical chairs at the Ministry of War passed unperceived. In July 1898 there was one new development, as Dreyfus began receiving Lucie's original letters, rather than the copies written by a government scribe he had received for the last year. Between declarations of love and dedication to the quest for exoneration, their letters often evoked the daily cares of any parent. Pierre, now age seven, caused his mother some concern because of his wilful nature; Alfred recommended against corporal punishment. At age five Jeanne seemed a more tractable child, but their parents doted upon them both. The fury of the Affair hardly touched the children, isolated from the world as they were by governesses, private tutors, and a large family, although drunken sailors frightened them once in Paris, and on another occasion a group threw rocks at them.

For nearly a year, since Esterhazy's public unmasking in November 1897, Lucie's letters had been hinting at progress in the case. Desperate for more definitive news, Dreyfus in September 1898 suffered a kind of moral and physical attack, lying for days in a semi-catatonic state. Recovering somewhat, he then wrote to the president of the Republic that he would cease writing if he had no response to his letters, a desperate assertion of power over the one aspect of his life he could control. When the government informed Lucie of his declaration she believed he meant he would not write to her either, and begged him not to deprive her of 'the only thing that is sweet in my life'. Yet Dreyfus had not intended that his wife should know of his threat, and wrote angrily to the prison administration demanding some reparation for his wife's suffering at the thought he had forsaken her. He then wrote Lucie a moving letter, vowing that 'if my voice ceased to be heard, it would mean that it had been extinguished forever, for if I have survived, it has been in order to insist on my honour – my property and the patrimony of our children – and in order to do my duty, as I have done it everywhere and always, and as it must always be done, when right and justice are on one's side, without ever fearing anything or anyone'.[9]

In November 1898 Dreyfus received the first concrete signs that he might not end his days on Devil's Island. Lucie hinted in a letter he received early in the month that the government was considering her request for revision. Then, on 16 November, he was handed a terse telegram from the prison administration telling him that the Criminal Chamber of the Cour de Cassation had accepted to look into her request for revision, and inviting him 'to produce your means of defence'. 'Finally the sky cleared', Dreyfus later wrote, 'I foresaw an end to this horrible martyrdom for myself and my family.' His conditions of imprisonment improved as well, and twice a day he was allowed to walk on a path outside the tall palisade around his hut. 'I saw the sea again, which I had not seen in more than two years, I saw again the meagre vegetation of the island; my eyes could rest upon something else besides the four walls of my prison.'

To prepare his defence Dreyfus asked permission to consult his lawyer Demange, but received no response from the government. Indeed, he had no news whatsoever for a month, then in late December 1898 received a copy of a report by Bard to the Criminal Chamber. Here for the first time he read with bewilderment of Ester-hazy and his acquittal, and of Henry's forgery, confession and suicide. Well might Dreyfus write that 'the meaning of many incidents escaped me'. On 5 January he was questioned upon orders of the Cour de Cassation about another incident he had little knowledge of, his alleged confession to Lebrun-Renault. 'Then the days and months passed without receiving any precise news', he later wrote, 'every month my wife's letters, often arriving after considerable delay, told me of her hope for a prompt end to our suffering, but I never saw that end. ...I knew nothing of the law of dispossession and could not understand the length of the inquiry, which seemed to be quite simple to me, since I knew only of the *bordereau*.' February turned to March, and then to April and May: 'each day, each hour, I expected a decision by the high court... the agonising and disturbing delay only accentuated my physical and mental exhaustion'.

An atmosphere of tense expectation also prevailed in France when the Cour de Cassation met to deliver its verdict on 3 June 1899. The courtroom was filled to bursting with partisans of all stripes, including Juarès, Clemenceau, Lazare, Mathieu and Leblois for the Dreyfusards, and many of the officers of the General Staff among the revisionists. Three alternatives faced the court: the appeal could be denied; Dreyfus could be remanded for another court martial; or he could be proclaimed innocent, preventing further prosecu-tion. Yet most Dreyfusards, including Lucie and Mathieu, actually preferred a retrial to exoneration, as it would allow Dreyfus to be found innocent by his peers in the army, rather than by a civilian court. The judges in their scarlet and ermine robes had already heard Ballot-Beaupré's summation, including his assertion that 'the army's position is not at issue before us; it is not under our jurisdiction; it is, thank Heavens! far above these discussions, which can in no way affect it; its honour, assuredly, does not demand that a condemned man who is innocent should continue to be held on Devil's Island'.[10] After thoroughly exploring every tortuous turn of the Affair over the last four years, Ballot-Beaupré had returned to the case of the *bordereau* with a simple question: 'is the *bordereau*, the main basis for the accusation and conviction, in Dreyfus's handwriting?' He paused, then answered, 'for myself, I have become convinced that Esterhazy and not Dreyfus wrote the *bordereau*'. The spectators had erupted with joy or consternation. Several of the judges had been in tears.

And now the court was to render its decision. The debate had been fierce in the deliberation room. First President Mazeau had had to compromise on the wording of the verdict in order to attain unanimity, which he believed essential for the credibility of the decision. But he had succeeded, and the verdict he read bore the signature of all forty-six judges. Mercier's illegal usage of the secret dossier was a decisive factor for the court, along with Henry's confession and suicide, since they cast doubt upon his testimony against Dreyfus in 1894. Other considerations also weighed upon the court, principally the testimony about the handwriting of the *bordereau*, the obvious inaccuracy of the police reports of 1894 depicting Dreyfus as a gambler and womanizer, and a half-dozen lesser points that collectively constituted the 'new evidence' needed for successful appeal under French law. Given all this, First President Mazeau intoned, his emotion-filled voice echoing in the tautly silent room, 'the court hereby rescinds and annuls the verdict rendered... against Alfred Dreyfus, and sends the accused before the Court Martial of Rennes'. Angry shouts erupted from anti-revisionists; Dreyfusards cheered and embraced.

Two days later, Monday, 5 June 1899, Dreyfus held in his hands the telegram he had waited four and a half years to read. 'Captain Dreyfus ceases to be subject to the regimen of deportation, becomes a simple suspect, is restored to his rank, and can wear his uniform', it said, 'Cruiser *Sfax* departs today from Fort-de-France under orders to retrieve the suspect from Devil's Island to return him to France.'

'My joy was enormous, unutterable', Dreyfus later wrote, 'I was finally escaping from this rack of tortures to which I had been nailed for five years, suffering from the martyrdom of my family and children as much as from my own. Happiness succeeded the horror of inexpressible anguish. At last my day of justice was dawning.'

Dreyfus immediately cabled Lucie, 'Heart and soul with you, children, everyone. Depart Friday. Waiting with immense joy the moment of supreme happiness of holding you in my arms. A thousand kisses.' He thought his retrial a formality, he thought his innocence recognized. Instead, he had yet to face his most demanding ordeal.

7

RENNES AND REHABILITATION
(1899–1906)

What sustained me... was the unshakeable faith that France would
one day proclaim my innocence to the world.[1]

The cruiser *Sfax* arrived off the coast of France on 30 June 1899
bearing the most famous prisoner the world had known since
Napoleon's exile on Saint Helena. The case of the *bordereau* had
become an Affair followed by millions from Moscow to Melbourne,
from high aristocrats to poor peasants, yet the prisoner himself knew
almost nothing about it. 'I remained in 1894, with the *bordereau* the
only document in the dossier', Dreyfus later wrote, 'I believed in the
good faith of General Boisdeffre, I believed in a head of state, Félix
Faure, who was wholly concerned with justice and truth.' Boisdeffre
had resigned in the aftermath of Henry's suicide nearly a year before,
while Faure had been dead four months. 'I believed that people had
recognized their error, I was expecting to find my family, and beyond
them my comrades who would be awaiting me with open arms, with
tears in their eyes.'

Instead he was bundled off the cruiser in the dead of night during
a driving rainstorm, badly injuring his legs when he had to jump into
the bobbing launch. Pride and his natural diffidence prevented him
from asking where he was, and nobody told him. The authorities had
arranged every detail of his arrival to prevent any incidents; a nationalist agitator had already hurried to stir up Brest, Dreyfus's rumoured
destination. Transferred to a carriage escorted by soldiers, then to a
special train, and then to another carriage, at dawn he finally stopped

129

in the courtyard of a prison. Only then did he learn that he had
arrived in Rennes, the stage for his second court martial, the most
celebrated trial of the century.

After this harrowing journey without sleep, shivering with fever
and chills, worn out by years in his equatorial prison, Dreyfus was
informed that he would soon see his wife. He even received a brief
message from her assuring him that 'I am close by, in the same city,
with my heart beating with joy and emotion'. 'Tears flooded my eyes',
Dreyfus later recalled, 'the tears that I had not known for so long.'
When shown to the room where his wife awaited he experienced
emotions 'too strong for human words to render the intensity. There
was everything, both joy and pain. We sought to read the signs of
our sufferings in each other's faces, we would have liked to say everything that was in our hearts, all the feelings repressed and suffocated
by the long years, and the words died upon our lips.' For her part,
Lucie refrained from speaking of 'a thousand things, of the children,
of the family, of those who love us both', for fear of overwhelming
her husband. There is a touch of disappointment in Dreyfus's
description of their meeting, perhaps inevitable after the years of
idealized anticipation. 'We contented ourselves with looking at each
other, putting in the looks we exchanged all the power of our affection and of our will. The presence of an infantry lieutenant, ordered
to remain during our encounters, also inhindered any intimacy.' A
police report noted laconically that 'the couple seems to have been
particularly reserved'.[2]

In the succeeding days Dreyfus had joyful reunions with his lawyer
('I threw myself into Demange's arms') and then his brother ('the
finest example of fraternal devotion'), but not his own children, who
were to be spared the spectacle of their father's second trial. Perhaps
too, it was decided that Dreyfus's physical degeneration – he was
gaunt and sickly, with several teeth missing so that he lisped slightly,
and had lost the habit of speech from years of enforced silence –
should be allowed to pass before they were to see their papa. Then
began a month of intensive preparations when Dreyfus had to master
the details of his own case. After the years of enforced inaction he
eagerly took charge of his defence, reading trial records and newspaper clippings late into the night. Dreyfus quickly lost his illusions
about the good faith of those who had condemned him and then kept
him imprisoned, they were 'so low and vile that they deserve only
pity'. To balance the temperate, courtly Demange, Mathieu had also

retained as counsel Fernand Labori, Zola's passionate defender.
Behind them stood the array of intellectuals, lawyers, and politicians
that constituted the Dreyfusard general staff. During the trial the
Auberge des Trois Marches, an inn near Rennes, served as their headquarters, where they shared comradeship and debated tactics. Many
arrived or left in groups, for the anti-Dreyfusard press grew ever more
savage, and the threat of violence lay heavily upon the city.

Well might the Dreyfusards take precautions, for violence had
already struck the new president of the Republic. The order by the
Cour de Cassation for a retrial had sent the nationalist and anti-
Semitic press into a paroxysm of vituperation. Articles advocated a
military coup to defend France from the 'Judaeo-Masonic syndicate'
that had bought the iniquitous decision, and the deputy Cassagnac
warned darkly that 'it is the Army that will have the last word'. The
day after the verdict President Loubet happened to be going to the
Auteuil racetrack near Paris, a tradition that gathered the elite of
French society. Troops had been stationed along his route to prevent
scenes, but security at the track itself was far less rigorous. When
Loubet arrived about 300 men and women – a mixture of aristocrats
and stableboys, according to Reinach – crowded around the base of
the presidential box shouting 'Resign!' and 'Down with Panama!', the
president's nickname on the right. Many wore a small blue flower as
a badge of anti-Semitism, others the white of royalism. Suddenly the
Baron Fernand Chevreau de Christiani broke from the group and
rushed up the steps towards the presidential box, wildly swinging his
walking stick. He managed to graze Loubet's top hat, knocking it
down upon his ears before two generals threw the baron from the
box to the grass below, where fighting had broken out between police
and demonstrators. By the time the scuffling ended perhaps fifty
people had been arrested, some of them nobles of the finest blood,
like Christiani. Within days fashionable jewellers on the Rue de Rivoli
were selling gold stick-pins in the form of a crumpled top hat. 'Having
lunched well, and spurred on by a bellicose lady', a society matron
explained, Christiani 'had betted he would dot President Loubet one
and shout "Down with Panama"'.[3] This wine-sodden attempt to
impress a lady cost the baron a four-year prison sentence.

The implications of Christiani's infantile outburst, like those of
Déroulède's farcical coup, were far more momentous than the events
themselves. For the second time anti-revisionists had publicly insulted
the president, symbolizing for many people Prime Minister Dupuy's

ineffectual defence of the Republic. The next day the Chamber voted
to post the verdict of the Cour de Cassation on all the town halls of
France, a rebuke to Loubet's attackers as well as atonement for the
similar posting of Cavaignac's forgery-ridden speech of July 1898. For
good measure the Chamber also voted its disdain for the 'hateful
machinations of the Royalist and clerical reaction'. These votes
signalled a new stage in the political evolution of the Affair. It was
not that a majority had been won over to Dreyfusism; rather, most
deputies supported with increasing militancy the institutions of the
maligned Republic, even if that meant associating themselves with a
Jew under indictment for treason. The political dimensions of the
Affair had eclipsed the case of the *bordereau*.

That same day, 5 June 1899, the Chamber also took up an even
more inflammatory question regarding the Affair. In order to attain
unanimity by the Cour de Cassation, President Mazeau had had to
accept wording in the verdict stating explicitly that Mercier had illegally sent the secret dossier to the 1894 judges. While true, this constituted a kind of 'poison pill' in the verdict, inserted by anti-revisionist
judges to influence the officers of the second court martial: if they
found Dreyfus innocent, then Mercier's guilt was proven. Taking their
cue from the Cour de Cassation, some in the Chamber, notably anti-
militarist socialists, sought Mercier's immediate indictment. Nationalists then turned the tables on Dupuy, asking whether he intended to
share responsibility, for he had also been prime minister at the time
of Mercier's felony. To avoid further complications, a majority in the
Chamber voted to postpone taking any action against Mercier until
after Dreyfus's second court martial. While politically expedient, this
was perhaps the worst outcome for Dreyfus, as it meant that the
judges at Rennes would be choosing between a once-convicted Jew
and a general still in active service.

Dupuy's government survived the assault on Loubet, but only by a
week. After the Auteuil incident rumours flew that agitators intended
to renew their attacks on the next race day. Republican and socialist
groups countered with plans for their own demonstration in support
of the president and the menaced Republic, forming a Committee of
Public Safety to lead the movement. Meanwhile, Loubet received
thousands of telegrams of support from the provinces, and on 11
June tens of thousands turned out for the march, many wearing the
republican badge of a red eglantine. In the evening skirmishes broke
out between the crowds and police, who were notoriously anti-

Dreyfusard, leading to a number of arrests. 'Seemingly indifferent when the Republic was under threat', one historian has noted, Dupuy 'demonstrated extraordinary zeal when it was being defended'.[4] The next day the Chamber voted that it would support 'only governments intent on defending vigorously the institutions of the Republic' and immediately voted down the Dupuy ministry.

As the politicians cobbled together a new government, developments on the legal front continued to favour the Dreyfusards. Even before the Cour de Cassation had ordered Dreyfus's retrial military authorities had arrested the unfortunate Du Paty de Clam, accused of forging the 'Speranza' and 'Blanche' telegrams sent to Picquart in Tunisia. The charges were later dropped, but it was sweet balm to many Dreyfusards to have him behind bars, at least for a time. Then on 4 June, the day after the Cour de Cassation verdict, Zola returned to France after nearly a year in Britain. Unable to speak or read English well, he had remained relatively isolated, spending his time writing, bicycling, and taking photographs. His long-time mistress and former linen maid Jeanne Rozerot and their two children had soon joined him, and his accommodating wife Alexandrine also visited when Jeanne was away. While abroad Zola had remained incognito, maintaining 'a patriotic silence' regarding the Affair. Upon his return he explained in *L'Aurore* that his only reason for self-exile had been to drag out the Affair, hoping for a break in the case of the *bordereau*, and he claimed vindication for all the assertions made in *J'accuse*. In unspoken reply to Maurras he cast the Dreyfusard cause as the one true patriotism. 'No empire, no matter how many weapons it brandishes, will be able to resist once France has given justice to the world, as it has already given liberty. I cannot picture any other role in history for France, and its glory will be more resplendent than any it has yet known.' He was certain Dreyfus would be found innocent, and that he himself would be exonerated in his retrial, set for late November, but noted that 'not until Picquart is free will the achievement be complete'.[5]

Zola did not have long to wait. On 9 June a civilian court released Picquart from prison, then dismissed the charge of forging the *petit bleu* for which Cavaignac had imprisoned him over a year before. The now enlarged Dreyfusard leadership gave Picquart a hero's welcome at a grand banquet, and he received thousands of congratulatory telegrams from around the world; artists and writers dedicated an *Homage des artistes à Picquart*, with original lithographs and thousands of signatures of well-wishers. With Zola back in Paris, Picquart free, and Dreyfus returned from 'the dry guillotine', the Dreyfusards had apparently triumphed. Like Dreyfus himself, some considered the Rennes trial to be a mere formality. Zola did not even attend the trial, nor did Clemenceau and Reinach (mainly to avoid provoking scenes), although Picquart was to be among those who met at the Auberge des Trois Marches.

Yet the greatest Dreyfusard victory in the summer of 1899 occurred in the political arena. For several years the Affair had contributed to a longer-term reordering of French political life, evident in the gradual coalescing of two heterogeneous camps. As the Dreyfusard and future prime minister Léon Blum observed, the Affair 'decomposed the existing combinations and alliances', creating a new political landscape. The polarizing effect of the Affair increasingly divided nationalists, anti-Semites, and conservative Catholics from moderate, radical, and socialist republicans. During the decade or so ending in 1899 most French governments had relied upon an 'opportunist' or 'progressist' coalition of moderates and conservatives; the next ten years would be dominated by radical ministries often supported by socialists. In the early and mid-1890s nationalists, anti-Semites, and socialists had conducted a simultaneous, if uncoordinated, attack on the Third Republic, but by the late 1890s many socialists concluded that defence of the republican form outweighed class warfare. Crucial in this regard was the whole-hearted commitment of Jaurès to the Dreyfusard cause in the summer of 1898. A coalition of socialist groups had already declared that the struggle for justice for the bourgeois Dreyfus was of no concern to the proletariat, and that socialist groups should stay out of the civil war raging within the dominant classes. In contrast, Jaurès now insisted that humanitarianism knew no class, and that the fight for Dreyfus was the fight for a just Republic, essential for the ultimate triumph of socialism. By 1899 Jaurès and the outrageous behaviour of the anti-revisionists had won over most socialists to the cause.

The summer of 1899 was the balance point in the ongoing restructuring of French political life, making replacing the fallen Dupuy ministry tremendously difficult. President Loubet first called upon several well-known, if uninspiring, figures, but all failed to find a majority. He then asked René Waldeck-Rousseau to form a government, a surprising choice since he had been in the Senate only six years, although he had served as minister of the interior for a brief period in the mid-1880s. A centrist with a reputation for integrity and level-headedness, Waldeck-Rousseau had the presence of mind to see that a traditional ministry composed of party chieftains could not hope to survive the rapidly shifting currents of French political life. Instead, he boldly sought to form a government that included men predominantly loyal to him, but representing a unique combination of parties and positions. For minister of commerce he selected Alexandre Millerand, the first socialist ever nominated for a cabinet post. Millerand began political life as a radical but had embraced the romantic socialism that predominated in France. Long on revolutionary rhetoric but relatively pragmatic in practice, French socialism at this time did not seriously threaten the capitalist order, although it frightened many in the bourgeoisie. Millerand himself may have looked like a raging bull, but his speeches were marked by reason rather than passion, making him particularly unthreatening to conservative sensibilities.

Bringing a socialist into his proposed cabinet was remarkable enough, but Waldeck-Rousseau had an even more canny move in mind. For the critical post of minister of war he selected retired general Gaston de Gallifet, an independent, iconoclastic nobleman well known both for his personal bravery and for summarily executing many insurgents of the Paris Commune in 1871. Waldeck-Rousseau's decision outraged socialists and others on the left, and seemed to contradict his selection of Millerand. Yet Gallifet was an inspired choice, for he combined haughty strength of will, sterling military credentials, and solid republican convictions. His dislike for many of the officers most closely associated with the Affair had rendered him open to Dreyfusard arguments, and he had already realized that the 1894 trial had been a sham.

Waldeck-Rousseau's apparently contradictory ministry was nearly stillborn. Millerand irritated the right, while Gallifet infuriated the left. Anti-Semites and radical nationalists called it a Dreyfusard ministry, and with reason: all the ministers were Dreyfusard, and Reinach had even helped conduct the necessary negotiations. Facing opposition from the anti-revisionist press and politicians, and from some socialists, on 19 June Waldeck-Rousseau withdrew. With no alternative at hand, however, Loubet felt obliged to renew his entreaties and Waldeck-Rousseau reluctantly agreed to present his ministry to the Chamber. When Waldeck-Rousseau strode to the podium on 26 June the deputies greeted him with so much angry shouting that he could hardly be heard. Some deputies cried out 'Murderer!' to Gallifet, who calmly replied, 'Murderer? Present'. Yet for most republicans there was no answering a socialist deputy's pronouncement that 'there is defence of the Republic; there is treason. Choose.' Former prime minister Brisson drove home the point, declaring, 'the government proposes to defend the Republic. I give it my vote. I ask all those on whom I may have any influence to vote, I do not say for the government, but for the Republic.' Reinach wrote that Brisson then raised his arms in the Freemason's distress signal in order to alert free-thinkers to the danger of a clericalist resurgence. The ministry gained a bare majority of twenty-five votes, with over sixty abstentions.

The narrow margin of victory did not mean that Waldeck-Rousseau led a weak government. Indeed, he and Gallifet immediately set about instituting the 'government of Republican defence' hoped for by many deputies and Dreyfusards. They replaced the prefect of police with a more vigorous republican, dismissed Zurlinden as military governor of Paris, and transferred Generals de Pellieux and Roget to provincial garrisons. The new minister of war also told Boisdeffre and Gonse that they should not expect to see further service, but that there would be no legal reprisals against them. These moves evoked little response from the army, for Gallifet had explicitly ordered 'silence in the ranks', but nationalists like Déroulède complained that the Dreyfusard ministry was undermining France's defence. Since his acquittal the feisty poet and deputy had continued conspiring with Assumptionists, royalists, and other enemies of the existing regime, among them Guérin of the Ligue Antisémitique. Guérin's headquarters on the rue Chabrol became their favoured meeting place, and by early August, in anticipation of the opening of Dreyfus's trial at Rennes, Déroulède had seemingly begun planning more mischief.

Informed by secret agents within the conspiracy, Waldeck-Rousseau called a hurried cabinet meeting to approve repressive measures. In the early hours of 12 August police arrested dozens of suspects, including Déroulède and the prinicpal agent of the Duc d'Orléans in Paris. The pretender himself had been once again on the verge of returning to France. Guérin managed to escape to his fortified Parisian headquarters, nicknamed 'Fort Chabrol'. Surrounded by police, he and a dozen comrades remained under seige throughout the Rennes trial. Waldeck-Rousseau had deliberately over-reacted to the alleged conspiracy, showing that he would tolerate no threat, however small, against the Republic. Gallifet did not wholly approve of this operation, complaining later that police had detained several members of his club. 'It isn't possible to belong to a club whose members are arrested – it isn't clubbable', he wrote to a friend, 'I've sent in my resignation from a club of which I have been a member for thirty-three years.'[6]

With Déroulède in jail and Guérin holed up in Fort Chabrol, Dreyfus's second trial could proceed with little fear of public disorder. For a month Rennes was to be the centre of a media circus unparalleled in the history of mass communications. Journalists and curiosity-seekers from around the globe crowded into every hotel, and new telephone and telegraph lines had been installed to handle the increased demand. With soldiers patrolling the principal streets and squares the city appeared more an army encampment than a staid provincial capital. Other soldiers guarded a security zone that included the prison, the high school where the trial would take place, and the house of a Protestant family where Lucie stayed – no hotel would welcome her for fear of disorder. Patrols looked for bombs in the basement of the high school's *salle des fêtes*, chosen because it could accommodate the large number of participants in the trial. The prosecution alone had called over seventy witnesses.

Anticipation gripped the courtroom opening day, 7 August 1899, as the spectators awaited Dreyfus's first public appearance.[7] Almost every figure of importance in the Affair was present, including Mme Henry, dressed in a mourning veil. 'Then all saw him, and the whole hall broke into a gasp', reported one observer, 'there came a little old man – an old, old man of thirty-nine.' The years on his 'torture rack' had emaciated Dreyfus, so that his knees poked sharply from his uniform trousers as he walked, despite the padding he wore to flesh out his uniform. Unable to keep down anything more than milk and eggs, he had strengthened himself with stimulants to get through the ordeal. He stood stiffly before the seven officers who would judge him, and when presented with the *bordereau* declared 'I say again that I am innocent, as I have always said it, as I cried out in 1894. For five years I have said that, my Colonel, now I say it again for the honour of my name and that of my children. I am innocent, my Colonel!' Yet his voice again had that strangled, flat sound many had noted in 1894, and did not inspire confidence. 'What was needed was an actor', Reinach explained, 'and he was a soldier.' Dreyfus went on to deny all the old charges of 1894, as well as the new charges of passing other secrets that had been added to the indictment. Hostile observers thought he was 'lying like a schoolboy', and 'splitting hairs with the dexterity of a wily attorney'.

The next three days the court met in closed session to consider the enormous dossier compiled against Dreyfus. Once again the 'scoundrel D' letter came under scrutiny, Panizzardi's letter to Schwartzkoppen allegedly referring to Dreyfus. Other documents, all equally unrelated to Dreyfus, received similarly close attention. A minor scandal blew up when Demange and Labori discovered that General Mercier had managed to insert in the dossier an inaccurate translation of a telegram from Panizzardi that seemed to incriminate Dreyfus. In the weeks before the trial Mercier had again become Dreyfus's most vocal accuser, recognizing, as he wrote in Rochefort's *L'Intransigeant*, that 'in this affair there is certainly a guilty man. And the guilty man is either him or me'. According to Reinach he also spread about the rumour that the *bordereau* was only a copy of an original document, upon which Kaiser Wilhelm himself had written comments to his spy, Dreyfus. Mercier supposedly let it be known that he had illegally shown the 1894 judges the secret dossier in order to avoid producing this 'annotated *bordereau*' in open court and risking a disastrous war with Germany. This 'annotated *bordereau*' had been mentioned in the anti-revisionist press several times over the course of the Affair, and may well have been one of Henry's legends to convince doubting superiors and politicians. In hindsight an ambiguous reference of December 1894 in Drumont's *La Libre Parole*, a paper with close ties to Henry, may have been about the 'annotated *bordereau*'. Yet the first certain mention was by Henry himself in November 1897 during a conversation with then Foreign Minister Paléologue, at the exact moment when the officers of the Statistical Section were colluding with Esterhazy to prevent reopening the case of the *bordereau*. Reinach, Mathieu, and Dreyfus himself believed that Henry had actually forged an 'annotated *bordereau*', but he had known that it could not be produced in public without being revealed as false. Instead, they believed that Henry, and later Mercier, showed a photograph of the forgery to selected persons to win them over.

Certainly reports about the 'annotated *bordereau*' filled the press in July and August 1899, and when Mercier came to the stand on 12 August many expected him to produce the devastating new evidence. Instead he spoke for over four hours on every other aspect of the Affair, not hesitating to bring into evidence information that had been shown false or irrelevant by the Cour de Cassation inquiry. He blithely assumed, as if uncontested, that the 'scoundrel D' letter could only refer to Dreyfus, that the mistranslated telegram implicated Dreyfus, and that Dreyfus was a known gambler. He next denounced the cosmopolitan syndicate, asserting that the Jews of Germany and England alone had sent 35 million francs for the cause. In justifying his illegal communication of the secret dossier to the 1894 judges he evoked, not the 'annotated *bordereau*', but the threat of war should the documents have become public. He described in great detail a 'tragic night' when the French army stood on the brink of mobilization against Germany, an event that never occurred, and that Mercier had trouble dating when contradicted by Casimir-Périer, president of the Republic in 1894.

Unfortunately for Dreyfus, Mercier's seeming command of detail and his imposing uniform made a strong impression, and the general's testimony was later supported on several points by other witnesses. Boisdeffre, for example, swore that he had indeed awaited orders for mobilization on some imprecise historic night. Only once did Mercier and Dreyfus exchange words, when Mercier concluded his testimony on a note of reason, saying 'if the least doubt crossed my mind, Gentlemen, I would be the first to declare before you to Captain Dreyfus: "I have been honestly mistaken."' Unable to contain his outrage, Dreyfus leapt to his feet and cried out, 'That is exactly what you ought to say!' When Mercier began again, 'I would come to say to Captain Dreyfus: "I have been honestly mistaken. I come with the same faith to admit it, and I shall do all in human power to repair it."' Dreyfus interrupted again with 'That is, indeed, your duty!' Still, Mercier calmly continued, 'My conviction since 1894 has not undergone the slightest change'.[8] Dreyfusards in the audience hissed and jeered the general as he left the stand, but he had the air of a man who had sadly, regretfully, done his duty.

Having given his testimony Mercier then became a *de facto* member of the prosecution. He maintained a constant vigil while prosecution witnesses gave their evidence, ready to help them out of difficulties or recall some neglected detail. Demange and Labori did their best to expose errors and omissions, but their handling of the defence was not without problems. Demange favoured a temperate defence, focused upon the facts of the case and designed to raise doubt in the minds of the judges. In contrast, Labori preached a crusade against the malefactors in the army who had sent an innocent man to Devil's

Island. The two approaches illustrated the divergent schools within Dreyfusism, one centred upon freeing Dreyfus, the other upon fighting larger political and social battles, and the contrast between them did not make for an effective legal strategy. Labori's tendentious questions and editorializing often provoked the presiding officer, while Demange was at pains to show that he respected the good faith of the judges and witnesses. At times the two barely spoke to each other, forcing Mathieu and Alfred to mediate between their own lawyers. Labori was so immersed in the trial that even a bullet could not keep him from the courtroom for long. On the morning of 14 August, as he and Picquart walked towards the *lycée*, someone behind them on the pavement shot the lawyer in the back, then ran away shouting 'I have killed a Dreyfus', or 'I have killed the Dreyfus'. Picquart chased the assailant but lost him the woods outside of town. Luckily, Labori's wound was not serious, and he returned to the trial in just over a week.[9]

The 1894 trial had lasted three days; by 1899 the Affair had grown so large that the Rennes court martial consumed five weeks. Witnesses testified for hours about whether Dreyfus had access to the information discussed in the *bordereau*, whether he knew he was going on manoeuvres as the document indicated, or whether he had acted alone or in collusion with Esterhazy. The question of Dreyfus's alleged confession to Lebrun-Renault occupied an entire session. The same officers who testified in 1894 that Dreyfus had been a gambling womanizer repeated their accusations, with even more precise details. Bertillon now argued that Dreyfus in the *bordereau* had copied his own writing, taking no account of Esterhazy's repeated confessions in the press that he had indeed written the document under Sandherr's orders. Esterhazy refused to testify, instead sending a letter from exile filled with the same tired lies he had been spreading for months. Picquart gave his usual crisp, thorough distillation of the Affair. For their part, most of the important army witnesses, like Boisdeffre, Billot, and Roget, testified that Dreyfus and Esterhazy were partners in treason, along with the shadowy Maurice Weil, whose wife monopolized so much of General Saussier's attention.

While the parade of witnesses continued at Rennes, Guérin and his dozen comrades remained surrounded in Fort Chabrol. Waldeck-Rousseau seemed content to let them stew, but on 20 August about 5,000 demonstrators, incited by the anti-Dreyfusard press, marched upon the building to relieve the siege. The hard-pressed police resorted to repeated mounted charges to break up the crowd, and the ensuing mêlée constituted the worst outbreak of street fighting in Paris since the insurrectionary Commune of 1871. Coming on top of Déroulède's coup and the attack on Loubet, the riot may have been decisive in discrediting anti-Dreyfusard extremism in the eyes of traditional conservatives.[10] Their sense of order and discipline could only be outraged by unruly and violent mobs shouting hateful slogans while attacking the police and the governing authorities. Indeed, a 'statist reflex', in which opinion rallied to the central government, powerfully aided Waldeck-Rousseau's efforts to curtail the anti-Dreyfusard, anti-republican agitation. Supported by the government and by the judiciary, Dreyfusards invoked law and order, while the anti-Dreyfusards increasingly appeared to stand for lawlessness and disorder. For the most part, socialists and republicans of the left and centre had already spurned anti-Dreyfusism, and now the August riot began to turn away some on the right, as well.

Meanwhile, the sheer volume of evidence presented at Rennes seemed to weigh against Dreyfus, and as the trial wound down Labori sought some decisive stroke to clarify the issues. At his request Waldeck-Rousseau twice asked the German government to allow Schwartzkoppen to testify. The Germans were quite content to let the French tear themselves apart, and would only reiterate that Germany had never had any dealings with Dreyfus. Labori then publicly appealed to both the Kaiser and the King of Italy for permission to question Schwartzkoppen and Panizzardi, a gamble that had an air of desperation. Yet neither side was sure of the outcome. At the last moment the prosecution called one Eugène Cernuski to testify, who claimed that a friend in the Austrian foreign ministry had confirmed that Dreyfus was a spy. Cernuski, revealed to be a small-time swindler, could not withstand Labori's spirited cross-examination, and feigning sickness did not appear for the second half of his deposition. On top of the inconclusive evidence this débâcle may have persuaded the prosecutor that the judges would hesitate to sentence Dreyfus to life imprisonment, and noted in his closing argument that they had the option of finding extenuating circumstances, allowing a reduced sentence.

The defence also encountered difficulties with its summation. In anticipation of the climactic session of 9 September 1899, police excluded women and soldiers from the courtroom, as they were thought to constitute a particular threat to good order. Picquart had already left town at the recommendation of the prefect in order to avoid becoming the target of violence should the judges acquit. By this time the rift between Labori and Demange divided the entire Dreyfusard leadership. Picquart and Clemenceau thought that Demange's strategy of merely raising a reasonable doubt would never overcome the judges's assumed predisposition to convict. Reinach, Bernard Lazare, and Mathieu Dreyfus believed instead that Labori's histrionics and harsh rhetoric only alienated the military judges, and argued that Demange should deliver the final statement. Angry at the sentiment against him, on the last day Labori refused to deliver the summation. In his place Demange presented a judicious exposition whose quiet solemnity moved some judges to tears. Still, the circumstances guaranteed that no matter what the outcome a large part of the Dreyfusard leadership would feel betrayed or prone to second-guessing. True to his strategy, Demange stressed the inconclusiveness of the evidence against Dreyfus. 'That doubt', he told the court, 'is enough for me. That doubt means acquittal.' He even concluded his exposition on an ingratiating note that iritated some Dreyfusards, telling the judges 'I have confidence in you because you are soldiers'. Dreyfus then rose to address the court. Physically and mentally exhausted by the gruelling ordeal he could only croak out a few broken phrases declaring his innocence and placing the fate of his children in the hands of the judges.

The judges deliberated an hour, then called the court back in session. In accordance with military judicial procedure Dreyfus waited in another room while the verdict was read: guilty, by a vote of five to two. The sentence was not life imprisonment, however, but ten years, for the judges had voted extenuating circumstances. Demange was too overcome to face Alfred, but when Labori brought the bad news he bore it stoically. 'Console my wife', were his only words. In contrast to the shattered Dreyfusards, many thousands celebrated throughout France, hailing victory over the Judaeo-Masonic syndicate. In Paris, demonstrators outside the offices of Drumont's La Libre Parole cheered and sang the 'Marseillaise' far into the night, while in Belfort a crowd shattered the windows of a house owned by Dreyfus's eldest brother. Abroad the reaction was far different. Crowds stoned several French consulates and there was talk of boycotting the 1900 Paris Exhibition.[11] Almost everywhere France and French justice were held in contempt; the nation that flattered itself as the centre of European culture was increasingly taken to be a land of prejudice and injustice, dominated by a stubborn military and a reactionary church.

Only two months before, Alfred and many of the Dreyfusards had thought their cause won. Now they had plunged again to the depths of defeat, but even so, they girded themselves for a new struggle. Zola set the tone, as he had with *J'accuse* after Esterhazy's acquittal in January 1898. 'I am terrified', he wrote in *L'Aurore* on 10 September, 'filled with the sacred awe of a man who witnesses the supernatural: rivers flowing backwards towards their sources and the earth toppling over under the sun. I cry out with consternation, for our noble and generous France has fallen to the bottom of the abyss.'[12] Rather than give in to despair, however, Mathieu redoubled his efforts to save his brother, especially since the verdict seemed to have destroyed Alfred's will to live. In the days after the verdict Alfred's health deteriorated rapidly, and Mathieu grew alarmed when Alfred for the first time asked to see his children, which sounded to Mathieu like the last request of a dying man. Alfred grew hysterical at the thought that he would have to go through another degradation ceremony, and Mathieu did not believe Alfred could survive it, but mercifully the court martial decided to dispense with that new humiliation. Given that there could be no hope for a successful appeal, Mathieu decided upon the only course that offered a chance for his brother: securing a presidential pardon.

Mathieu could count upon the support of President Loubet and Prime Minister Waldeck-Rousseau, since both wanted an end to the crisis that had gripped France for the last eighteen months. For Waldeck-Rousseau the pardon was to be but a prelude to a general amnesty for all those who may have committed crimes related to the Affair, which he believed necessary for reconciliation and social peace. Yet opposition to the pardon arose from a unexpected quarter. The radical wing of the Dreyfusard movment, represented in its various guises by Clemenceau and Jaurès, thought requesting a pardon was tantamount to defeat. For them the Affair was larger than Dreyfus, it was a sacred fight for their visions of the Republic, a heroic struggle whose outcome would shape France for decades to come. Jaurès had no illusions that victory would bring the advent of socialism, but he did hope that the vindication would lead to a more just, humane, and progressive society. Clemenceau's goals were somewhat more pragmatic and limited, since he sought to bloody the nose of the militarists and clericals he had fought against all his life. 'You are sacrificing the cause of all the oppressed to one man's interests', he told Mathieu and Reinach. Picquart, with his steely sense of discipline, agreed. Clemenceau also recognized, as did Reinach, that a pardon would end the 'heroic' phase of the Affair, for the cause would no longer have a suffering martyr. In part because of this, Labori, the crusader for justice, was the most bitterly opposed of all, even suggesting that Alfred had betrayed Dreyfusism. 'It is not given to everyone to be a hero', he remarked unworthily. But in an emotional summit meeting of the Dreyfusard leadership none wished to stand in the way of Alfred's freedom, for Mathieu would act only if supported unanimously. Clemenceau was the last to concede. 'If I were the brother', he admitted, 'I would accept.'

Dreyfus himself was the final obstacle to the pardon. For him, it reeked of pity, not vindication, and while a pardon could bring him freedom, it would not restore his honour. 'I had no need of mercy', he later wrote, 'I was thirsty for justice.' Yet the lure of freedom, and particularly the prospect of ending the suffering of his family, won out in the end. To meet any objections from the radical Dreyfusards, Mathieu had Jaurès compose a statement accepting a pardon which affirmed Alfred's determination to seek judicial exoneration. 'The government of the Republic grants me my freedom', Jaurès wrote on Alfred's behalf, 'It means nothing to me without my honour. Beginning today, I shall continue to seek reparation for the terrible judicial error from which I still suffer.'

Having waited several weeks so as to make the pardon more palatable to the army, on 19 September 1899 President Loubet signed Dreyfus's pardon; that same day, Scheurer-Kestner died at his home at Thann, after having done so much to help vindicate his fellow Alsatian. The next day, accompanied by a police escort, Alfred and Mathieu began the final leg of the journey that had begun five years before, when Alfred had set out on 15 October 1894 for what he had thought was a routine inspection. The journey had taken him from Du Paty's phantasmagorical interrogations through half a dozen prisons and courtrooms, and had set him upon a desert island as the only prisoner of a purpose-built compound, the despised object of national and anti-Semitic fury. The way back had brought Alfred to the brink of despair – and even death – after the verdict at Rennes. Yet finally, on 21 September 1899, Alfred and Mathieu arrived at Carpentras, the home of their sister just north of Avignon, where they hoped to find peace and renewal.

Surrounded by his family, seeing his children for the first time in five years, Alfred had ended one journey but was determined to begin another: the road to rehabilitation. While less lonely than the struggle for revision, it was nonetheless a path of heartbreaking tragedy, as the Dreyfusard cause disintegrated into recrimination and acrimony. For the pardon of September 1899 had indeed ended the heroic era of the grand Affair. As Léon Blum recognized, 'the spell had been broken'. Personal, political, and tactical differences among the Dreyfusards had already exploded at the Rennes trial; the pardon and the amnesty definitively shattered the Dreyfusard leadership. Clemenceau, Picquart and Labori came to believe that Reinach – a close associate of Waldeck-Rousseau – had convinced Mathieu and Alfred to accept the pardon and amnesty in order to buy tranquillity for the government. At one point Picquart even refused to shake the hand of Mathieu or Demange, and Labori eventually broke off all relations with the Dreyfus family. Clemenceau the radical and Jaurès the socialist eventually returned to their feuding over political questions. Indeed, the duel between the two would shape French politics until the outbreak of the Great War. These emotionally wrenching schisms found expression in the press, with each side accusing the other of betraying the cause. Alfred attempted to reconcile the parties, but finally returned to his accustomed detachment.

What most angered Clemenceau and Picquart was that the amnesty sought by Waldeck-Rousseau would prevent civil or criminal proceedings against the officers whose crimes had caused and perpetuated the Affair. Picquart had been drummed out of the army, yet Mercier was free to seek, and gain, election to the Senate in 1900 – where Clemenceau joined him in 1902. The long-anticipated amnesty, which finally became law in late 1900, also adjourned several lesser cases related to the Affair: Zola's retrial for *J'accuse*, the suit pitting Mme Henry and Reinach, and a case brought by Picquart against a newspaper for publishing a fake photograph of him meeting with Schwartzkoppen, to cite only three. In his zeal to protect the Republic, however, Waldeck-Rousseau made certain that the amnesty did not cover the conspiracy among the royalists, Déroulède, and Guérin, and in November 1899 the High Court of the Senate tried them and eighteen others. Most were acquitted, but Déroulède was sentenced to ten years' exile, while Guérin's obstinance at 'Fort Chabrol' brought him a ten-year prison sentence. Waldeck-Rousseau also disbanded the Assumptionist order and its newspaper *La Croix*, a favourite target of anti-clericalist republicans. Although disavowed by several bishops, the anti-Semitic order had insisted that it represented the true voice of Catholics in France. These measures effectively pulled the teeth of the radical nationalists and anti-Semites. Drumont still fulminated against the Jews and their lap-dogs in the government, but the fire had gone out of the anti-revisionists. The Dreyfusards were almost as quiet, in part because of the loss of Zola, who in 1902 was accidentally asphyxiated by the gas from a faulty room heater.

Despite opposition from the Dreyfusards, the amnesty bill slowly made its way through the legislature. 'No one wishes more ardently than I for peace, for the reconciliation of all good Frenchmen, for the end of the shocking virulence of which I was the first victim,' Dreyfus wrote to the chair of the committee handling the amnesty, yet, 'it benefits only scoundrels who abused the good faith of the judges; who knowingly had an innocent man condemned through lies, perjury, and forgery; and who cast me into the abyss.' Meanwhile, Dreyfus painstakingly collected material for his appeal of the Rennes verdict. Since French law required new evidence or proof of perjury for a successful appeal, Alfred, Mathieu, Demange, Jaurès, and Reinach – the remnants of the former Dreyfusard general staff – concentrated upon two avenues. The first lay in attacking the credibility of Cernuski, whose last-minute testimony they believed had turned the tide against Dreyfus. They uncovered some evidence that the Statistical Section had paid Cernuski, and succeeded in later having several officers arrested for a time, but nothing could be proven. Ironically, the second avenue had even less foundation in fact, but was eventually successful. The much-reduced Dreyfusard leadership was already convinced that Henry had forged a copy of the *bordereau* allegedly annotated by Kaiser Wilhelm; they now came to believe that Mercier, as in 1894, had illegally sent documents to the judges at Rennes, including the 'annotated *bordereau*'. Dreyfus culled mountains of newspaper clippings and volumes of court testimony searching for traces of the elusive document but made little headway. At last a break came when a friend of Mathieu's reported that one of the judges had confirmed the existence of the annotated *bordereau*. The judge immediately denied the story, but when Jaurès later heard the tale he leapt upon this opportunity to revive the Affair in the Chamber of Deputies in April 1903.

By this time Waldeck-Rousseau had retired, and he would soon die of cancer. Gallifet had preceded him in resigning, in part from disgust at the game of politics, in part because he felt his influence in the cabinet was declining. The new prime minister was Emile Combes, a rigid anti-Catholic and former seminarian whose minister of war was the equally anti-clerical former head of the Ecole Polytechnique, General Louis André. Their government rested upon a *bloc des gauches* coalition of radicals and socialists in order to carry on the fight against the Catholic church, and Jaurès himself had been elected vice-president of the Chamber, so when he came to the rostrum he could expect a sympathetic hearing by a good part of the deputies. Over the course of two days he mustered all his formidable oratorical skills to expose the improprieties in the Affair, raising enough doubt about the Rennes verdict that Minister of War André declared to the Chamber that he would open a new inquiry. The case of the *bordereau* had risen again.

For seven months André meticulously sifted through the enormous dossier of the Affair. His research proved that Schwartzkoppen had been receiving information long before Dreyfus had become a *stagiaire*, and more decisively, that Henry or others had falsified several documents taken as authentic by the Rennes court martial. With inside information about André's findings, Dreyfus in November 1903 formally petitioned for revision of the Rennes verdict. In March 1904 the Criminal Chamber of the Cour de Cassation once again took up the case of the *bordereau*. In contrast to 1899, however, most of the expert witnesses and officers now sided with Dreyfus: only Bertillon maintained that the *bordereau* was an auto-forgery. Testimony proved that Dreyfus could not have written that he was just leaving for manoeuvres and that he could not have furnished some of the information mentioned. Also in contrast to 1899 there was little public interest in the proceedings, in part because the review dragged on for month after dreary month. Finally, in 1906 the Criminal Chamber transmitted the case to the Cour de Cassation in conformity with the 1899 law of dispossession, and the entire matter had to be thoroughly reviewed yet again.

The wheels of justice always ground slowly, but there were also political considerations behind this majestic pace. Prime Minister Combes was perfectly happy to use the Affair against his opponents, yet did not want a potentially unpopular verdict to cloud his prospects in the 1906 elections. In the event, his government fell beforehand anyway, over an episode that stemmed directly from the Dreyfus Affair. In order to reassert control over the army and reduce the allegedly dominant influence of the church over the higher officers,

Gallifet and then André had reaffirmed that only the minister of war could promote officers to the rank of general, and not the military's own commission on rank. André had established *fichiers*, or card files, to evaluate the republican and secular credentials of candidates that eventually included information on some 25,000 individuals. The Freemasons supplied much of this material, particularly concerning religious opinions and practices. Although legal, when this fact became public in the autumn of 1904 many took this as evidence of the Judaeo-Masonic syndicate denounced for so long by the anti-revisionists. An outraged nationalist deputy slapped André in the face during one tumultuous meeting of the Chamber; Déroulède and Barrès hailed this violence as an act of heroism. André later resigned, although his fate was less dire than his attacker, who committed suicide in order to avoid trial. Combes did not long survive his minister of war, resigning in January 1905. Two other governments took office before the elections of May 1906 ended the ministerial – and judicial – impasse.

In July 1906 the Cour de Cassation finally rendered its conclusive verdict on the case of the *bordereau*, some twelve years after the troublesome document had been gathered from Schwartzkoppen's wastebasket. For the last time the principal Dreyfusards gathered in a courtroom to witness the end of the drama. 'In the final analysis, of the accusations against Dreyfus there is nothing that remains standing', the decision read, 'the annulment of the Court-Martial's verdict leaves no charge that may be qualified as a crime or misdemeanour against him.' The court not only unanimously annulled the Rennes verdict, it even declared that a third court martial was not in order, sparing the disastrous possibility of a third conviction. 'It was the end of my torment which had lasted twelve years, the end of my anguish over the future of my children', Dreyfus later wrote. For good measure, the court decreed that its decision would be published in the *Journal Officiel* of the Republic, as well as in fifty-five newspapers to be chosen by Dreyfus; all of France was to know that the once-reviled officer was indeed innocent. In the days that followed Dreyfus received congratulations from around the world, and celebrated his vindication with an ever-growing following of family, friends, and well-wishers. Drumont, Rochefort, and Barrès made their customary denunciations, but no one by this time was paying them much attention.

A kind of political apotheosis completed the judicial victory of the Dreyfusard cause. On 13 July 1906 the Chamber almost unanimously voted to reinstate Dreyfus into the army with promotion to the rank of major, and Picquart was made a brigadier-general. In the Senate, Mercier had the temerity to speak against the reinstatement and was shouted down by the disgusted senators, one of whom threatened that if not for the amnesty Mercier would be occupying Dreyfus's now vacant prison cell. Shortly thereafter the Council of the Legion of Honour unanimously decided to induct Dreyfus as 'rightful compensation for a soldier who has endured a unique martydom'. The Senate also voted to place a bust of Auguste Scheurer-Kestner in its gallery of honour, along with that of another deceased Dreyfusard notable, Ludovic Trarieux. To complete the Dreyfusard triumph, upon a motion from Jaurès the Chamber decided that Zola's ashes would be ceremoniously transferred to the Pantheon, France's temple to her most honoured children. The controversial novelist had indeed been prescient – although almost a decade too early – when he concluded his November 1897 article praising Scheurer-Kestner's crusade for Dreyfus with the defiant words, 'Truth is on the march, and nothing will stop it'.

CONCLUSION

Everything begins in *mystique* and ends in politics.[1]

On 21 July 1906 Alfred Dreyfus stood again at attention in a courtyard of the Ecole Militaire, just as he had done nearly twelve years
before while undergoing the degrading ritual of exclusion from the
army. Once more, soldiers in parade dress lined the courtyard while
again the bugle and drum marked the stages of a solemn rite. Upon
this occasion, however, instead of 'Death to the traitor!' and 'Down
with the Jews!' a small group of spectators shouted 'Long live the
Republic! Long live Dreyfus!' while Dreyfus was knighted a member
of the Legion of Honour. 'My mind, disorientated, returned to memo-
ries of twelve years', he later wrote, 'the way the mob howled, the
terrible ceremony, my stripes torn unjustly from my uniform, my
sword broken and lying in pieces at my feet.' The presiding general
dubbed Dreyfus three times on the shoulders with his sword, then
embraced the overwhelmed *chevalier*. Unlike the first ceremony, Lucie
Dreyfus looked on from a window, and after the soldiers had filed
out she greeted her newly elevated husband, who forgot himself to
the extent of kissing her before the surrounding well-wishers. Mathieu
stood by, and Picquart, too, was there, warmly shaking Dreyfus's hand.
Someone cried out 'Long live Picquart', but the newly minted
brigadier-general replied, 'No, Long live Dreyfus!' to which Alfred
responded, 'No! Long live the Republic! Long live truth!' At one point
Dreyfus was so overcome that he nearly collapsed, but he soon recovered, and left the courtyard still ringing with acclamation. 'What a
splendid day of restitution this was', he declared, 'for France and for
the Republic!'[2]

Although the Affair was over, its dying embers could still flare into
violence. Just days before Dreyfus entered the Legion of Honour,
Gonse and Picquart had met on the field of honour to settle their

differences in a duel; Gonse missed, and Picquart did not fire. More seriously, during the ceremonial translation of Zola's ashes to the Pantheon in September 1908 an anti-Semitic nationalist, inspired by the violent rhetoric of Action Française, shot twice at Dreyfus, wounding him on the arm. His attacker was acquitted on the grounds that he had acted in a moment of passion. Violence had always accompanied the struggle, most egregiously during the demonstrations against Zola and Jews throughout France in January 1898, but also including the shooting of Labori at Rennes, the attack on Loubet at Auteuil, the numerous duels between partisans (thirty-one according to one count), and the several episodes of fistfights in the Chamber – to which could be added the threatened violence in the Chamber against Prime Minister Jospin upon the centenary of *J'accuse* in January 1998. The Affair left victims in its wake wherever it passed, most prominent among them Alfred Dreyfus and his family, but also Picquart, imprisoned for nearly a year, and even Henry, victim of his own deception. Ruined careers (Forzinetti dismissed, professors revoked), court-martialled officers (Dreyfus, Picquart and Du Paty, among others), and even broken marriages (the husband of Picquart's mistress divorced her when General de Pellieux told him of the liaison; Mme Esterhazy divorced her husband for living openly with Pays) accompanied the crisis.

The tragedy was all the greater because many of the guilty paid little for their crimes. Esterhazy endured only a few difficult years in his English exile, impoverished and embittered, railing at the Jews who had destroyed him and the army that had betrayed him. Soon the death of an uncle brought him a small annuity, however, and his still formidable talents with women and words began to assert themselves once again. Marguérite Pays broke with him when he refused to marry her, but other women lent money and consolation, and he eventually found steady employment as a journalist under a variety of pseudonyms. As count 'Jean de Voilement' he settled down to a comfortable home in Harpenden (Hertfordshire) with an evidently well-off companion whom he may even have married. Yet Esterhazy's fury at the army never died, and during the Great War he wrote articles so hostile to the Allied cause that his editor in France was nearly shot for subversion. He died in 1923, still proclaiming that he had written the *bordereau* under Sandherr's direction; even this greatest of rogues sought to maintain a figleaf of honour in his disgrace.

Henry and Mercier must vie for the title of the one most responsible for the conviction and continued imprisonment of an innocent man; Sandherr's share of responsibility can never be known, while Du Paty was more an inventive dupe than an orchestrator. Henry paid with his life and Du Paty with his career, although in 1912 Minister of War Millerand returned him to the reserves, for which Millerand was hounded from office by the left in the Chamber. Du Paty went on to die a hero's death in 1916. Yet Mercier served serenely in the Senate until 1920 and expired the next year, still convinced of his rectitude. For the most part the other officers – Gonse, Boisdeffre, Billot, de Pellieux, Roget, Lauth, Gribelin – who lied or kept silent to protect Mercier and the honour of the army were more weak and misguided than culpable. Wrong-headed to the end, Bertillon spent his last years upholding his anthropometrical system of identification against the encroachments of fingerprinting. All of them contributed their part to the fiasco, but in relatively modest measure. A courageous declaration by then Minister of War Billot in the autumn of 1897 would have probably spared France the ordeal, but he, and the others, had been convinced of Dreyfus's guilt by Henry's forgeries and Mercier's assurances. A baleful reasoning dictated much of the Affair: why destroy illustrious careers and undermine the army just because a traitor had been irregularly convicted? The necessity of protecting individual rights, especially when guilt is thought certain, has never been so clearly demonstrated.

Esterhazy's treason was a crime against the state; Henry and Mercier committed crimes against an individual; the campaign of racism carried out by radical anti-Dreyfusards rose instead to the level of crime against humanity. Dreyfus was convicted in the case of the *bordereau* only in part because he was a Jew, but the Affair was almost wholly dependent upon the fact that he was. The anti-Semitism of Drumont's *La Parole Libre*, Rochefort's *L'Intransigeant*, the Assomptionists' *La Croix*, and Guérin's *L'Antijuif* poisoned political discourse, while Déroulède, Barrès, Maurras, and the Duc d'Orléans and other opponents of the Third Republic sought to reap the political benefits. Certainly not all anti-Dreyfusards were anti-Semitic; the complexities and distortions of the facts understandably led to opposing conclusions. And certainly Dreyfusards like Hervé and Grouhier, and even upon occasion Clemenceau and Jaurès, attacked the Catholic church, the army, or their anti-Dreyfusard opponents with brutality and maliciousness. Yet the race hatred spread by the radical anti-Dreyfusards condemns them as the most guilty of all the participants in the Affair, even if they had no role in the injustice of the case of the *bordereau*. For the most part these radical anti-Dreyfusards also fared well after the Affair, although Drumont seemed cursed by his role. Having associated himself so closely with the vanquished cause of anti-Dreyfusism he lost his previous influence, dying in poverty and obscurity in 1918. It is true that Déroulède also paid a price. Waldeck-Rousseau forced him into exile for conspiring against the Republic in 1899, and after his return he failed to regain his former place in the Chamber.

Charles Maurras, who had done so much to rally anti-Dreyfusard spirits after Henry's suicide, had a different destiny. As the leader of Action Française he became the most prominent figure on the radical right, espousing authoritarian monarchism and vehement anti-Semitism. Maurras advocated force to attain his ends, and the street violence of his supporters earned the movement attention beyond its actual strength. Action Française was only the first of the proto-fascist parties to rise in France, yet Maurras always held pride of place and he was hailed by Philippe Pétain, leader of the collaborationist Vichy regime from 1940 to 1944, as 'the most French of Frenchmen' despite his desire for accommodation with Germany.[3] Given his condemnation of Dreyfus the fate of Maurras was ironically fitting: after the Second World War he was convicted of intelligence with the enemy.

The price was high, but the victory was won: Dreyfus had been freed after nearly five years in prison, and after twelve years had regained his honour – although it was only in 1995, a century after the first court martial, that the army officially recognized that Dreyfus was innocent. Everywhere the Dreyfusards and their allies were triumphant. A radical-dominated Chamber had declared the separation of church and state in 1905; that same year Jaurès and other socialists had united in a single party for the first time, creating the French Section of the International Workingman's Association; and in October 1906 Clemenceau formed his first government, calling upon none other than Picquart to be his minister of war. Yet the Dreyfusard victory did not bring about the reign of progressive humanism Jaurès sought, nor did it mean that the clerical and royalist dragons had been slain, as Clemenceau had hoped.

Indeed, the bickering among the Dreyfusard victors and the degeneration of Dreyfusism into a mere political dispute led the Catholic

Dreyfusard Charles Péguy to sigh with resignation that 'Everything begins in *mystique* but ends in politics'. This perhaps underestimates the significance of the Affair, for it decisively contributed to reshaping both the right and left. Traditionally the right had advocated order; after the Affair the extreme right increasingly fomented disorder. Late nineteenth-century socialists had sought revolution; after the Affair socialists could be counted upon to support the 'bourgeois' parliamentary Republic when it was threatened. The real revolutionaries of the latter Third Republic were the integral nationalists, the racial anti-Semites, and the various fascists who repudiated the grand legacies of the French Revolution that had become the foundations of French society and politics. In this they were more revolutionary than the French Communist Party that split with the socialists after the First World War; the French Communist Party always considered its work to be fulfilling, not renouncing, the promise of the Revolution.

The Affair contributed to this political transformation in two main ways: by reorienting the politics of anti-Semitism, and by definitively establishing the Republic in France. As early as December 1898 the Radicals excluded militant nationalists and anti-Semites from their party. Similarly, when Jaurès brought most of the socialists of 1898 and 1899 around to Dreyfusism he rooted the left in the most profound humanitarian traditions of France, in large measure breaking the hold of anti-Semitism upon socialism in France. It is not coincidental that the first Jewish prime minister in France was a socialist, nor that the first socialist prime minister was a Jew. Conversely, the radical anti-Dreyfusards tied large segments of monarchist, militant Catholic, and anti-republican opinion to the abusive and destructive doctrines of racial anti-Semitism. Because of the fundamental contradiction between anti-Semitism and the highest ideals of the French revolutionary tradition, socialism could never fully take up the progressive work of the Revolution without first divesting itself of the remnants of anti-Semitism. Nor could the extreme right such as the Action Française (or more recently, the National Front) present a coherent alternative in keeping with French political culture so long as it retained the legacy of racism and xenophobia embodied in the embrace of radical anti-Dreyfusism. The French anti-racist movement SOS Racism, for example, has accused the radical-right National Front of having never accepted the French Revolution or the innocence of Dreyfus. Anti-revisionism and anti-Semitism grew inextricably intwined in the late 1890s; for a time they rose together, but they also collapsed together. Drumont and the other radical anti-Dreyfusards succeeded only in discrediting their cause. As a result of the Affair the extreme right grew more unified but less viable, while the left for the most part jettisoned a prejudice fraught with liabilities.

Thus the reorienting of anti-Semitism during the Affair helped clarify the political landscape on the left and far right, reordering the constellation of political forces in the Chamber. Although the Radicals and the socialists arrived late to Dreyfusism, their meeting in the Dreyfusard movement definitively settled the governmental form of the French state. Founded in defeat after the Franco-Prussian War, the Third Republic survived the 1870s mainly because monarchists could not agree upon a candidate to the throne, while in the 1880s the inconsequential Boulanger had nearly toppled the regime. Seen in this light Déroulède's attempted coup and Waldeck-Rousseau's subsequent 'government of Republican defence' stands as a pivotal point in French political life. The coalition of centre, moderate right, and left embodied in Waldeck-Rousseau, Gallifet, and Millerand was essentially that of the *Union sacré* that held France together during the early years of the First World War, and not greatly dissimilar from the Popular Front ministry that preserved parliamentary government in France during the crisis of the 1930s.

Few of the leading Dreyfusards would live to see their companion in arms Blum leading France at the head of the Popular Front. Scheurer-Kestener, Trarieux, and Zola had died even before the final victory in 1906. Jaurès led the struggle against the repressive labour policies of Clemenceau's government, then became the most prominent voice against the growth of militarism in France. He was assassinated by a deranged right-wing extremist during the crisis of July 1914, a destiny in keeping with the rhetorical violence that had infected French political culture during the Affair. Clemenceau returned to power at the age of seventy-five during the darkest moment of French fortunes in the Great War, earning the nickname of 'the tiger' for his ruthless prosecution of the war effort, and of pacifists and other opponents. He was given a hero's funeral upon his death in 1929. For both Jaurès and Clemenceau the Affair had provided the essential context for their ascent to become the most significant French political figures of the early twentieth century.

Clemenceau's former minister of war, Picquart, has a more ambiguous historical reputation. He displayed great courage and fortitude in the struggle against the General Staff, but after Rennes he bitterly turned against Alfred, Mathieu, Reinach, and others for what he considered their connivance at the amnesty. He died in 1914 after being thrown from his horse. His fellow rejectionist Labori briefly reconciled with the Dreyfus family in 1914, but soon returned to his resentments. In contrast, Dreyfus's other lawyer, Demange, remained steadfastly loyal throughout, and continued to take up unpopular cases. In 1919, for example, he defended the Radical deputy Joseph Caillaux, who favoured a negotiated peace, against accusations of conniving with the enemy, pitting Demange against his former comrade in Dreyfusism, Prime Minister Clemenceau.

Demange was perhaps the first person outside the Dreyfus family who proclaimed Dreyfus to be innocent – along with prison warden Forzinetti, who suspected as much from the moment of Alfred's incarceration. Bernard Lazare, however, was the first Dreyfusard. Even before Dreyfus's trial the young anarchist had written the first articles denouncing the anti-Semitic origins of the case of the *bordereau*. His politics and militant stand against anti-Semitism separated him from most of the other Dreyfusards, but especially in the early years of 1895 and 1896 he was crucial in forging the eventual victory. His evolution is indicative of one response among Jews to the Affair: originally he advocated Jewish assimilation, but the hatred displayed by anti-Dreyfusards convinced him that Jews would never be accepted by a large part of the French nation. He then turned to Zionism, an ancient dream that had been given new impetus by Theodore Herzl, for whom the Affair had also confirmed the need for a Jewish state. Lazare's response was that of a small minority, however; more common was that of Joseph Reinach. For him the Affair only reinforced the need for a strong Republic to protect the rights of all citizens. His *Histoire de l'Affaire Dreyfus*, completed in 1911, is a monument of moderate Dreyfusism and republican conviction.

With the passing of Reinach in 1921, Demange in 1925, Clemenceau in 1929, and Mathieu in 1930, nearly all the most prominent Dreyfusards had gone; all, that is, except Alfred himself. Perhaps the stubborn stolidity that had allowed him to endure Devil's Island accounts for his longevity. After the ceremony inducting him into the Legion of Honour he had attempted to return to obscurity. His reinstatement into the army had been at a rank lower than he would normally have attained, so he served only a year before retiring to live a generally uneventful life amidst his family and small group of friends. For a time he grew quite interested in syndicalism, even giving a lecture on the topic before a group of workers who were no doubt more interested in seeing the former prisoner of Devil's Island than hearing about the problem of labour from a rich bourgeois. He re-entered the artillery during the Great War, even at age fifty-eight serving at the front during the crisis of 1917, not far from where his son Pierre also fought. He and Pierre survived the war, unlike the sons of Mathieu and Reinach.[4]

Filled with joy at the return of his native Alsace to France, after the war Dreyfus again retreated into his family. He would only occasionally allow his name to be associated with larger causes, as when he signed a petition protesting the executions of Sacco and Vanzetti, the American anarchists convicted on dubious evidence in 1927 of robbery and murder. Even in his last years he still suffered occasionally from fevers and chills, as well as from nightmares of being chained to his cot, wrists and ankles bleeding, while parasites crawled over his flesh. He had left Devil's Island in 1899, but he would never be free of it. He died in July 1935, and was buried upon Bastille Day, a fitting occasion for a man who made a cult of patriotism and of an officer's honour. Lucie Dreyfus remained the only survivor of the original inner circle, and her fate, like that of her husband, further illuminates the disparate destinies of French Jews. During the Second World War she assumed a new name and was hidden in a convent, a courageous example of Christian charity towards a family that had suffered so much from its absence. Yet she was among the lucky ones. Many in the extended Dreyfus, Hadamard and Reinach families, including grandchildren of Alfred and Lucie, died in the camps of the Holocaust. Ironically – or perhaps fittingly? – the son of Du Paty de Clam helped carry out these atrocities as 'commissaire aux questions juives' beginning in February 1944.[5]

The collaborationist Vichy regime which was directly responsible for many of these deaths resurrected much of the anti-Dreyfusard rhetoric condeming Jews and Freemasons, adding only fervent anti-Communism to the mix. The defeat of Vichy constituted, then, a second defeat of anti-Dreyfusism and anti-Semitism in France, although anti-Semitic incidents still occasionally arise, and the continued strength of anti-immigrant parties in France and Europe demonstrates that the fear of 'alien' elements in the nation is still very much alive. Indeed, the case of the *bordereau* became a towering

Affair because it translated and crystallized the most profound evolutions in French and European society: the tension between personal rights and the prerogatives of the state; the clash of progressive individualism and organic solidarities; the struggle between liberal ideals and traditional culture; the problem of reconciling equality and diversity. This Affair during a *belle époque* a hundred years past evoked enduring tensions within the Western tradition, which is why it continues to engender new legacies and new lessons during our own *fin de siècle*.

NOTES

PREFACE

1. For a recent example see André Figueras, *Ce Canaille de Dreyfus* (Paris: Publications André Figueras, 1982).
2. Michel de Lombarès, *L'Affaire Dreyfus: La Clef du Mystère* (Paris: Robert Laffont, 1972); Robert Elliot Kaplan, *The Forgotten Crisis: The fin-de-siècle Crisis of Democracy in France* (Oxford: Berg, 1995); Henri Guillemin, *L'Enigme Esterhazy* (Paris: Gallimard, 1962). Jean Doise argues that Dreyfus was indeed innocent, but that the real 'traitor' was acting upon orders of the French General Staff in order to confuse the Germans, *Un Secret bien gardé: histoire militaire de l'affaire Dreyfus* (Paris: Seuil, 1994).

1 IN SEARCH OF A TRAITOR (1894)

1. From the *bordereau*, or note, offering information to the German military attaché in Paris.
2. Cited in Jean-Denis Bredin, *The Affair: The Case of Alfred Dreyfus*, trans. Jeffrey Mehlman (New York: George Braziller, 1986; French edn 1983), 49.
3. Count Maximilien von Schwartzkoppen, *Les Carnets de Schwartzkoppen: La Verité sur Dreyfus* (Paris: Reider, 1930).
4. For accounts that argue the *bordereau* did not arrive by the 'ordinary path' see Maurice Baumont, *Aux Sources de l'Affaire Dreyfus* (Paris: Productions de Paris, 1959); Guy Chapman, *The Dreyfus Case: A Reassessment* (London: Rupert Hart-Davis, 1955); Guillemin, *L'Enigme Esterhazy*; and Joseph Reinach, *Histoire de l'Affaire Dreyfus*, 7 vols. (Paris: La Revue Blanche, 1901–1911). Bredin, *The Affair*, Douglas Johnson, *France and the Dreyfus Affair* (New York: Walker, 1966), and Marcel Thomas, *L'Affaire sans Dreyfus* (Paris: Fayard, 1961) find the ordinary path most probable.
5. Allan Mitchell (1980) 'The Xenophobic Style: French Counterespionage and the Emergence of the Dreyfus Affair', *Journal of Modern History* **52**(3): 414–25.
6. Marr published the influential anti-Semitic book *Sieg des Judenthums über das Germanenthum (The Victory of Jewdom over Germandom)* in 1879.
7. Michael Marrus, *The Politics of Assimilation: The Jewish Community in France*

at the Time of the Dreyfus Affair (Oxford: Oxford University Press, 1980); Albert S. Lindemann, The Jew Accused: Three Anti-Semitic Affairs (Dreyfus, Beilis, Frank), 1894–1915 (New York: Cambridge University Press, 1991).

8. Eugen Weber, France: Fin-de-siècle (Cambridge: Harvard University Press), 130.

9. See Zeev Sternhell in The Jews in Modern France, ed. Frances Malino and Bernard Wasserstein (Hanover, NH: Brandeis University Press, 1985).

10. Michael Burns, Dreyfus: A Family Affair, 1789–1945 (New York: Harper-Collins, 1991), 91.

11. D. L. Lewis, Prisoners of Honor: The Dreyfus Affair (New York, William Murrow, 1973), 21.

12. It is still unfair to suggest that 'many of Dreyfus's ills came originally from his own defects', Johnson, France and the Dreyfus Affair, 43.

13. Cited in Bredin, The Affair, 51.

14. From Du Paty's unpublished notes, cited in Thomas, L'Affaire sans Dreyfus, 144.

15. Johnson, France and the Dreyfus Affair, 17 and Benjamin Martin, 'The Dreyfus Affair and the Corruption of the French Legal System', in Norman L. Kleeblatt, The Dreyfus Affair: Art, Truth, and Justice (Berkeley: University of California Press, 1897), 38.

16. Louis Snyder, The Dreyfus Case: A Documentary History (Rutgers University Press: New Brunswick, NJ, 1973), 14.

17. Alfred Dreyfus, Five Years of My Life, 1894–99 (New York: McClure, Phillips, 1901), 8.

18. Bredin, The Affair, 57; Reinach, Histoire de l'Affaire Dreyfus, 1: 120.

2 A TRIAL, AN EXILE (1894–1895)

1. Dreyfus to his wife Lucie, 5 January 1895.

2. Both accounts may be found in Dreyfus, Five Years, 11 and 42.

3. Burns, Dreyfus: A Family Affair, 113.

4. Bredin, The Affair, 70.

5. Most recently by Burns, Dreyfus: A Family Affair.

6. Dreyfus, Five Years, 1. He added that his childhood had 'passed happily amid the gentle influences of a mother and sisters, a kind father devoted to his children, and the companionship of older brothers'.

7. Burns, Dreyfus: A Family Affair, 67 and 78.

8. Translated in Bredin, The Affair, 86.

9. Dreyfus, Five Years, 13.

10. Enquête de la Cour de Cassation, 2 vols (Paris: Stock, 1899), 1: 255.

11. Reinach and Bredin believe Mercier knew as well, and Thomas does not exclude the possibility. Martin in Kleeblatt argues that the Statistical Section duped Mercier.

12. Burns, Dreyfus: A Family Affair, 116; Bredin, The Affair, 79.

13. Lewis, Prisoners of Honor, 96.

14. Bredin, The Affair, 94.

15. Burns, Dreyfus: A Family Affair, 137; accounts of Henry's exact words vary.

16. Chapman, The Dreyfus Case, 188.

17. Eric Cahm, *The Dreyfus Affair in French Society and Politics* (New York: Longman, 1996; French edn, 1994), 21.
18. Jérôme Hélie, 'L'arche sainte fracturé' in *La France de L'Affaire Dreyfus*, ed. Pierre Birnbaum (Paris: Gallimard, 1994), 238.
19. Burns, *Dreyfus: a Family Affair*, 143
20. Dreyfus, *Five Years*, 50.
21. Bredin, *The Affair*, 8.
22. *La Cocarde, Le Jour, Le Temps*, 6 January 1895; evening papers carried the next day's date. See also Reinach, *Histoire*, 1: 519; Patrice Boussel, *L'Affaire Dreyfus et La Presse* (Paris: Armand Colin, 1960), 78.
23. *Le Figaro*, 6 January 1995.
24. Burns, *Dreyfus: A Family Affair*, 162.

3 THE *PETIT BLEU* (1896–1897)

1. Lieutenant-Colonel Picquart's response to General Gonse's request that he remain silent about evidence exonerating Dreyfus; Gonse denied Picquart's account. Reinach, *Histoire de l'Affaire Dreyfus*, 2: 359; *Cour de Cassation*, 1: 249.
2. *Cour de Cassation*, 1: 132, 143; Picquart said he did not read the secret dossier until the summer of 1896.
3. *Cour de Cassation*, 1: 408, deposition by Curé, who explained that what he meant was that Esterhazy was intelligent, an explanation that does not ring true.
4. Mathieu Dreyfus, *L'Affaire Dreyfus telle que j'ai vécue* (Paris: Grasset, 1978), 93.
5. Burns, *Dreyfus: A Family Affair*, 187.
6. This group's existence became public in 1902, giving fresh support to those who believed Dreyfusards were part of a secret Jewish cabal; Paula Hyman, 'The French Jewish Community from Emancipation to the Dreyfus Affair', in Kleeblatt, 31–2.
7. Translated in Bredin, *The Affair*, 137.
8. Alfred Dreyfus, *Cinq Années de ma vie* (Paris, 1899), 169.
9. Reinach, *Histoire de l'Affaire Dreyfus*, 2: 80.
10. Schwartzkoppen, *Carnets*, 10.
11. Marcel Thomas, *Esterhazy, ou l'envers de l'Affaire Dreyfus* (Paris: Vernal, 1989), 184.
12. Thomas, *L'Affaire sans Dreyfus*, 217.
13. Reinach, *Histoire de l'Affaire Dreyfus*, 2: 359.
14. Lauth agreed with Gribelin, *Cour de Cassation*, 1: 432, 415.
15. See Thomas, *L'Affaire sans Dreyfus*, 354; Reinach, *Histoire de l'Affaire Dreyfus*, 2: 421; Bredin, *The Affair*, 174.
16. Reinach, *Histoire de l'Affaire Dreyfus*, 2: 436.
17. *Cour de Cassation*, 1: 309.
18. Reinach, *Histoire de l'Affaire Dreyfus*, 2: 436.
19. Marcel Thomas, *Esterhazy*, 250; Boussel, *L'Affaire Dreyfus et la presse*, 119.
20. Translated in Bredin, *The Affair*, 182.

4   A SUCCESSFUL COLLUSION (AUTUMN 1897)

1. Esterhazy's account of a conversation with Du Paty at the beginning of his collusion with officers of the General Staff, translated in Snyder, *The Dreyfus Case*, 133.
2. Bredin, *The Affair*, 190.
3. Du Paty testimony in April 1899 in *Cour de Cassation*, 2: 31. Boisdeffre in September 1898 admitted knowing that some officers wanted to warn Esterhazy, but claimed he had no role in the collusion; *Cour de Cassation*, 2: 210.
4. Schwartzkoppen recounted this conversation to Panizzardi, and they both later repeated it to various diplomats; it is also found in Schwartzkoppen, *Carnets*, 173.
5. This tale has partisans to this day, since it has the advantage of explaining why the officers colluded with Esterhazy; see Kaplan, *Forgotten Crisis*; Guillemin, *L'Enigme Esterhazy*; de Lombarès, *L'Affaire Dreyfus*; Doise, *Un Secret bien gardé*.
6. Translated in Snyder, *The Dreyfus Case*, 138.
7. Auguste Scheurer-Kestner, *Mémoires d'un sénateur dreyfussard*, Strasbourg: Bueb et Remaux, 1988), 139.
8. Translated in Cahm, *The Dreyfus Affair*, 43.
9. Johnson, *France and the Dreyfus Affair*, 93.
10. Dreyfus, *Cinq Années*, 191.
11. Translated in Burns, *Dreyfus: A Family Affair*, 209.
12. Bredin, *The Affair*, 211.
13. Chapman, *The Dreyfus Case*, 165, 166.
14. Richard Griffiths, *The Use of Abuse: The Polemics of the Dreyfus Affair and Its Aftermath* (Oxford: Berg, 1991), 5.
15. Bredin, *The Affair*, 223.
16. Translated in Snyder, *The Dreyfus Case*, 145, 146.
17. Reinach, *Histoire de L'Affaire Dreyfus*, 3: 187.
18. Bredin, *The Affair*, 228; Chapman, *The Dreyfus Case*, 169.
19. Scheurer-Kestner, *Mémoires*, 225.
20. Translated in Snyder, *The Dreyfus Case*, 168.
21. Cahm, *The Dreyfus Affair*, 59.
22. Scheurer-Kestner, *Mémoires*, 249.
23. Reinach, *Histoire de l'Affaire Dreyfus*, 3: 211.

5   THE GRAND *AFFAIRE* (1898)

1. Gabriel Monod, cited in Baumont, *Aux Sources*, 226;
2. Stephen Wilson (1973) 'The Anti-Semitic Riots of 1898 in France', *Historical Journal* **16**(4): 789–806, and *Ideology and Experience Anti-Semitism in France at the Time of the Dreyfus Affair* (Rutherford, New Jersey: Fairleigh Dickinson University Press, 1982); Eugen Weber, 'Reflections on the Jews in France', in Malino and Wasserstein, *The Jews in Modern France*, 8–27; Nancy Fitch (1992) 'Mass Culture, Mass Parliamentary Politics, and Modern Anti-Semitism: The Dreyfus Affair in Rural France', *American*

Historical Review, **97**(6): 55–95.

3. Weber in Malino and Wasserstein, *The Jews in Modern France*, 24; Wilson 'The Anti-Semitic Riots', 793.

4. Michael Burns, *Rural Society and French Politics: Boulangism and the Dreyfus Affair* (Princeton: Princeton University Press, 1984), 137; Jocelyn George, 'Provinciales: la France des quatre coins', in *La France de L'Affaire Dreyfus*, ed. Pierre Birnbaum (Paris: Gallimard, 1994).

5. Reinach, *Histoire de l'Affaire Dreyfus*, 3: 310.

6. *Cour de Cassation*, 2: 168.

7. Dreyfus, *Cinq Années*, 196, 203; Reinach, *Histoire de l'Affaire Dreyfus*, 3: 336.

8. The trial may be followed in its entirety in *Procès Zola*, and in Reinach, 3: 339ff.

9. Reinach, *Histoire de l'Affaire Dreyfus*, 3: 440.

10. Jeremy Jennings, ed., *Intellectuals in Twentieth-Century France: Mandarins and Samurais* (New York: St Martin's Press, 1993), 44.

11. Christophe Charle, 'Champ littéraire et champ du pouvoir: Les Ecrivains et l'Affaire Dreyfus', *Annales ESC* (March–April 1977), 245, and *La Naissance des 'intellectuels', 1880–1900* (Paris: Editions de Minuit, 1990); Phillip Cate, 'The Paris Cry: Graphic Artists and the Dreyfus Affair', in Kleeblatt, *The Dreyfus Affair*.

12. Maurras cited in Griffiths, *The Use of Abuse*, 25; Goguel cited in Bredin, *The Affair*, 543.

13. Voltaire had successfully argued for the judicial rehabilitation of Calas, a Protestant wrongly executed for murdering his son; Reinach, *Histoire de l'Affaire Dreyfus*, 3: 383.

14. Susan Rubin Sulieman, 'The Literary Significance of the Dreyfus Affair', in Kleeblatt, *The Dreyfus Affair*, 128; Griffiths, *The Use of Abuse*, xii.

15. Deposition by Bertulus, *Cour de Cassation*, 2: 20; Reinach, *Histoire de l'Affaire Dreyfus*, 4: 76. Bredin, *The Affair*, 322 and Thomas, *Esterhazy*, 329, doubt Bertulus's story, but a clerk later testified that from the next room he heard Henry cry out, 'the honour of the army! Save the honour of the army!'

6 IN THE BALANCE (1898–1899)

1. The nationalist Paul Déroulède, calling for a *coup d'état*.

2. Maurras and Barrès quoted in Griffiths, *The Use of Abuse*, 25.

3. Snyder, *The Dreyfus Case*, 223; Reinach, *Histoire de l'Affaire Dreyfus*, 4: 252.

4. Reinach, *Histoire de l'Affaire Dreyfus*, 4: 324.

5. Bredin, *The Affair*, 361.

6. Jean-Marie Mayeur and Madeleine Reberioux, *The Third Republic from its Origins to the Great War, 1871–1914*, trans. J. R. Foster (Cambridge: Cambridge University Press, 1984; French edn, 1973), 190, Benjamin Martin, *Crime and Criminal Justice under the Third Republic: The Shame of Marianne* (Baton Rouge: Louisiana State University Press, 1990), and Bredin, *The Affair*, 524, find justice was in no way blind, while Jean-Pierre Royer, 'La magistrature déchirée', in *La France de l'Affaire Dreyfus*, ed.

Pierre Birnbaum (Paris: Gallimard, 1994), 255, Pierre Miquel, *L'Affaire Dreyfus* (Paris: PUF, 1992), and Gérard Masson, *Les Juges et Le Pouvoir* (Paris: Moreau and Syros, 1977), argue the contrary.

7. Stephen Wilson, 'Le monument Henry; la structure de l'antisémitisme en France, 1898–1899', *Annales ESC*, March–April, 1977; Bredin, *The Affair*, 350.

8. David B. Ralston, *The Army of the Republic: The Place of the Military in the Political Evolution of France, 1871–1914* (Cambridge: MIT Press, 1967), 223.

9. Dreyfus, *Cinq Années*, 214.

10. Cahm, *The Dreyfus Affair*, 150.

7 RENNES AND REHABILITATION (1899–1906)

1. Alfred Dreyfus, translated in Bredin, *The Affair*, 481.

2. Burns, *Dreyfus: A Family Affair*, 221.

3. Chapman, *The Dreyfus Case*, 266.

4. Bredin, *The Affair*, 386.

5. Translated in Emile Zola, *The Dreyfus Affair: 'J'accuse' and Other Writings*, ed. Alain Pagès, trans. Eleanor Levieux (New Haven: Yale University Press, 1996), 132.

6. Chapman, *The Dreyfus Case*, 284.

7. The trial may be followed in full in *Conseil de guerre de Rennes, Le procès Dreyfus* (Paris: Stock, 1900).

8. Translated in Snyder, *The Dreyfus Case*, 283.

9. In his anger Jaurès implied the army was behind the attack, writing that 'to convict Dreyfus in 1894 the General Staff suppressed the defence; this time, it found it more simple to suppress the defender'; Reinach, *Histoire de l'Affaire Dreyfus*, 5: 360.

10. Jean-Marc Berlière, 'La généalolgie d'une double tradition policière', in *La France de l'Affaire Dreyfus* (Paris: Gallimard, 1994), 211.

11. Burns, *Dreyfus: A Family Affair*, 260.

12. Translated in Zola, *The Dreyfus Affair*, 137.

CONCLUSION

1. From Charles Péguy's disillusioned complaint about the Affair, *Notre jeunesse* (Paris: Gallimard, 1913).

2. Snyder, *The Dreyfus Case*, 376; Bredin, *The Affair*, 484. Reinach was resentful that few of the loyal Dreyfusards had been invited, but Dreyfus – and the army – sought to keep the ceremony brief and simple; Reinach, *Histoire de l'Affaire Dreyfus*, 5: 502.

3. For the debate on the nature and origins of French fascism see Zeev Sternhell, *La Droite révolutionnaire, 1885–1914: Les Origines françaises du fascisme* (Paris: Seuil, 1978).

4. Burns, *Dreyfus, A Family Affair*, 363ff.

5. Pierre Birnbaum, *L'Affaire Dreyfus: La République en péril* (Paris: Gallimard, 1994), 95.

GUIDE FOR FURTHER READING

The best recent extended treatment in English is Jean-Denis Bredin, *The Affair: The Case of Alfred Dreyfus*, trans. Jeffrey Mehlman (New York: George Braziller, 1986; French edn, 1983). It may be supplemented by Eric Cahm, *The Dreyfus Affair in French Society and Politics* (New York: Longman, 1996; French edn, 1994) since Cahm is particularly strong on the role of particular political, social, and intellectual groups and organizations. Douglas Johnson, *France and the Dreyfus Affair* (New York: Walker, 1966) is sometimes indulgent towards the General Staff but is scrupulous and reliable. Guy Chapman, *The Dreyfus Case: A Reassessment* (London: Rupert Hart-Davis, 1955) is an older account emphasizing the political contexts of the Affair, while D. L. Lewis, *Prisoners of Honor: The Dreyfus Affair* (New York: William Murrow, 1973) is engaging but partisan. The most important documents have been translated in Louis Snyder, *The Dreyfus Case: A Documentary History* (New Brunswick, New Jersey: Rutgers University Press, 1973).

The Affair as seen by Alfred Dreyfus himself may be followed in Alfred Dreyfus, *Five Years of My Life, 1894–99* (New York: McClure, Phillips, 1901), and *The Letters of Captain Alfred Dreyfus to his Wife*, trans. L. G. Moreau (New York: Harper & Row, 1899). Michael Burns: *Dreyfus: A Family Affair, 1789–1945* (New York: HarperCollins, 1991) reveals the impact of the Affair on the Dreyfus family.

On anti-Semitism see Michael Marrus, *The Politics of Assimilation: The Jewish Community in France at the Time of the Dreyfus Affair* (Oxford: Oxford University Press, 1980); Albert S. Lindemann, *The Jew Accused: Three Anti-Semitic Affairs (Dreyfus, Beilis, Frank), 1894–1915* (New York: Cambridge University Press, 1991); Sander Gilman, *The Jew's Body* (New York: Routledge, 1991); Frances Malino and Bernard Wasserstein, eds, *The Jews in Modern France* (Hanover, NH: University Press of New England, 1985); Stephen Wilson, *Ideology and Experience: Antisemitism in France at the time of the Dreyfus Affair* (Rutherford, New Jersey: Fairleigh Dickinson University Press, 1982); Nelly Wilson, *Bernard Lazare: Antisemitism and the Problem of Jewish Identity in Late Nineteenth-century France* (Cambridge: Cambridge University Press, 1978).

For intellectuals see Richard Griffiths, *The Use of Abuse: The Polemics of the Dreyfus Affair and Its Aftermath* (Oxford: Berg, 1991); Norman L. Kleeblatt, ed., *The Dreyfus Affair: Art, Truth, and Justice* (Berkeley: University of California Press, 1987); Jeremy Jennings, ed., *Intellectuals in Twentieth-Century France: Mandarins and Samurais* (New York: St Martin's Press, 1993); Emile Zola, *The Dreyfus Affair: 'J'accuse' and Other Writings*, ed. Alain Pagès, trans. Eleanor Levieux (New Haven: Yale University Press, 1996).

Among the many fine treatments of the larger context of *belle époque* politics are: Robert Elliot Kaplan, *Forgotten Crisis: The Fin-de-Siècle Crisis of Democracy in France* (Oxford: Berg, 1995); Michael Sutton, *Nationalism, Positivism, and Catholicism: The Politics of Charles Maurras and French Catholics, 1890–1914* (Cambridge: Cambridge University Press, 1983); Michael Burns, *Rural Society and French Politics: Boulangism and the Dreyfus Affair, 1886–1900* (Princeton: Princeton University Press, 1984); Zeev Sternhell, *The Birth of Fascist Ideology*, trans. David Maisel (Princeton: Princeton University Press, 1994); Richard D. Sonn, *Anarchism and Cultural Politics in Fin-de-Siècle France* (Lincoln: University of Nebraska Press, 1989).

For society and culture see: Charles Rearick, *Pleasures of the Belle Epoque* (New Haven: Yale University Press, 1988); Herman Lebovics, *True France: The Wars over Cultural Identity, 1900–45* (Ithaca: Cornell University Press, 1992); Ruth Harris, *Murders and Madness: Medicine, Law, and Society in the Fin-de-Siècle* (Oxford: Oxford University Press, 1989); Robert A. Nye, *Crime, Madness, and Politics in Modern France: The Medical Concept of National Decline* (Princeton: Princeton University Press, 1984); Eugen Weber, *France: Fin-de-Siècle* (Cambridge: Harvard University Press, 1986); Debora Silverman, *Art Nouveau in Fin-de-Siècle France: Politics, Psychology, and Style* (Berkeley: University of California Press, 1989) and the still useful Roger Shattuck, *The Banquet Years: The Arts in France, 1885–1918* (New York: Harcourt, 1958).

INDEX

107, 112, 114, 118–9, 122, 134–5, 142, 144–6, 156
Rennes 127, 130, 134; trial 137–42
Renoir 99
Ribot, Alexander 35
riots 88–90
Roche, Jules 14, 23
Rochefort, Henri 58, 79, 92, 102, 124, 148, 152
Rodin 99
Roget, Gaudérique 106, 112, 122, 136, 140, 152
Rothschilds 48, 58
royalists 121–2, 132; *see also* d'Orléans, Duc de
Rozerot, Jeanne 133

S
Sacco and Vanzetti 157
Saint-Cyr 13, 40
Sandherr, Jean-Conrad 3–5, 8–9, 12, 29, 39, 84, 107, 119, 152; and forgeries 22–3; anti-Semitism 8, 33, 41
Saussier, Félix 9–10, 12, 14, 19, 32, 41, 45, 50, 55–6, 72–3, 107, 112, 140
Scheurer-Kestner, Auguste 43, 75, 78–81, 83–4, 99, 149, 155; joins Dreyfusards 63–6, 74; and Billot 63, 67, 71–2
Schwartzkoppen, Maximilien, and *bordereau* 1–2, 9, 39, 42, 141; and 'scoundrel D' letter 9, 22, 29, 45; and Panizzardi 1, 4, 9, 53; espionage 2, 26, 80, 147; and Esterhazy 48–9, 57, 70
'scoundrel D' letter 5, 9, 11, 22, 29, 45, 54, 72, 103, 138
secret dossier 29–30, 38, 48, 50, 53, 55, 61, 91, 94, 119, 127
Sfax 127, 129
Signac 99
social Darwinism 6, 90
socialism x, 82–3, 91, 104, 132, 134–5, 154
SOS Racism 154
'Speranza' letter 59, 69, *see also* forgeries
'Speranza' telegram 73, 80, 93, 102–3
stagiaires 4–5, 21

Statistical Section, and *bordereau* 3–5, 9, 16, 22–3, 25, 28–9, 40; and *petit bleu* 39, 46–7, 50, 57; versus Picquart 60, 62; collusion with Esterhazy 66–74, 78; de Pellieux inquiry 80–1; Ravary inquiry 81–2; Esterhazy trial 84–6; Zola trial 95–8
Steinheil, Marguérite 121
'syndicate' ix, 24, 50, 78–9, 83, 85, 91, 114, 118, 121, 131, 139, 142, 148

T
Times (London) 100
Trarieux, Ludovic 63, 99, 102, 104–5, 149, 155
Treaty of Frankfurt (1871) 20
Tribune (Chicago) 100

U
'Uhlan' letter, 81–2, 93, *see also* forgeries

V
Val-Carlos, Marquis de 23–4, 28–9, 38, 52, 96
Veiled Lady 72, 78, 85, 88, 93
'Vidi' article 73–4
Ville Saint Nazaire 36
Voltaire 99

W
Waldeck-Rousseau, René 24, 27, 134–6, 140–1, 153, 155; pardon and amnesty 143–6
Weil, Maurice 41, 46–8, 55, 58, 60–1, 140
Weiss letter 51; *see also* forgeries
Weyler letter 51, 59; *see also* forgeries
Wilhelm II 4, 34, 80, 120, 138

Z
Zionism 33, 156
Zola, Alexandrine 133
Zola, Emile ix, 56, 78–9, 100, 104, 109, 143, 145–6, 149, 155; and anti-Semitism 43, 83–4; joins Dreyfusards 75–6; *J'accuse* 87–9; trial 91–8, 102; exile 104, 107; returns to France 133–4; *see also J'accuse*
Zurlinden, Emile 35, 111–12, 114, 116, 136